FROM NIGHTMARE TO FREEDOM

Healing After The Holocaust

By Lillian Judd and Dennis L. Judd

For my son Dennis and in loving memory of my parents, sister,
my husband Emil and my son Jirka-Irv

From Nightmare To Freedom – Healing After The Holocaust

Copyright ©2011 by Judd House Publisher

ISBN 978-9833847-0-0

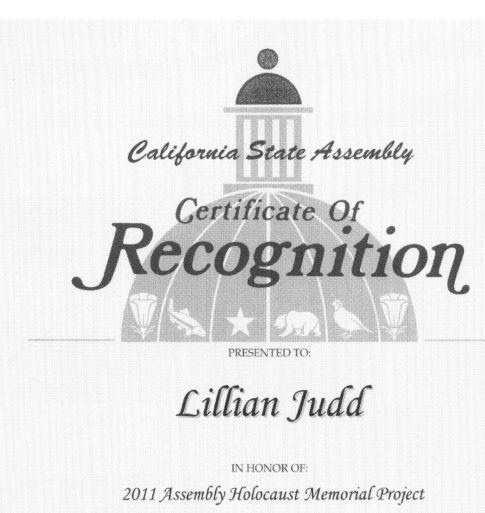

California State Assembly

Certificate Of

Recognition

PRESENTED TO:

Lillian Judd

IN HONOR OF:

2011 Assembly Holocaust Memorial Project

California State Assembly Chambers

Sacramento, California

May 2nd, 2011

MEMBER OF THE ASSEMBLY
7th ASSEMBLY DISTRICT
CALIFORNIA STATE LEGISLATURE

Lillian Judd, a Czechoslovakian- born Holocaust survivor, pulls up her sleeve to show an assembly of Pomolita middle school students the tattoo she received in a concentration camp during World War II

POEM FOR LILLIAN JUDD

Being torn from her home, caused her heartache and pain
Branded like cattle her wrist was inflamed
Her father beaten in front of her eyes,
Hate filled her heart witnessing his brutal demise.
Stripped of pride and long locks of hair,
Hissing gases from hell caused toxic fumes of despair
Remembering terror and inflicting pain
Praying to God to keep her sane.
False hopes about mother kept her alive,
The bonds of sisterhood helped her to survive.
After this tragedy she had to find faith in "me".
Releasing her hate finally helped her feel free.

By: Brittany, Bryan, Chris and Joey
Mountain Shadows Middle School
May 26, 2006

Lillian's Acknowledgments

I need to first thank my son, Dennis Judd, my partner in this book for all the time he has put in over the last 10 years. If it weren't for Dennis, this book would never have been finished. I also feel very close to Dennis' wife, Anna, who contributed to the editing, and with whom I share a deep feeling place. My grandchildren, Sarah and Daniel, keep me going, I love them both.

I want to acknowledge Al and Susan Batzdorff, for their editing assistance, and careful attention that I not lose my "accent" as I told my story.

To the people at the Holocaust Alliance, especially Myrna Goodman, Ph.D., thank you for your telling me to look for a publisher and agent and that perhaps my story would be good as a school text book.,

To all the teachers from the middle schools, high schools, junior college, and universities who invited me to speak to their classes. To all the students who listened and who were impacted by my story and sent me beautiful thank you notes.

My appreciation to Mel Hecker of the United States Holocaust Memorial Museum, who invited me to Washington, read my document, and gave me valuable feedback and encouraged me to publish.

To my friend, Joslyn Metzger who kept encouraging me, and Sylvia Sucher who coordinated my school speaking engagements for many years, actually accompanying me to them.

I spoke to Rotary groups, juvenile hall, churches, and synagogues, to anyone that invited me. I am most grateful for their interest in bringing this Holocaust story out.

The writing of this book completed my personal therapy without a therapist. I found my peace in writing this story. I hope your reading it will give you an understanding of what anger and hate and prejudice can bring out in people so that we can replace hatred with love and create a hate-free, genocide-free future.

Recognition

Special thanks to "The United States Holocaust Museum" for giving us the rights to republish the photos from "The Auschwitz" Album, and providing the Nazi documentation of prisoner #A -10946- Lili Klein.

Special thanks to "Sonoma West Publishers", "The Press Democrat", and "The Ukiah Daily Journal" for all the support and help they provided by giving us the authorization to use the articles they published about Lillian Judd.

Special thanks to Christopher Chung, the photographer for "The Press Democrat" who took the photo used on the front cover of the book during Lillian's Bat Mitzvah when she turned 80 years old.

Special thanks to Sarah Baldik, the photographer for "The Ukiah Daily Journal" who took the photo when Lillian Judd was giving a presentation in 2011 to students at Ukiah High School.

Special thanks to Professor Elaine Leeder, Dean of the School of Social Sciences at Sonoma State University for writing the Forward to our book, to Joslyn Metzger for her help proofreading this book, and to Demitrius Handelih for his help enhancing the photography.

A special appreciation to all the professors and the students who wrote so many letters to Lillian Judd; and to Brittany, Bryan, Chris and Joey for their poem in honor of Lillian Judd.

Dedication

In honor of my son Dennis and his wife Anna,

and my grandchildren Sarah and Daniel.

In loving memory of my parents Hajnal and Elemer,

and my sisters Renee and Irene who were killed at Auschwitz,

In loving memory of my sister Herczi who survived the camps with me,

my dear brother Leonard who brought us to America,

and in memory of my husband Emil and our son Irving.

Table of Contents

Foreword

Elaine Leeder, MSW, MPH, PhD

Professor of Sociology

Dean of the School of Social Sciences

Sonoma State University

In the year 2000 I was honored to be a student at the US Holocaust Memorial Museum in Washington D.C. where I studied how to teach the Holocaust to college students. In 2004 I was invited back to assist in the teaching of college professors on teaching the Holocaust at primarily Latino universities in the US. During both those educational experiences I had the privilege of working with Holocaust survivors and scholars on pedagogy and teaching methodology. We discussed such difficult subjects as what makes good people do evil things, how does one survive atrocities that are incomprehensible and how to teach a new generation about the Holocaust and other genocides. As part of our education we read numerous Holocaust survivor memoirs, poignant and moving tales of suffering and struggle. Each tells a unique story, no two quite the same; each has a tone and set of emotions that are often remarkable, horrifying and yet hopeful. My reading was profound because during that time I also learned about the details of my own family in Lithuania and how they spent their final hours at a pit outside of a small town called Kupiskis. The Holocaust, always in the background of my life, now took center stage. I began teaching about the Holocaust at my university and reaching hundreds of students to try to influence future generations so that the phrase "Never again" would have real meaning.

In the year 2001, I had the honor of meeting Lillian Judd and was moved beyond words when I read her profound and deeply touching story. Lillian experienced losses and suffering that none of us should ever have to confront. Yet she has a wonderful sense of life and joie de vive. I have danced with her at a reunion for Holocaust survivors and at her own Bat Mitzvah, which she finally got to celebrate at the age of 80.

Lillian Judd is an example of the incredible strength of human spirit. She shows us that there is life after genocide; that the experience of loss and horrific suffering does not have to define an entire life. Lillian Judd is a great inspiration to virtually everyone she meets on her way.

From Nightmare To Freedom tells Lillian's tale in explicit detail. Beyond Lillian's unique tale there are valuable and timely lessons for the reader to take away. Lillian makes her story truly relevant to the pressing issues we are facing in our lives today. It is our task on a daily basis to fight intolerance and injustice. Lillian Judd's book encourages us all to reach out and make a difference in another person's life. This book serves as a striking testimonial to both survival and the possibility of good to exist even in the most evil of circumstances. It is a tale of devastation and yet it is even more so a tale of hope. Lillian's book raises questions and provides answers for generations to come.

As the son of a Holocaust survivor, Dennis Judd has been a "memorial candle" for his family. Dennis is working hard, in his own way, on repairing the pain of those around him. As a child of survivors, Dennis has a heavy burden of forgiving and remembering. The literature on children of survivors indicates that some become depressed and helpless in the face of their family's trauma. Dennis has not been cowed by his family's experience. Instead, he has been empowered by it. It will always be imprinted in Dennis' identity. It makes Dennis passionate about continuing the mission of his mother Lillian - of educating the younger generations about the Holocaust and about his individual family story of survival.

Lillian's son, Dennis Judd, is actively involved in preserving his mother's story. He has always been truly dedicated to keeping the memories of his parents, aunts and uncles, who went through concentration camps alive. He interviewed them all and videotaped their stories for future generations.

Dennis Judd wrote a chapter explaining the feelings of the second generation of Holocaust survivors, which has greatly enhanced the book. Dennis spent countless hours researching the archives of the United States Holocaust Memorial Museum and found Nazi documentation of prisoner A-10946 (Lillian) and actual photographs taken as the train with Lillian's family on board, arrived at Auschwitz, all of which are included in this book. It gave another dimension to his mother's personal story, and also put it into a proper historical documentary framework, which makes this book even more valuable as a teaching tool for schools and colleges, and any social organization interested in serious learning about the Holocaust.

Children of survivor's have to transcend trauma and not be numbed into silence by their cultural heritage. Many families, like Dennis' did make it out and have shown the Nazis and Hitler that there is life after genocide. They have proven that Hitler did not annihilate an entire people. In fact, they are alive, having children and grandchildren, and thriving in spite of the trauma.

Please open your hearts and prepare to be transformed by this very special book. Give yourself permission to cry and be deeply touched by the sorrows Lillian so vividly describes. Savor the moments of joy that survivors were able to find even in the hard life they had after the war. Laugh at some adventures Lillian had. Feel greatly empowered by experiencing with Lillian the triumphs of simple people, just like you and I, who were able to preserve their spirit in spite of it all.

I hope that when you finish this book, you will join the ranks of those who have made a firm resolution to personally stand up against any prejudice and hatred, which you might encounter in your life. Our actions would be the best tribute to the memory of those who perished in the Holocaust. Together, we can make it a safer world. Should you get complacent and discouraged do return to Lillian's story and allow it to reenergize you and motivate your work in preventing atrocities in the world.

Preface

The last day of the Jewish holiday Shavuot is the day our family designated to hold as our "Memorial Day" in memory of our parents, sisters and brothers. It is a very depressing day for me. I don't remember taking it as hard in the past years as I do now. All through the years I had nightmares on and off about some episodes in the camps but have never dreamt about my family. Last night I had a very vivid nightmare.

We had just arrived at Auschwitz-Birkenau in the box cars. We heard a big commotion as the German soldiers kept opening the doors shouting: "Alles rous ohne packeten" (Everybody out without packages). We were scared, and tried to obey by jumping out as fast as possible. I helped my dad coming down,

I saw my father reach for his briefcase which held his prayer objects, which he used every day. At that moment a German S.S. soldier hit him with his rifle-butt with such force that my father collapsed to the ground, covered with blood. I screamed and woke up shaking all over. It seemed so real, in spite of the forty two years that have since gone by. I could not get it out of my mind. Never before could I talk about my experiences, but now I decided to put it down on paper.

As I started to write, it felt as if I was unloading my inner burden and I felt lighter and lighter with each page I completed. I am not a writer, but it was the best therapy for me. From this nightmare, freedom came to me. Now I can go on with my life.

Part I: Carpathian Beginnings

At the end of the 1800's, my grandfather and grandmother "Friedman" lived in the village of Radvancz-Ungvar located in the Carpathian Mountains. My mother, Hajnal Friedman, was born in 1897 in the same house as I was born. Only at that time, the territory was under Austro-Hungarian rule. She was raised and educated in Hungarian. She was also fluent in German, Yiddish and Ukrainian.

Sometime around the turn of the twentieth century, after my mother was born, Grandfather Friedman left Radvancz for the United States with the idea of making a better living for his family. He stayed with his brother Charlie who had already emigrated. It was thought that America was the golden country where the dollars grew on trees. He made some money with hard work, and came back home to Radvancz. He and grandmother had another baby and off he went to America again. I am not sure how many times this happened, but out of the family of six children (four boys and two girls), four were born after my mother. My Grandfather passed away on one of his trips back to Radvancz.

As the story goes, my mother was a beautiful girl with jet black hair and very expressive brown eyes. Her skin was like porcelain and she had a pretty smile that showed even teeth. She was pampered by her mother and her older brothers. There was great love among the brothers and sisters. Mother used to tell us about her oldest brother, Willy, who always watched over her. He visited her at work and brought her a shiny apple or an orange, a very special treat.

Mother had a better education than her siblings. She finished high school and a two-year business course to become a secretary. She also learned to sew, a skill that turned out to be very helpful in the years to come.

Young Love

When World War I broke out, Mother worked as a secretary for a high-ranking Austro-Hungarian officer and with what she earned, helped maintain her family. She met a young man, and after a short acquaintance, they decided to go steady and it appeared to be a very serious relationship between them. They had a great romance for four years. As often happened in Europe, the young man's mother did not approve of her son marrying a poor working girl. The fact that she was beautiful and talented in every way and that they were deeply in love did not make any difference to her. Apparently the young man did not have much backbone, because in the end he married another girl, someone who was introduced to him by a matchmaker.

Mother felt jilted and very sad. I do not think she ever got over it, but after a while she was invited to a wedding and decided to go. There she met my father, Elemer Klein. He was tall, blue-eyed, and blond, a very handsome young man. Neighbors said he was much better looking than her first love.

Father was born in a village called Botfalva and was raised in the neighboring village of Doboruska, located about 15 kilometers from Radvancz. His family spoke Hungarian and Yiddish. Father served in the Austro-Hungarian Army during World War I. He was wounded in his leg during battle.

The Establishment of Czechoslovakia

In 1918 with the end of World War I, the Austro-Hungarian Empire was split apart. As a result of this, a new nation was established in the mountainous heart of Europe. Czechoslovakia was created through the efforts of Thomas Garyk (Garrique) Masaryk. Masaryk was elected as the first president of Czechoslovakia in 1920. The new government was liberal and democratic, modeled after the United States. The country consisted of four sections, each having its' own capital city: *Czechy's (Czech's)* capital was *Praha* (Prague); *Morava's* (Moravia's) capital, *Brno*; *Slovensko's* (Slovakia's) capital, *Bratislava*; and *Podkarpatske Rus*,(Zakarpatska Ukraina) capital *Uzhorod*. The name of our village changed from Radvancz to Radvanka.

Languages spoken were Czech, Slovak, Ukrainian, German, Hungarian and Yiddish. The official language was Czech. Neither of my parents ever managed to learn the Czech language, and they were not the only ones. The older generation maintained certain resentment toward the Czech government and always compared life to what it used to be like under the Hungarian government. Refusing to learn the Czech language was their form of rebellion.

Mother and Father went out a few times and quickly became serious about each other. I believe that Father fell in love with Mother, but I have a feeling that on my mother's side it may have been considered a marriage on the rebound. They married in 1920, and mother soon became pregnant.

Soon after, the long awaited affidavit from Mom's Uncle Charlie arrived for Mother's family, to go to America. Because she was newly married, and pregnant with her first child, Mother decided to stay in Europe. It was either that, or leave for America without her husband. So, my grandmother, my four uncles and my aunt immigrated to America leaving my mother. From the beginning, Mother missed her family. She felt abandoned, and perhaps in the long run it affected her married life.

Mom's brothers all ended up living in different states. Uncle Willy and family lived in Pittsburgh, Pennsylvania. Uncle Adolf and family settled in Bronx, New York. Uncle Joe and family lived in Ohio. Uncle Morris and family lived in Detroit, Michigan. I do not know where my Aunt Ester and family lived, but she was the sibling who kept up the regular correspondence with Mother.

The New Addition

Mother and Father's first child, Leonard, was born in 1921 with great difficulty. Mother almost died delivering him after laboring for thirty-six hours. The midwife was present from the first labor pain, but she could not deliver the baby, and Mother was getting weak. A doctor was called in, and the two of them worked hard to bring the baby into the world.

Mother used to tell us how she heard the midwife begging the doctor to save the mother and let the baby go. The doctor said, "Let's try to save the mother *and* the baby." When the baby boy was finally taken out, he was not breathing. The doctor submerged the baby by turns from warm into cold water until it cried out. All was well.

My parents had five children, one son and four daughters. They waited at least three years between babies. I was born in 1923. The next child was Herczi, born in 1926. Renee was born in 1930, and Iren in 1935.

Leonard (about 5 years old)

Lili (2 years) and Leonard (5 years)

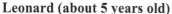

As I remember, my parents were arguing a lot. The fact that my father never could make a good, or even a fair living, might have been a factor. Father started out as a buyer of livestock. He was the unluckiest person on earth. Poor man, whatever he started never came out right. Later he opened a butcher shop which was built on our property facing the street. At least he did not have to pay rent.

I do not know if it was because of a lack of business knowledge, guts, or money, or maybe all three, but Father's business was not successful. The shop was not outfitted to store merchandise properly; it did not have an icehouse. As a result, he could not kill and refrigerate a whole steer. He had to buy quarters of beef from the big butchers for resale, and therefore made less money.

Business was also difficult to conduct because of a language barrier; many of the customers spoke Ukrainian and my father spoke Hungarian. Another problem was that most of Father's customers were peasants from nearby villages passing through to go to church on Sunday. On their way home they would buy meat for dinner. He would often sell the meat to them on credit. By the time he closed the shop at the end of the day he had hardly enough cash to maintain us through the week. On Saturday evenings he had to walk to the villages and hustle to collect on the bills for meat purchased a week or two before, so he could pay for the meat he was to buy Sunday morning. Sometimes the peasants did not have any money for him so they would pay with a chicken or some produce they had grown (which we did not need, because we had our own). He would get home around eleven o'clock at night, very tired from all the walking and *schlepping* (carrying).

Mother's family in America would sometimes send us a few dollars and packages of used clothing. My mother was able to take them apart and make new beautiful outfits for herself and her family. She was a tremendously skilled seamstress. She could make the old look like new, and we were always envied for the dresses she made for us.

Since we owned a house on a large parcel (about an acre), we were almost self-sufficient in providing our own food. We had enough land to supply us with wheat for flour, and there was room for a large vegetable garden where we grew potatoes, corn, cucumbers, onions, carrots, and beans. Some years weren't as good as others because of drought or pests, but we survived. We had a couple of dairy cows in the stalls, chickens for eggs and meat, some turkeys, and a lot of pigeons. The cows supplied us with enough milk to make all of the dairy products we needed for the family with some left over to sell to neighbors. The milk was kept in large pitchers next to a covered window in the living room. After two or three days it became sour, just right to spoon off the cream (*tejfel*) on top for making butter in our wooden churn. Mother would churn the cream into butter. Buttermilk (*iro*) was the residue left after the butter was removed from the churn. The sour milk that remained in the pitcher was like yogurt (*aludtej*), and Mother made cheese out of it. The buttermilk and yogurt were richer because the milk was not stripped of its fat. It was used as it came out of the cow.

Sour milk and all of the dairy products were a real treat in our house. Thursdays were declared meatless days in my family, so we could enjoy the dairy foods we loved so much. A special Thursday night meal was hot mashed potatoes with fried onions and *aludtej* (yogurt). We drank *iro* (buttermilk) with the meal or even between meals. The remaining milk, cheese and butter were stored in the *shpaiz*, the cool walk-in closet near the kitchen. We had to be careful not to mix up the dairy with meat, which was forbidden because my family observed the Jewish dietary laws.

Money was always scarce, even though we had all the food we needed. I never had a store-bought doll or toys, but then, neither did any of my friends, so we did not miss anything. When a few of us got together and wanted to play with a doll, we made our own. Someone's grandmother showed us how. We took two sticks (a short one and a long one) and some old clothing that we could cut up, a pair of scissors and off we were, busy for a whole afternoon making dolls. The next day we were occupied with making dresses and finding cardboard boxes for dollhouses. Later, when we were older, we made our own games and cards out of old cardboard, even yo-yo's from wooden spools. We always found something to do and had fun at little or no cost.

Our home was comfortable enough. It was basically a 700 square foot one bedroom home without electricity, running water, or an indoor bathroom. Some families in the area had larger homes than ours, but most of the houses were smaller. Ours had a good-sized kitchen with a wood-burning stove, a large table, and enough chairs to accommodate up to seven people. There was also a large brass bed in the kitchen, where my sister Herczi and I slept.

Next to the kitchen was a small room that was always a few degrees cooler than the rest of the house. It looked something like a walk-in closet, with a cement floor and shelves lining the walls, we called it "THE SHPAIZ" Mother used this room to store perishable foods. The sauerkraut she made (a tremendous project) was kept in there over the winter, along with various kinds of homemade preserves and the *lekvar* (a dense, dark plum spread) mother would make when plums were in season. There were no supermarkets at that time, so if we wanted to have some fruit or vegetables in the winter we had to prepare ahead.

On the other side of the kitchen, were two rooms. One was a large room mother and father shared as a bedroom with my two youngest sisters, Renee and Iren. The other, a slightly smaller room that was used for entertaining guests, was where my brother Leonard slept. When I was in my early teens, I received my mother's permission to switch rooms. My parents had nice furniture, and I did not think it was being used to its best advantage. I made a beautiful living/dining room out of the bedroom and turned the guest room into the bedroom. This way we did not have to go through the bedroom to reach the living room.

In those days, few people had electricity, indoor plumbing or bathrooms in their homes. Most of us had to use outhouses in the backyard. It was no picnic when we had to go into the cold and dark backyard on a winter night. Usually mornings were cold in the wintertime, and the fire had to be started early if we wanted to wash. We had to pump enough water out of the well and carry it in buckets into the house, where we would warm it up in a large pot that was always sitting on the cooler side of the stove.

Because we had no bathroom, baths were taken in the living room using a large basin (called the *lavor*) filled with warm water. For my bath I would set the basin on a wooden chair by the wood-burning stove, pour some of the water into it, and use a piece of soap I would take from the kitchen. If I had any shampoo, I would use that, or else I would just use the bar soap to wash my hair. I would strip down to the waist and start by first washing my hair and face and then the rest of my upper body. When I was done, I would dry myself with a towel, move the basin from the chair to the floor and wash the rest of my body. After I got dressed I felt clean and refreshed.

Our well, which was located in front of our house, served a lot of purposes besides providing our water for drinking, cooking, and bathing. It was also where the cows were brought daily from their stalls to drink. On the right side of the house Mother had her vegetable garden. It always looked so nice and neat. Across from the vegetable garden were the fruit orchards where my father planted and maintained the most delicious choice of fruits – meaty Italian plums, big, juicy peaches, and sweet apricots. Behind the house were the cows' stalls, and next to them, a hill of smelly manure was kept for fertilizer to be used on the fields in spring.

Lili (5), Hajnal (31), Herczi (2), Leonard (8)

The New Adventure 1928 off to America

It was during this time in my early childhood that arrangements for our family to leave Czechoslovakia for America began to be made. Mother's family, who had already immigrated, missed her very much, and she missed them. It was decided that her brothers would arrange for us to go to America.

About 1928, Mother received a letter from the American Consulate advising us to prepare for the journey to Prague for the medical examinations. We were given a month to get ready to leave for America. Leonard was eight years old, I was five, and Herczi a very cute two-year old.

On the day of departure, there was a big commotion at our house. My Aunt Regina from my father's side came to our house early in the morning to help us get packed and ready to leave. She was going to stay in our house until we got in touch with her and let her know we were on our way to the new country. Neighbors and friends came out to wish us well. It was a tearful good-bye.

We were taken by horse and buggy to the train station, where we boarded the train to Prague. We slept and ate on the train, and the days passed quickly. As I looked out the window, the scenery went by so fast it made me dizzy.

I don't remember how many days we were on the train, when one early morning we were awakened by loud yelling. "*Horke parky!* Fresh hot dogs and drinks!" We were in Prague. I had never seen so many people in my life. Somebody met us at the station and led us to a tall building, but on the way, my parents bought us some hot dogs with lots of mustard on the bun. We ended up in a large hall filled with many other families sitting clustered together on the floor. "Sit down there," said the man who had brought us, pointing to a corner of the floor. Mother spread out a blanket she carried and we all sat down to wait our turn for the examination.

As it turned out, we waited on that floor for two nights and almost three days. During this long wait, my parents let us eat the *wurshtlies* (their name for the hot dogs), but because the hot dogs weren't kosher, they couldn't eat them. They had to go to the store to buy some sardines, bread and lemon for themselves. It was hard. Everyone sat, and slept, and worried together about what the future would bring.

On the third day, they first called in the children, then Mother, and finally, Father. We were given shots and were ready to go, but had to wait a long time for Father to join us. When they called us in, it was to give us bad news. Father still favored the leg that was wounded in World War I. As he got older, the limp got worse and more noticeable.

Eventually he had to use a cane to make walking easier. Since our father had an injured leg, they did not think he could make a living for us in America, and he was turned down. We would not be allowed to go.

This was a great shock. Mother cried all the way home. She was so disappointed and yet she did not think of leaving Father behind. She could have taken us and gone to America and later, when she became a citizen, she could have brought him out. Apparently she didn't think of that at the time.

We returned to our home in Radvanka and to the life we had led before. My aunt went home. I saw my mother crying now and then, but as time passed, it seemed to be forgotten that we had ever tried to leave our home. It was not strange to hear again the ringing of cow bells from a distance in the mornings as all of the cows from the village were herded by the village herder to pasture. People had to pay for this service. The dust and the smells chased everyone into their homes. This was repeated at dusk, when the cows were returned to their stalls. From our front yard we had fun watching cows returning to their proper gate. They seemed to remember where they belonged.

Preparation for Sabbath

My father had to sell lots of meat to feed and clothe so many of us. Our mother took care of all the chores around the house, and she worked very hard. She had to see to it that the cows were milked, the butter churned, and the cheese made. Sometimes we had more butter and cheese than we needed, and our neighbor was always happy to buy the extras.

Mother was busiest toward the end of the week when she had to start with the baking. We had wooden containers that were used for bread. Every Wednesday evening, Mother mixed the flour, yeast and water and kneaded the dough to make bread. It was left overnight to rise. She woke up very early in the morning to form four large breads the size of a wheel, so that they would last through the week. Mother never forgot to make a few small ones for us, for breakfast. By the time we got up to go to school, she had a delicious roll for each of us, which we enjoyed with fresh butter.

On Thursday evening the procedure started all over, except one container held the *challah* dough and the other the sweet dough. By morning the dough rose up to the top of the containers and was ready to prepare for baking. On Friday morning we woke up to the Shabbat fragrances. The cheese rolls, the poppy seed cake, the *challah*, which my mother braided out of seven long pieces of dough, and the other goodies smelled heavenly. The chicken soup was cooking on the stove for diner. The roast beef, potato *kugel* and *cholent*, (bean, barley, onions, seasonings and meat) were ready for the oven. In our house there was no cooking on Shabbat. My parents kept a kosher home, strictly observing the dietary laws according to the Jewish tradition, and we were also taught to follow the rules. On Fridays after sundown Shabbat began. In the winter time, a non-Jewish woman was hired to come in every hour or so to add wood to the stove so we would not freeze, because we were not allowed to do it ourselves. If she came late for any reason, and the fire would burn out, she would have to start it up all over. It took a long time before the kitchen got warm again.

Ever since I can remember, we always had a large brick built-in oven in the kitchen. After all was baked and cooked, and the coals were raked to the side, we used to lie on the top of the oven and it kept us warm and comfortable. The *cholent* and the *kugel* were placed inside for the next day. Just as the sun was setting, it was left to cook overnight, and it kept hot for the Shabbat.

I loved Friday evenings. Mother washed and changed her dress, and she looked beautiful. She spread a white damask tablecloth on the table. The *challahs* were covered with a special hand-embroidered cloth, and she set the candelabra with the candles in the middle. When the sun was setting, displaying the bright red, yellow and orange colors around us, and as darkness was just about approaching, Mother called us in. She was ready to light the candles and say the blessings, and bless each of us separately. Father went to the synagogue, and when he came back, we had a nice din er. Everything was always delicious.

Mother and Father sat down to read after dinner and relaxed. We went out to the square and played tag or hide and seek, until we were out of breath. It was a good way to get together with boys and girls of the neighborhood and also to work off the big heavy dinner. Soon it was time to go in. We were always looking forward to the next day.

Many years later when it was hard to think back and remember, some memories came back to me like the Friday evenings. It was beautiful; also we had more and better food than on weekdays. I often think about it, even today.

Learning Experiences

Every season brought a different pastime our way. In spring, we walked to the Uz River, on our way to the forest, through grassy fields speckled with colorful wild flowers. In the forest we would roam, picking violets, lilies of the valley, and other early spring flowers. Later in the season, we would pick wild strawberries to bring home and eat with sour cream. A neighbor I liked very much, and whom I called "Mariska Neni" (Aunt Mariska), taught me which mushrooms were edible and which were poisonous. She also taught me how to fish in the Uz River with homemade poles.

Spring turned into summer and it brought even more of nature's bounties. Our fruit trees were loaded with wonderful fruit ready for harvest. The mulberries on our old mulberry tree became ripe in this season, turning from green to white. Neighbors would come over to help us eat them. Someone would climb the tree and two others would hold out a tablecloth by its corners to catch the berries as the person in the tree shook the branches. The berries were very good fresh, but could not be saved for the winter in any manner.

In the fall the air became cool. Trees burst into color before shedding their leaves for the winter. We had two large walnut trees close to the fence and there were always some walnuts on the ground to be picked up.

Next door to us lived a family with three young boys. Their property was twice as wide as ours, with fruit trees growing from one end to the other. We always bought apples from them, since they had so many kinds. I loved to walk down to the very end of our yard. On the way down we sometimes saw the neighbor's youngest son. We would tease him, and he would get angry and throw apples over the fence at us. That was what we wanted! We would laugh, and the more we laughed, the angrier he got, and the more apples he would throw at us.

Fall kept us very busy. Most of the villagers would have corn to husk and tie up to dry. Everyone would take turns, inviting neighbors to come over to help. The hosts of the affair would prepare food and drinks. A large pot of fresh corn cooked on the stove, and there was a lot of singing and joking all through the evening.

Grapes were also harvested in fall. A few people in the neighborhood owned vineyards and would invite people from the area to pick the grapes when they were ripe. Some people paid for the work; with others, the pay was just all of the grapes you could eat.

A yearly ritual in fall at our house was making *lekvar*. We would buy large quantities of plums to make this sweet plum spread. (Our own plums were considered delicacies and would only be eaten fresh.) We would invite some neighbors to help us make the *lekvar*. We would wash the plums in large tubs of water pumped out of the well. Once they were cleaned, we would open each one using our thumbs, and take out the pit. A large hole was dug in the front yard and wood was placed in the bottom of it. The kettle was positioned on top of the wood, which was then ignited.. The plums were then placed into a kettle that held an X-shaped piece of wood designed to keep them from sticking to the bottom and burning on the hot fire. We were seated about ten feet away, so the hot syrup wouldn't splash us. Because of our distance from the pot, we used a long pole for stirring. Trading off the task in shifts, we constantly pushed and pulled the pole to swivel the X-shaped wood in the pot, moving the plums back and forth. Wood would be added throughout the hours-long cooking process to keep the fire hot.

11

On those evenings we had a party going. It was a tiring job to stir the plums, so we made the best of it. We would sing and talk, sometimes even dancing late into the night, until the *lekvar* was cooked and fully thickened. The next morning Mother stored the *lekva*r in jars or crock pots and put it away for the winter and we shoveled dirt back into the hole. We would scrub the kettle clean, clean the X-shape plum turner and the long poles, and we'd pass all of this along to the next family interested in making *lekvar* for the winter.

Home Made Sauerkraut

Another fall ritual was making sauerkraut. Father would buy a hundred heads of cabbage from the farmers, and we would borrow a cabbage shredder. (The cabbage shredder would make its rounds through the village as households took turns making their year's supply of sauerkraut.) Some friends would come over to help. To begin, Mother would spread a white tablecloth on the kitchen floor and place the shredder in the center of it. Then we would wash and clean all those cabbages. Mother and Father would shred the heads into large bowls. As they were filled, the bowls would then be dumped into a huge barrel. When the bottom of the barrel was substantially covered with shredded cabbage, whole heads would be placed on top for making stuffed cabbage in the winter. Some apples were placed into the barrel. Next would come another thick layer of shredded cabbage. Coarse salt and bay leaves were sprinkled on the cabbage and then it was pressed down well. To do this pressing, Mother would wash her feet and put on a pair of long, white socks. She'd climb into the barrel and dance on the cabbage to soften it up and press it down. After this, more whole apples were put into the barrel, and more layers were added, always followed by the dancing, until the barrel was completely filled. The next job was to lay a wooden cover on top of the barrel and weigh it down with a large rock. It took three men to put this rock into place. We could all rest now.

After a few days, the cabbage would start to ferment. A grayish foam would appear on the surface, and Mother had to skim it off every day for a couple of weeks. It smelled very bad, like rotting vegetables. After the foam disappeared it would begin to smell like – and become - sauerkraut that would last for the whole winter. And the apples were delicious!

Preparation for the winter continued. The large container of *schmaltz* (goose fat) was placed into the *shpaiz,* and the vegetables and grains from the field were harvested and stored. Mother made us some warm clothes and most of the time we needed shoes and some warm socks as the weather changed.

We had quite a few rain storms before the weather got cold enough for snow. The rain was needed for the fields to get a deep soaking, but it also made the streets muddy.

Soon the wind became colder and snow would follow, and we felt the chill even before that.

The roads were not paved at that time in our section, so after the rains we had puddles the size of a pond on the lower side of the street. We just walked around it, because one did not know how deep the water was. Sometimes it covered our ankles.

The puddles were where the geese usually congregated, bathing very noisily. The gander made the biggest and loudest splashes, really showing off. He was a lot larger than the rest of them.

Once I was coming home from my friend's house, when a goose or gander started chasing me and, of course, caught up with me and bit my back side. That was quite embarrassing and painful. I was walking by, minding my own business. I saw the geese from a distance playing with each other in the puddle. I did not expect to be attacked by them; it had never happened before. From then on, I went around a block to avoid them. I had a mark on my lower back for a long time.

Stuffing the Geese

My Uncle Willy sent money every year from America so in return, we would send him some goose fat. In the fall Mother started by buying the geese and they were force fed as soon as the first snow came down.

I was afraid to go near them. I did not forget my lesson. I remember how every week one goose was started on the process of gaining weight. Twice or maybe three times a day a woman came over. She would sit on a pad on the floor and take the goose, making it lie down in front of her; she put one of her legs on the bird's back and the other one under its breast so that the goose could not move. The mouth was forcefully opened and handful after handful of corn was stuffed into it. The poor bird tried to fight off the cruelty, but it did not have a chance. This went on for two or three weeks. It was spaced so that every week one goose was ready for slaughter. On Thursdays, we took a goose to the shochet. (He was a very learned and trained person who had to cut the necks of the birds or animals in a special way to assure they were kosher and therefore edible for Jewish people.)

Mother prepared a terrific meal for the Sabbath from its meat and rendered the fat and placed it into a metal urn with the liver and some of the *grivens* (fried skin). The lid was locked and the urn was kept buried under the snow until the next week when the whole process was repeated with another goose.

Something happened with the last bird. While being stuffed with the corn it started to choke. I was told that a kernel went down the wrong pipe and now the goose could not breathe. We had to rush it to the *shochet*, who was usually able to dislodge the blockage, but this time he could not do it, so he had to cut its throat, and luckily it was kosher.

In a couple of months the urn was filled with the rendered fat and sealed; by then the contents were frozen solid. It was ready to be mailed. It took weeks before it reached its destination and was enjoyed tremendously by the whole family in America.

Winter Games

My brother Leonard (we called him Loli) was my mother's favorite, the only son among four daughters. He had been spoiled and the girls were always jealous. When Lolika (endearing term) got new skates, we would tease him for being Mom's pet, and at the same time wished that we were in his shoes. He got away with lots of things that we could not.

One winter my brother Loli talked me into helping him pump some water out of the well and pour it over our front yard to make a hockey field. As we were pouring, the water froze almost immediately. The next morning it was covered by snow. When my father saw what we had done, he was furious. It would be treacherous to feed the cows now. They could slip and break a leg, and that would be the end of them. The food would have to be hand-carried to them in buckets, and that was risky, too.

Eventually things quieted down and Leonard and I went out to sweep the snow off the ice so he could teach me to play hockey. He had ice skates and I did not. He made hockey sticks out of branches, and we used a wooden spool for the puck. I was supposed to hit the puck to him sort of slow, so it would slide on the ice, but somehow it went flying and hit him in the eye. That scared the daylights out of me, but he was not hurt and he just told me to be more careful. After that I did not feel like playing that game anymore.

School

It was close to my sixth birthday, and the time had come for my parents to decide which school to send me to. There were several choices, and some close by our house. Across the street was the Russian school, where my brother was a student. He was taught the *azbuka* (Russian alphabet) and the Czech language was only secondary. The other school was a few blocks away, and Slovak was taught there for four years, but since there was no high school to continue, it wasn't practical. All the above-mentioned schooling and books were provided by the Czechoslovakian government and it was free to us. The Hebrew School had a good reputation. It was a private establishment and the parents had to pay tuition. It cost too much for my parents.

Mother inquired further and came up with the Jewish School, which was different than the Hebrew School. It offered religious and secular education for four years, and after that the students were prepared for high school. It was also run by the government. I was accepted in that school in spite of not being six years old until October twenty ninth.

It took me almost two hours walking each way; it was hard at times, especially in winter when it was very cold and I had to walk on the river bank. The cold wind blew across the frozen river; I really had to move fast in order not to freeze to death. In the long run it was worth it.

My Seventh Birthday

The winter was cold in 1930 and started early. It was only October and people were shivering, although they were bundled up in their winter clothes. As I entered our house I had a special feeling, as if something was different, but I didn't know what. I forgot about my birthday. I was seven years old.

Father surprised me with something I had always wanted. He gave me a homemade sleigh. So many of my friends had their own that I had felt pretty left out in the winter time. Now I could hardly wait for the snow to come. Every morning when I woke up, the first thing was to run to the window and check for snow. My face must have shown the disappointment I felt when I came away from the window. I did not have to wait too long. One morning when I looked out, it seemed as if beyond our window there was a different world. The sun was radiant and the white snow sparkled as if millions of diamonds were covering the ground. It looked like a wonderland.

I ran to find my father, gave him a big hug and a kiss and thanked him for the hundredth time for the beautiful sleigh he had given me. I also asked him if he would like to come up to the hill and watch me ride down. He came with me, but told me that he could stay only for a short time because he was busy that morning. We walked to the hill together and since there were already a few boys and girls that I could join, Father said that he would watch me from below as I came down. That was okay with me. It was hard to walk uphill in the fresh snow, but we all made it. I sat on my sleigh, but did not know how to control it. I must have thought that it knew its way down. It sure did, and it went its own way. So many times I was sure that I would collide with someone or something, but somehow I found out that if I grabbed the rope that was tied to the front and pulled it to one side or the other I could make the sleigh go where I wanted it to go. This was a great discovery. I had so much fun that morning, I almost forgot that I still had school to attend in the afternoon, and I was almost late. I ran home and could not even eat my lunch from all the excitement I felt. I changed clothes, because after the snow had melted, I was wet. I picked up my books and a snack and ran to school. I got there just in time.

In class everyone was talking at the same time, until the teacher, Mrs. Horowitz, arrived. Then everything went quiet. She demanded and got lots of respect from all her students. I was always quiet in class, and never talked to anyone unless I was spoken to first. I was in shock when the teacher asked me what I had been up to. I really did not know what she meant, until she asked me why my cheeks were so red. What was I doing? I told her about my early morning sleigh ride experience. Mrs. Horowitz must have liked the subject well enough. She went on talking about a similar sleigh ride in her young life. Then she asked other children to talk about the snow and what they liked to do. I was beginning to realize how easy it was to become the center of attention without even trying.

Mother came home from the city a little bit later, and she gave me a box, and said, "Do you know that today is your birthday?" I said, "Yes, it is my 7th birthday!" In our house we did not celebrate birthdays, but our parents always tried to give us something on that day. It was always something we needed. This time I did not know what to expect. I did not really need anything special. Mom asked me to open the package. I opened it and there was a pair of shoes for me. I had never seen such beautiful shoes. They looked pretty much like the ones worn for ice skating, but the leather was hand-decorated and it looked special. (As I see it now, my mom must have liked them a lot as well.) In seconds they were on my feet, and they were a little snug. It hurt some part of my feet, but my mom said that these were the last shoes in this style and if they did not fit we could take them back, but we would have to choose another kind. I loved those shoes and did not want to give them up, so I said they fit pretty good and thanked her for the present.

I will never forget those shoes. They were high laced. I felt like a ballerina in them, but when I walked home from school wearing them, I suffered. I had to stop often to keep my foot from hurting. Soon I had blisters, and corns started to form on my small toes. When mom caught me limping, she wanted to know why. I had to tell her.

Mom was very upset because by then she could not replace the shoes. She did not let me wear them anymore. I had to wear my old shoes and, come to think of it, I never found out what happened to my beautiful shoes, but I still wear their marks on my feet. What a price for vanity!

Renee

My sister Renee was born in 1930; I was 7 years old and did not yet know about where babies came from. I only remember that a fat lady came to our house, and chased us out and said go play outside. She did not want us in the house. I was very scared and did not understand why my mother was screaming inside. We were not allowed to go in. Later, our neighbor, Aunt Mariska came over (she was not really our aunt, but we called all our elders "Aunt" and "Uncle") and took care of us. After a while I did not hear Mom scream anymore and shortly I heard a baby cry. Aunt Mariska gathered us together and told us that we had a new baby sister. I was so confused, wondering how all this came about. Nobody had time to answer my questions until later, when I was allowed to see the new baby. At first she seemed so ugly and wrinkled, that I could not look at her, and did not want to be close to her.

A day or two later Mother called me over as she was feeding the baby and told me to look at my beautiful sister. She was beautiful with her rosy cheeks and blue eyes. How did this big change happen? She called her Reisele Renee after my grandma. I was allowed to hold her. From that time on I spent lots of time with her. I loved her and I was happy to have another sister.

A couple of years later, my sister Herczi was old enough to start school, so we walked together. By then I was in second grade. Many times as we were walking home, a couple of gentile boys, just somewhat older than we were, started to chase us and throw stones at us.

One day my brother and I were skating on the street which was padded with snow, when those same boys were coming toward us walking home from school. I told my brother that they were always beating up on us. He caught both of them and banged them lightly one against the other and told them that he would give them a good beating if they ever bothered us again. I was very impressed with the results, because they never even came near us after that.

All through the four years of elementary school I was a shy little girl, very skinny, and a terrible eater. I remember that mother used to bribe me to finish my meat; she even gave me money. I also overheard her saying that she was worried about me, because I was so skinny, and she said that I was a homely kid. I grew up believing it and felt ugly. Many years later I found a picture here in America of my brother, my sister and I, and I think that Mother was right. I had an ugly haircut and I did not look very pretty.

If I Could Ride

I was about ten years old when riding a bicycle was my deepest desire. I did not have a bicycle, but I wanted to learn how to ride one. I bothered my father so much that he finally agreed to borrow one from the grocer across the street. Because of my father's bad leg he could not run after me and hold me, as I had seen some other fathers do.

I had a bike to practice on, but I was on my own. Too short to reach over the bar, I tried to ride it by pushing my leg under the bar. I found a quiet street and tried and tried, but each time I fell down. Sometimes the bike fell on top of me. I did not care that my knees and elbows were scraped, as long as the bike was not broken. I did not give up, and after a while I was able to turn the pedal twice and then three times, before I toppled over and then each time it lasted longer, until I was able to stay on for a longer time. My happiness almost complete, I was able to ride the bike back to the grocer, and thanked him for letting me use it. When he told me that I could borrow it any time, I was in seventh heaven. It took a week or more before I was able to ride again. Ugly scabs formed on my knees and elbows, and I had to wait until they healed. That did not hold me back too long. Even before I was healed, I borrowed the bike again. I was riding it, but now I did not fall as often as before. I still managed to scrape the scabs off and I was bleeding. It was time to quit. When I came home my mother wanted to know what happened and made me soak my sores, so that they would not get infected.

Infection set in first on my elbows, and then on my knees. I was in lots of pain, and couldn't even think of bike riding at the time. My arm was swollen, and I remember seeing a blue streak going from my elbow upwards. I showed it to my mother, and she took me to the doctor right away. There I was given a shot and some other treatment, and the blue slowly disappeared. I did not sleep much that night. The sores felt as if someone had been hitting them with a sledge hammer. It took a few weeks before they were completely healed. I did not try bike riding again for a long time.

Teenage Memories

When Iren Feigele was born, she was named after Mom's grandmother. Renee was 5 years old, Herczi was 10 and I was a big girl of 12. This time Aunt Mariska was sitting with me while Mom was in labor with the midwife, explaining to me some facts of life. Soon we heard the baby cry. She had lots of black hair and dark eyes. Now there were five of us, I had three sisters and a brother.

Also, when I was about twelve years old I had to have an operation on my neck, because of an abscess that had to be drained. After an examination, the doctors were talking in front of me and I heard them say that they should have waited with the operation a little longer; the wound was not healing as they thought it should. I was given some kind of radiation treatment, and after that everything was fine, except that I grew a streak of gray hair on the front of my head. It did not bother me at all, but when I got a little older, about sixteen, my mother thought I should do something about it.

One day on my way home from work, I stopped at a beauty shop and asked the owner if he could dye my gray hair to match the brown. I guess he saw that I didn't go to beauty shops too often and I didn't know anything about hair treatments or dyeing, so he felt he could tell me anything he wanted. He told me that he had to treat all my hair gradually, and he proceeded to work on it. The resulting color was a rusty red. I was afraid to go home.

When my mother saw me, she was furious. She asked me, "Why had I let him ruin my hair the way he did." I didn't know what was he doing, until I saw the results and then it was too late. He told me that he would bleach it out gradually, before he could put the brown color on properly. What did I know? I believed him. I thought I could wash the dye out with a strong solution, so I took ashes and tied them in a cloth and placed them into a large pot filled with water. Then I boiled it for several hours until it became very strong bleach. The women used to use it to bleach out the white linen when they were washing clothes. I took that bleach and washed my hair in it. Well, after my hair dried, it was bright orange. I didn't want to go on the street, I looked like a freak, but Mother said we were going to see that beautician right then, and we went. When he saw me he was shocked. He couldn't figure out what had happened. When I told him, he couldn't believe his ears. Of course he said that he couldn't do anything with it for awhile, and later he would bleach it out. Anyway, after awhile he made me into a honey blonde and since my hair is naturally dark, he had a sucker every two weeks for touch-ups. After a few visits, his wife asked me if I could do her alterations for the family in exchange for their work, which wasn't too bad after all.

Leonard's Journey to America

Aunt Esther was my mother's younger sister. In 1920, together with my grandmother and uncles, she immigrated to America. Throughout the years, Aunt Esther and Mother kept in close contact. They exchanged their children's photographs and I remember her sending pictures of her two little girls. Somehow I still remember their pretty little faces. Aunt Esther died at a very young age of cancer. Later, when my grandmother past away, my four uncles got together and decided to try and bring us to America again. Since my father had been refused entry before, because of his wounded leg, they planned to start with the oldest child. Their plan was to bring us out one by one, as we would reach a certain age. Since my brother Leonard was the oldest in the family, they sent him an Affidavit first. Mother was instructed to register the document at the American Consulate.

A long time went by before mom was notified by the Consulate that they were beginning to process the Affidavit. However, now they wanted more documents. Mother worked hard to obtain all the papers the Consulate asked for. As soon as she mailed in the requested documents, they wanted more. It seemed as if there would be no end to it. This process took a good couple of years.

In 1938 I finished high school. I had completed four years of elementary school, and four years of high school. With that, the mandatory schooling had been finished. I was planning to attend the gymnasium for further education.

The Happy House

There lived a family not too far from our house, which was known among us as "the happy house." They were the Hirschbergers. That house was always full of life. Yachet Neni (Aunt Jetti) was a nice old lady. Her husband was a morose man, who worked hard and was a good provider; he also liked to hit the bottle now and then but he was harmless. They had quite a few children who were already grown, and all but three daughters and a son lived in America. One of the daughters was married and lived elsewhere with her own family; the other two lived at home even after they were married. They always had guests in the house, and every time I went there with my mother, they were either dancing or playing cards and seemed to have lots of fun. That home was better furnished than anybody else is in the community. It always looked elegant and immaculate. I loved to visit there; it was always filled with good stuff. Yachet Neni always gave us some delicious cakes and milk while we were in her house. She liked Mother a lot, her daughters Bela and Blanka were just a little younger than my mother and so they came to our house often. As a matter of fact, Blanka used to baby-sit for us every time when Mother went to see a Yiddish play that came to town. Mother mostly went with Bela; she was closer to Mom's age.

Later both sisters left for America. Yachet Neni was very lonely after that, and she came to our house frequently, crying all the time. Her son was working for the Electric Company, therefore they had electricity in their house; we didn't. When my brother Leonard left for America, Mother would cry all the time, and it helped when Yachet Neni came over and they talked. She became my mother's advisor.

Uzhorod - Overtaken

In 1938, Great Britain and Germany made a deal to give Czechoslovakia to Germany. In the same year the Hungarian army, which was allied with the Germans, marched in and occupied Uzhorod without a battle. I am sorry to say that the older generation was very glad to see them. Jews and Gentiles alike were waving the

Hungarian flags welcoming them. They were happy, believing that now everything would be the way it used to be before World War I.

Under Czechoslovakian law, when a healthy boy became 20 years old, he had to enlist in the army. After the Hungarian occupation, the Czech soldiers in our part of the country were transferred into the Hungarian Army. All Jewish soldiers, however, were taken out of the army and placed into Forced Labor Camps. There, they were forced, as slaves, to dig ditches, build streets and work in mines. The Hungarian government next began to round up all able Jewish men from 18 to 45 years of age. These men were also sent to the Forced Labor Camps. On occasion, a laborer would be allowed to come home for a three or four day leave. There were hardly any men left at home, only the old, the very young, or the disabled remained.

Soon disappointment came after disappointment. First the change in currency came. We had to give seven Czech crowns for one Hungarian Pengo; that was bad, but still not the worst. Next, the Hungarian soldiers bought up almost everything from the local stores for very little money and shipped it to the motherland, as they called Hungary. That forced the prices up for us. The merchants had to reorder the merchandise and pay Hungarian money, which made everything very expensive.

Leonard's Escape

Toward the end of that year, Mother received the Visa and the Passport for Leonard, who was 17 years old. Everyone seemed to be happy and envious at the same time. This was a big happening at that time to get permission from the new regime to leave the country. Only Mother had cried all the time, "Her only son was leaving".

In 1939 Mother and Leonard were waiting to find out, where and when he would board the Ship. The Hungarian Army had taken over our city, and who knew if they would honor the arrangements made for his departure? Luckily, they did, and when the time had arrived for Leonard to leave, Mother, Father, Herczi, Renee, Iren, and I walked to the train station. Quite a few of Leonard's friends were there also. We all wished him a good trip and a happy and successful life in America. We all cried a lot but Mother could not stop crying for weeks.

Leonard took the train all the way to Nazi occupied France where, by some miracle, he was able to board the last ship out, which happened to be the Queen Mary. His passport was stamped with Nazi swastika. He arrived safely to Detroit, Michigan, where Uncle Morris and family were waiting for him. At first we received letters and money from Leonard, but soon the letters came opened and censured; shortly after that, they stopped altogether.

Leonard's Passport Book

**Swastika in Leonard's Passport when he left occupied France on the Queen Mary.
He was one of the last of the Jews let out of Europe by the Nazi's.**

**The Klein's 1942/43 (Left to Right) Herczi 16, Hajnal 46,
Iren 5, Renee 12, Elemer 47, Lili 19**

The Klein girls (about 1944)

My World Turned Upside - Down

One day as I was walking home from school with some friends, I saw Ruzenka my schoolmate running toward us, telling us in tears about the orders her family received to pack up and leave Uzhorod. Ruzenka's family, which was not Jewish, had transferred from Prague, shortly after the establishment of Czechoslovakia in 1918. Her father worked for the Czech government. They had lived in Uzhorod, for almost two decades, establishing a nice family and livelihood. Now they were being forced to leave. That was a great shock to me, because my family was never in with politics we never talked about the war. I was actually very ignorant about what was going on in the world. At the age of fourteen I did not fully understood the situation, but I learned real fast.

When the Hungarians took over our part of Czechoslovakia, they came out with different orders daily. More and more restrictions and hardships were placed on the Jewish people. We had to prove that our great grandfathers lived in Hungary and therefore we also belonged there. We had kilograms of papers to prove all that plus my father served under the Austro-Hungarian Army, where he got injured. In spite of that, his license to operate his small butcher shop was revoked with all the other Jewish owners.

In the dark of the night, large military trucks came in and picked up families that had lived there for decades. At some point their ancestors had come from Russia or Poland. We assumed that they were taken back to where they came from, but no one knew anything for sure. They just disappeared.

One such family was the Hershkovic family. Mr. Hershkovic was a tall hefty man, honest and a good neighbor. He had a large family of about ten children. I often visited them as a child to say hello every now and then. I used to like being in their large and warm kitchen where they were cooking a lot. The smell of food was very nice. Their oldest son was about 3 years older than I. He was a very nice young man. Mrs. Hershkovic was very proud of him. He got married a couple months before the whole family was taken away. I do not know how many more families were taken at the same time, but I missed them. No one ever heard of them. They just vanished.

Poor Jews where were they taken? No one knew what to do about it, so nothing was done. Later we found out that they were taken to Poland to be killed, and that some Polish gentiles were very happy to help the Nazis do that.

Some of the boys from the Labor Camps were allowed to come home for a few days once in a while, and told us about what they had seen on the Polish border. The Nazis brought the bulldozers and dug a large deep hole, forced the old men, (many with beard) women and children to strip and line up around the edge of the hole. The Nazis machine-gunned them from behind and they all fell into the hole. The bulldozer quickly covered them with the dirt. Some were dead some were injured, and alive, all were covered with the heavy dirt. From time to time more of these horrible stories were filtering out. On a Friday evening my dad came home from the temple with tears in his eyes. The Rabbi told the congregation about how many of the non Hungarian Jewish families that had been taken away, were lined up by the river and machine gunned down by the S.S. soldiers into the river. At the services, he forbade us to eat fish, because they might have been feeding off the Jewish bodies. Everyone said Kaddish for the killed Jews and cried. We hoped and prayed that this would not happen to us, since we were so far from Poland.

My family had no plans for the future; it was almost as if they were just waiting in limbo for what may come. They just never talked about what will happen to us. With four young girls and no money, it was hard enough to survive, let alone plan an escape. I never heard them talking about any of it even when we got together with the Jewish relatives and friends.

After the Hungarian occupation, the Czech schools were closed right after my graduation. Everything became Hungarian. I did not want to go to school anymore. I hated the new regime.

According to the system in our part of Europe, the boys and girls at 14 were ready to choose a profession or trade. Some decided to continue their studies and went on to higher schooling, while others entered an apprenticeship. It was hard to decide at that age what trade to choose and be contented doing it the rest of your life. Usually the parents helped with the decision and also with locating a suitable master, with whom they signed a contract for two or three years. There was not that big of a choice available. Tailor-seamstress, barber-beauty operator, salesperson, baker, shoemaker, butcher, etc. The deal was that the master would teach the trade and in exchange the apprentice would obey and respect him and work for the duration of the contract. I had to make up my mind, and took my mother's advice to become a seamstress.

Mother found me a seamstress shop, where I was signed up at fourteen as an apprentice for two years without any pay. I had to walk a long way to work in the morning, then walk home for lunch and come back to work all afternoon until six. There was no fun for me at work but I did not give it up.

I never liked sewing very much, but I created a fantasy and that kept me going. Since we were always hoping to go to America, I dreamt that someday I would be a good seamstress and a fashion designer and when I came to America I would open a fancy salon. The wealthy clients would come from all over to view my line, and we would serve tea and cookies, and ultimately I would become very, very successful.

The first year of my apprenticeship was a waste of time. The boss did not trust a young girl or boy with any work pertaining to the trade he was to teach. For instance, in tailoring, most of the time an apprentice was not allowed to do much more than ripping out the helper's mistakes. (A helper was a person who was working for pay.) The rest of one's time was used being a servant, running errands for his family, babysitting for his kids, or sometimes even cleaning house.

In order to receive the certificate of accomplishment at the end of our term, we had to attend trade school twice weekly. Once apprenticeship was completed, the next step was to find a job as a helper if the boss you already had did not retain you. The pay was small, but as time went on and experience was acquired, your salary would be raised. After about three or four years working as a helper, one was ready to open his or her own shop, and so the cycle started all over again.

The Changes Came Gradually and Systematically

The time came very soon when all Jewish licenses were revoked. Jewish store owners had to stand by and watch as they were being robbed legally. A gentile person, usually someone we knew and had helped all our life, was placed as manager into every Jewish store and gradually it was taken over by him, merchandise and all. To add insult to injury, the former proprietors had to stay and teach the new owners the business before they were dismissed.

When I became sixteen years old, I met a young man by the name of Laczi Klein and we became close friends. We dated a lot and thought we were in love. My mother set a curfew, we had to be home by eight in the evening and we were. We used to go to afternoon dances or to the movies or just walking up and down the river bank, which was pretty crowded on a Saturday afternoon. All the boys and girls were out. We always had a pleasant time.

One time Laczi and his friend Willie Lebovic took me out for dinner. We went to a fancy place called Jaczicks. They served outdoors in a beautiful garden setting with music playing all night long. I was so impressed; I had never been in a restaurant like this. When Willie asked me if he could order dinner for me, I happily agreed. When the food was brought to the table, my plate looked as delicious as it tasted. I had no idea what I was eating but it sure was good. Afterwards when we were eating our rich dessert, Willy wanted to know how I liked my dinner. I told him that it was great. Then he told me that it was pork. I told him that he shouldn't have done that, knowing I was Kosher. It spoiled the whole evening. That was the very first time I ever tasted pork as it was against my religion to eat it.

Laczi was a couple of years older than I. We thought everything was just perfect between us and that someday soon, when the war would end, we would get married. My parents liked him, and his family liked me. However, when Laczi turned 20, he was taken to a forced labor camp by the Hungarians.

Initially, the boys from the camps were allowed to come home on furloughs. I went out dancing either with Laczi or with one of our friends when Laczi was away. The time had come when our gentile friends, who became Nazi sympathizers, stood up and shouted, "Jews out!" We were outnumbered, but even if we had not been, there was not much we could do. So we walked out of the dance hall and never went back. We made house parties where our Jewish friends got together. We would sing and dance and make our own fun.

On Sundays, we went to dances given at the dancing school which were attended mostly by Jewish youngsters. I remember they had a white gypsy orchestra, all young boys, who were very talented musicians. (The gypsies lived a secluded life by the river Ung. Most of them had dark complexion, but there were some white gypsies also between them.) Once in a while they held dances in the evening also. My mother accompanied me on those occasions, since I wasn't allowed to go out in the evening without a chaperon.

A new law came out in around 1943, stating that the men from the labor camps were no longer being given furloughs. On occasion, they might be let out for a few days in the event of a family emergency. So everyone tried to use every opportunity to bring their loved ones home, even for such a short time. Even I took advantage of the situation. When a friend of mine suddenly lost her husband, I sent a telegram to Laczi which read, "Come at once. Steve passed away." He got a four-day leave and came home, but before he could go back. I had to get a copy of the death certificate to prove that he had a good reason. Other than that we lived quietly and always tried to remain in the background.

I Loved to Dance and I Still Do

It seemed that we got use to our misery and adapted to it. After all, we were teenagers and needed an outlet. My friends and I got together on Sunday afternoons in the hall of the dancing school. Music was provided by the White Gypsy Junior Orchestra and we danced the time away.

One Sunday afternoon, whom did I see dancing with a young man next to me, but my sister Herczi! She was wearing my dress and my shoes and she seemed to be having a great time. Herczi was growing up, and she turned out to be a very pretty little girl. Well developed in the right places, she was a daring little thing.

At first I was angry with her for taking my clothes without asking and I was sure Mother did not know of her being there. She would not have allowed her to go. She always used to say that she could not afford two grown daughters at the same time.

Somehow, Herczi persuaded Mother to let her go, so after that we began going to the dances together. Once, there was to be a masquerade party and we both got dressed in costume and walked to the place, only to find out that it was the wrong date. It was embarrassing.

I always had a lot of fun at those dances. I was quite popular and not a bad dancer. One day as I was dancing with a friend and neighbor, Schwartz Patyu, the band leader tapped my partner's shoulder, and he finished the dance with me. I was embarrassed. He was a gypsy and what would people say? But he was cute and a good dancer. He asked me which was my favorite song and I told him "La Paloma." After that, whenever I came through the door, he stopped whatever the band was playing and started on La Paloma. Everybody teased me about it, but it was fun. At least we could forget our problems for those few hours.

Life in General

Life was pretty hard for us. My father could not sell meat, and money was scarce. Now we were short of food as well, because Mother was forced to sell most of it so she could buy us shoes for the winter. We never even tasted butter, sour cream, fresh green vegetables, eggs or other goodies any more. All were sold, since the cash was needed for other necessities.

My mother was a great seamstress. Poor thing, she never owned a tape measure, chalk or pins, but she was always able to cut out a dress and sew it up in no time. I, on the other hand, was taught a more complex approach to sewing which included basting, measuring and two or three fittings, before I could finish a garment inside and out. Consequently, it took me much longer than my mother to sew a dress. Now that I was not working at a job any more, Mother and I decided to join forces and let some people know surreptitiously that we were open for business.

By then a good piece of material for a dress was not available at the stores. Everything that was sold was synthetic. Sometimes the material fell apart after the garment was washed. I befriended a Jewish man who had owned a fabric store before the Hungarians took it from him. He had a private inventory of quality cloth material that he had hidden in his home. He sold me some for a price that allowed me to make a few Pengo profit when I sold it. I showed the material to some gentile people I thought I could trust and they became very excited about it. I told them I could only sell it if they would let me make their dresses for them. I was able to make about five dresses this way.

I saved the scrap leftover materials and ripped up old clothing and steamed it so that I could use it to make my own clothing. I designed my own styles, and received many compliments.

There were a couple of gentile housewives who asked me to make some of my designs for them. They paid my price for the first one and then went to their gentile seamstresses to make copies of my designs. It was a losing battle.

Life under the Hungarians was brutal in more ways than one. Anti-Semitism was raging. The favorite subject of cartoonists was Jews with exaggerated noses. Social life for Jews was becoming non-existent. I found work as a helper. By now most people worked without a license, since they had to eat and feed their children, but heaven help the one who was reported. That person was taken away and in most cases the family would not even know where. They were treated like criminals and the news media really had a field day printing all kinds of atrocities about the black marketing Jew.

The time went by, and every now and then as I was going to work I saw some Jewish young people thrown into the "Black Limousine" by the Hungarian fascist party officers. In most cases those people were never seen again. Occasionally they let somebody out. I often wondered if it was done so that they would tell about the terrible torture those unfortunate youngsters had to go through. Mostly they were accused of being Communists, or someone reported them for listening to a foreign radio broadcast or whatever. One was guilty until proven innocent, exactly the opposite as in the United States. When people are oppressed and abused, the way we were in those days, they live one day at a time in fear.

I remember a third cousin; I didn't even know him, just knew of him. He was arrested for allegedly belonging to the underground partisan group. I do not know if he was reported by someone or what happened, but he was taken into the "Kem Elharito Building" where the spies were taken. There the Hungarians tortured the accused prisoners to make them talk. This poor boy was put through the most inhumane tortures that only a madman could invent. Afterwards, when his whole body was raw and bloody, they brought in his parents. The mother was very ill, but they made her come in to see him in that dreadful condition. No matter what had been done to him, he would not confess or tell on his comrades. The effect on the parents and the rest of the Jewish community was terrible.

Some people ran off and tried to cross over to Russia, where some were shot by the Russians as spies. There was no future for us. A few people left for Palestine, but that took cash and lots of idealism, because you had to enter illegally; and one never knew how and where they would end up.

By that time some of my friends had left for Budapest and found work there. God, how I would have liked to go, but my mother never permitted any of us to leave home. She felt that we were more secure at home together. As it happened, most of those who were in Budapest stayed there all through the war, and were saved from going to the concentration camps.

Taking Chances and Paying For It

It had been a long time since the Jewish community had had any meat. Kosher slaughtering was forbidden and so the Jews had to make do without meat. My father, with the help of two young men, decided to slaughter a cow kosher, so that the people in the community would have meat for the approaching Jewish holiday. As I came home that day, I saw a long line of people leading up to our front door. First of all, it scared me out of my wits. I thought something had happened to someone in my family, but when I found out that they were waiting for the illegal meat, I got very angry and questioned them and warned them of the fact that we could all go to jail if we were caught. I brought out a piece of paper and a pencil and took their order and promised to deliver the meat to their homes. Only then were they willing to leave.

In the big scare we forgot to fill one order for a very unfriendly neighbor, but by then there was nothing left even for us. This person became very angry and made all kinds of threats. I pleaded with him to be understanding, but there was nothing we could do about it. Soon we cleaned up all the mess and the two boys came over to help me deliver the meat. It was a risky business. We put the orders on our bicycles, some of the blood was dripping out of the packages, if someone had seen it, and we would have been in big trouble. Well, we thanked God for helping us get through with that messy deal, only it was a bit too soon, because the boys Larry and Patyu still had to deliver the skin to the dealer. I remember that they rented a wagon and a horse for that purpose, only they did not go very far before they were stopped. The police (kakas tolas csendor) brought them back to the house, and they started to search the house for the hind quarters which is not kosher and which was to be sold to the gentiles the next day.

I remember Mother giving me all the money they had taken in that day telling me to try and bribe the officer, because by now we were in big trouble. The officer must have been a decent person because he said to me: "Miss, save your money. There is nothing I can do. We are here, because someone reported your father and we just have to look until we find the meat so we can take it as evidence." And they did find it. At that point they forced my father into the wagon and asked him who else was involved with him. Poor Father was so scared that he probably would have told them about the boys. At this point I even surprised myself with my fast thinking up a white lie, which I blurted out immediately. I told the officers that there was no one at all; the cows got loose in the stall and began to fight, one cow stabbed the other with its horn so deep that she would have died anyway, so my Father cut her throat so that at least the meat would be edible, and since it was too much for us, we tried to sell some of it. I do not know if the officers believed me, but they wrote what I said in their report. We stuck to that story all through.

My father was taken to jail. At first we did not know where, and we were advised by someone to go to a certain party who could help free my father quickly. His name was Roth Naczi. I looked him up and talked to him. His first question was: How much money do you have? My answer was, "250 pengos." He said it wasn't enough. 300 more pengos were needed and that it was not for him, but for the officials who would help us. So we had no choice but to sell a cow and raise the money that way. Needless to say, we gave him all the money he asked for and we were waiting for some results. Days went by and nothing happened, he kept on stalling us and the days became weeks.

My poor Father was locked up like a criminal and the news media did their usual things reporting on the front page how Elemer Klein, the Jew, was caught black-marketing, when all he wanted to do was feed his starving family. It was in the newspaper that he was held in the city jail. Herczi and I went to the jail to find out if we could see Father. A nice and friendly police man was the guard, and he took us in. Poor Father was in very bad shape. He hardly ate anything, because it was not Kosher. Mother started to cook lunches and dinners for him and we took it to him every day.

Well at this point, things were deteriorating and we did not know where to turn. Since I was the eldest now at home, the entire burden was on my shoulders. Herczi helped mother at home and that was hard work. I kept going after Roth Naczi and since I could not show him the resentment and anger I felt toward him, I pleaded with him to help us. I don't think he knew how, but apparently he wanted to get rid of me, so, lucky for me, he sent me to see Mr. Szilagyi, a real gentleman. He was a very influential and respected Jew even in those days. He used to own a big hotel in our town which he had to give up. A learned and charitable man, he had at one time been very prosperous.

I will never forget the time when I went to see Mr. Szilagyi for the first time. I was petrified and started to sob so hard that he could not understand me at all. He was so gentle as he said to me; "Let's start all over and please calm down so that I could understand what you're saying and see if I could help you." Somehow I did just that, and later he told me to come back the next day and he would think of something. My hopes were up again, and I went home.

Now, the terrible journey had just begun. All this time we were taking food to the jail for my father, so he could observe the dietary laws, as he did not eat the food they gave him. During this time we got to know the police captain and the other personnel quite well; they let us in most any time. My sister Herczi and I were the ones going in and out, visiting my father a few times every day. Meantime mother was trying to make a go of things at home. Herczi helped a lot, Renee was number four and she was an apprentice in a photo studio, and Iren the youngest one was too young to do much, but everyone pitched in with something.

Next morning I met with Mr. Szilagyi. This was one of many meetings to come and he never took a penny from me. Mr. Szilagyi said we would have to try an appeal process to get father out, however, we had to act fast because all prisoners held in local jails without any trial, would be sent to a concentration camp, from which they were never seen again. So we first had to figure out a way to keep father from being transported to the camp. He gave me an address and the name of a Hungarian doctor, who was the chief physician for all of the local jails. The doctor could help keep father from being transported if he could determine that my father could not travel because of illness.

I went to see this doctor, whose name I don't remember anymore; he had so many titles that I had to practice all night so that I could address him the right way. I came to his big fancy house shaking in my boots, to find out that he was not in. To my luck, a man I knew well was cleaning the windows and he told me when to come back so that I could find him at home.

I came the next day and sure enough the doctor was in. I tried to introduce myself to him and planned to tell him my problems the way Mr. Szilagyi instructed me to do, but I was so scared of him that I started to cry, and I was again given time to collect myself, so that I could talk to him.

I told him the story of how my mother was becoming ill and the whole burden was resting heavily on my shoulders and the children were crying at home because they were hungry and miserable. I think he felt sorry for me, because he promised to see my father the next morning at the line-up. He instructed me to wait for him in front of the jail building and he would tell me then, what he wanted me to do. I waited and waited, but he didn't show.

I was there again the next morning, and met him in front of the jail. He told me to come to his house that afternoon to talk about it. I went home and told my mother what he said.

Mother thought I should take something special to the doctor to gain his favor. So she picked a large basket of peaches and under which she put five kilograms of sugar, which at that time was next to impossible to get.

Well, I don't know whether the gift worked on the doctor or he did what he did out of the goodness in his heart, as I found out he was truly a very good person. He told me to tell my father that he should complain about his health and fake faintness the next morning at the daily exercises. That way he could single him out, talk to him and examine him in his office.

The next morning he examined my father, and noticed something wrong with his leg. As I mentioned earlier, my father was shot in the leg in the First World War, and as a result, he walked with a limp. The doctor was then able to require that my father not be transported.

The doctor next, advised me to have someone knowledgeable write an appeal and include information about his war wound and the fact that he was not committing any crime, since he was only trying to feed his family and did not want to watch all that meat go to waste.

We knew a man in our community who was highly educated and a fine elderly gentleman. He knew my father well and also the rest of the family. He agreed to write the necessary document, and he wrote it well. I remember him, a tall slim man with a long beard. His name was, I believe, Kontros Bacsi. I passed his house daily, and if he was outside, I always used to greet him and he replied very cheerfully.

The next day I took the document first to Mr. Szilagyi and after he read it and was real pleased with it, he told me to make sure that the doctor signed it. I met the doctor and he promised to sign it, but first I needed to take the document to the police captain to begin the appeal process before he could sign it. I had to pay a fee for that, and the captain said "Miss, you are wasting your time and money. Nobody ever got off for a crime of black marketing." The Hungarians called my father's deeds a crime of black marketing.

All through this time I was in touch with the doctor and with Mr. Szilagyi and acted on their advice. After I talked with the doctor, he assured me that he would do his best. He would state in a letter that my father was too ill to travel on the train, and would not reach his destination alive. As I look back now, for the life of me I am unable to understand their reasoning. Judging from their actions, I don't think that they cared if we lived or died. Yet, this letter possibly saved my father's life at that point.

A couple of days later, I met with Mr. Szilagyi, and he told me that I would have to go to Budapest and talk to, or rather appeal to, the judge and beg for my father's freedom. He said; "Do not go to the Joint, (an aid society for Jews; the Joint Distribution Committee) because they will send with you an attorney, and the judge will throw out both of you."

He told me to go alone and, in the name of my young sisters and ill mother, beg for his help. He also told me that there were two judges handling these cases, one a cruel person and the other more lenient. It would depend on my luck which one I might get. He also told me their names and their long titles. In parting he told me to keep in close contact with him, so that he could tell me when to leave.

Budapest is the capital city of Hungary. I had never been further than ten kilometers from my home before (except the brief trip to Prague, when I was only 5 years old), and now I had to go to a large city all by myself. It was scary.

The day came quickly when Mr. Szilagyi sent for me, and when I went to see him, he informed me that the next evening I would have to leave on the train and travel all night, so that I could arrive in Budapest in the morning.

Food was scarce, especially good food, so the big preparations began. My mother made fried chicken and some cakes for me. I found out the addresses of some friends that lived in Budapest. I thought that this way I would have some place to leave my suitcase, while I would have to run around. I left on the train at about six in the evening toward the unknown.

I must admit, the trip itself was quite an experience. The train compartment was very comfortable, with benches around the walls and in the middle. It was not over-crowded and after a while people became friendly and talked to their neighbors. I sat in a spot where I was facing everybody, and next to me sat a young man, who introduced himself and asked where I was from. As we started to talk, he told me that his uncle in Budapest held a very high government position and that he was staying with him. He was saying how much he would like to get together with me while I stayed in Budapest and if I would give him the address of the people I am visiting, he would see to it that I would get a formal invitation to his uncle's house. Of course I did not tell him the reason I was going there, and he assumed that I was on vacation. Each time we stopped at a station, he always jumped off the train and brought back with him whatever that particular station was offering - cherries, nuts, candies, drinks. I felt flattered with all this attention, and as we were nearing our destination, I tried to tell him that he would never see me again, and he kept saying that he wanted to show me the city as it should be seen. He was very good-looking, and, as naive as I was, I felt that there had to be some strings attached to his interest in me. Who knows? At that point I did not trust any man.

To tell him he could not see me, I did not think it would be fair of me, after all the nice things he did for me on the train, without giving any reason. He treated me like a lady, so I told him that he would not want me to come to his uncle's house, because I was Jewish. He did not believe me. It is true that I had long wavy blond hair and a medium light complexion. I was often told by gentiles that I did not look Jewish. I had no idea why or how a Jew looked different. Some Jewish people had longer noses, or mostly dark hair and dark eyes. One must realize that most of the gentiles were blond with blue eyes, so a person with dark curly hair, dark eyes and maybe a hooked nose would stand out. However, I would say that only a small percentage would fit that description, but that was how the Hungarian cartoonists portrayed a Jew. As I said, he did not believe me, and his answer was: "Sure, if you are Jewish, I am Mohammedan." He was laughing as if he had just heard a good joke.

When we arrived in Budapest, it was about eight o'clock in the morning. People were rushing back and forth. I was shaking inside and fought with myself to remain calm on the outside. I did not want anyone to see how scared I was, especially not him. He gave me his telephone number and asked me to call him later in the day. He also told me whom to ask for directions when needed, and we parted company forever.

I took the street car to the first address of a very good friend of ours. When my boyfriend had to go to the labor camp, his friend moved to Budapest, and found himself a job. Unfortunately, he and his landlady had already left for work, so no one was at home. I found the same situation at two other addresses. I was getting increasingly frustrated, but I had one more place to try. It was the address of Bert Harvey, a boy I grew up with. I went up to that apartment, praying that someone should be home, because it was my last resort.

I was lucky; the landlady was at home with a friend who was not working. I cannot describe the feeling in my heart as I rang the door bell. The door was opened by a very pleasant lady maybe in her middle age; she had a pretty smile on her face when she asked me how she could help me. I introduced myself quickly and told her that I was looking for a friend, and I needed a place to leave my suitcase while I took care of some business. I told them my story, and they were very sympathetic and helpful.

She called Bert, and I talked with him. He was to come home at seven in the evening and offered to take me out at that time. Things started to happen. The lady of the house had to go to work, but she told me I was welcome to spend the night if I needed to. Her friend also turned out to be a jewel; she volunteered to go with me to the courthouse. I do not know how I could have found it by myself. As it was, this lady turned out to be my friend also. Both were strangers to me, who had never laid eyes on me before and probably knew that they would not see me again.

Well, the two of us started out for the office where I was to see the judge. As I was approaching his door, I noticed his name and realized that my luck must have run out, because the name on the door belonged to the so called mean judge. I had been scared to death to begin with, but now I felt sure that all was lost. I had no choice, I had to go on.

Shivering all over, I went in with a copy of the petition in my hand preparing myself for the worst. I introduced myself and started to tell him the reason for my visit. I knew I was talking too fast, but I wanted to cover all I had to say, before I broke down in tears. What I did not know was that the man was hard of hearing and therefore didn't understand very much of what I was telling him. Sometimes people that can't hear have a tendency to speak louder than necessary and that actually happened here. He shouted at me to slow down and speak louder. By then I was in tears; I handed him the petition while trying to tell him about how my father was arrested and mother was ill, and there was no one to help us, which was true enough, and I pleaded with him to pardon my father. I guess he was not as bad as his reputation portrayed him, because he did have compassion after all. He really felt sorry for me. He tried to calm me down and said, "I remember the case. I reviewed it the other day and sent it back to Ungvar." By now I really thought all was over and started to cry uncontrollably. He informed me at that point that there was no reason to cry, he only sent it back because it lacked the signature of the chief doctor in Ungvar. He promised that when the document came back, he would do the best he could. I asked him if he thought that I should wait in Budapest until he had made his decision.

He answered me with a question: "Do you have any close relatives here with whom you can stay?" I had to tell him I had no one. "In that case," he said it almost like an order, "take the next train home and see to it that the doctor signs the petition and mails it back to me as soon as possible, and then I will see what I can do for you."

Well, I did not know what to believe; I was not at all sure whether I had accomplished anything. My new friend kept encouraging me and told me over and over that all would be well. I decided to take the next train home, so she took me to the station and before I left, I gave her most of the food I had. When she saw the fried chicken, her eyes just opened wide and she said that she had not had anything like that in a long time. I asked her to say goodbye to Bert and the landlady for me and to give my thanks to both, but I especially owed my thanks to her, and I let her know how grateful I was. We said our goodbyes and I boarded the train for home.

By now I had been on the road round the clock without any sleep, so I just slept through the night on the train. I arrived at home about six in the morning, with mixed feelings. I was angry at that doctor for not keeping his word, I felt guilty for not being able to do better after all the money that was spent on this trip.

As I walked home from the station, some early risers were out in the street, and since everyone in Radvanka knew everyone else's business, I was approached by several people. They all wanted to know what I had accomplished. Sadly I had to tell them that I did not know yet. As soon as I got home and told my mother what had happened, I went right to sleep. It seemed as if I had hardly fallen asleep, when my mother woke me up and told me it was time to get up, because it was one thirty and I had to meet the doctor at two o'clock. I could hardly keep my eyes open, but I got dressed, hopped on my bicycle and was on my way.

Luckily for me, my boyfriend Laci had left me his bike when he was taken to the forced labor camp. It was a racer, and I loved to ride on it fast. I had long blond hair and it just swayed when I was riding against the wind.

I waited for the doctor in front of the jail for an hour, but he did not come. By then I was exhausted physically and emotionally. I went home in tears. The next day I was waiting for him at two o'clock again, but this time he came and told me right away that he had already mailed the documents back and now all I had to do was wait for the reply.

About two weeks later, I received a message from the police captain that he wanted to see me. I went to his office and saw a long line of women waiting to see him, so I stood behind the last one and waited my turn. All of a sudden I was grabbed roughly out of the line, and when I looked up, I saw the captain and he took me with him to the office. He asked me what I was doing in that line, I told him that I was waiting for my turn to see him. He looked at me and said: "Don't you know who those women are?" Of course I did not, so he explained that they were the city prostitutes waiting for their checkups. This was embarrassing…

Afterwards, he pulled out some documents and said, "This is your father's release. Congratulations to you. To my knowledge you are the first one who has actually been able to obtain a release for the same crime."

The next day my father was free. The news spread fast and people came to our house to ask me how I did it. They had relatives who were arrested for the same or a similar crime and were paying large amounts of money to attorneys and saw no results. How can one answer questions like that? It was luck and lots of hard work. It was luck to be able to get the help of Mr. Szilagyi, and the fact that I was a young girl pleading for my father's freedom and life, helped.

Learning to Swim

In Uzhorod the winters were very cold and summers were hot especially when it did not rain for a while. This incident happened to me on a day sometime in July; it was extremely hot that day and also at night. I decided to do something to cool off. I could not swim and it was embarrassing just to sit in the water, so I took my bathing suit with me and before I left work, I changed into it and walked toward home on the river bank. When I came to a spot where hardly any people were present, I decided that this would be as good a place as any to try swimming on my own. I went down to the water, took my wrap off and went in. At first it was pleasant, but as I went in deeper, I was scared. By then the water reached my waistline and I tried to make the swimming motions I had practiced so many times on the grass. Well, I knew that rivers can be treacherous, unlike a swimming pool, also that this river had been known to claim several lives every season, but I was determined to try to learn how to swim. Little did I know that the reason for this spot not being crowded was that there was a strong current and everybody who had a little sense knew enough to stay away from it.

Before I realized what was happening to me, I felt an undertow pulling me down. I was unable to stop and lost control altogether. Needless to say, I panicked. I had not counted on this, so I did not know what to do. My ego did not let me cry out for help, so I swallowed more water than I wanted to. (Maybe that is the reason why I don't like water to this day.)

Everything was happening much too fast, all the things that I had not done yet, the life I had not enjoyed yet, how would my parents take my death, all these thoughts came to mind in that instant. I was sure that this was the end and that there was no way out. I went under a couple of times yet never uttered a sound, a cry for help.

I started to pray to God for help and forgiveness; I know He must have heard me, because just about that moment I reached a large rock, grabbed on to it and was saved. I was shaking all over for a long time and never have I forgotten that incident. With God's help I made it that time.

I am still terrified of the water even though all this happened about 60 years ago. Since then, I managed to learn to swim a little, enough to be safe in the water but I can't submerge my face, and while I can swim across the width of the pool I cannot swim across the length.

In 1944 Purim was celebrated in a subdued way. Everyone felt a certain tension in the air. In our household we had to do without a lot of things, especially when it came to food. This year Mother could not afford to bake too many cakes, but as she was a proud soul, she managed to bake some and faked the rest. For example, she waited until someone sent the cakes to her first and then used those cakes to add to her own. Luckily for us, Mother was a very good housekeeper and did the best she could with what she had, to feed us.

A couple of days after Purim, Yachet Neni came to visit and talked to my mother for a long time. The next day I got a big surprise. Mother bought me a beautiful camel coat; she said it was for Passover. To this day I can't figure out where she got the money for it, but I did find out that Yachet Neni had something to do with it. They both felt that I was a big girl and should be dressed accordingly. I was very grateful to both of them.

I didn't have my new coat for more than a week, when the order came out that all Jews must wear a yellow Star of David on their lapels. So, one went on my coat also.

Lili and Hajnal (Mom) just before all Jews
were required to wear the yellow star.

Mother had a beautiful hand-embroidered bedspread made of organdy, which had a yellow lining. I had a great idea, I asked mother's permission to use the lining to make stars out of it and sell them. She told me to go ahead, I made the first sample from cardboard and after that I made the stars for most of the Jewish people in the area. For myself, I even made a scarf to match the star. Needless to say, the money came in handy.

By that time we heard rumors that the S.S. soldiers were in the nearby villages and had raped several Jewish girls, so, naturally, we were scared of them.

One day I decided to visit my prosperous great aunt, who lived about a good hour's walk from our house. I asked my girlfriend to come along with me. The street was pretty deserted at the time, and as we were walking, we saw two S.S. officers coming toward us. We were scared stiff, but forced ourselves to walk on. As they were passing us, they started to laugh and made a few remarks about the star on my coat and the scarf. We felt so relieved that the remarks did not bother us at all.

Passover

Once again the Jewish mothers were very busy at this time with preparations for Passover. The houses were painted and scrubbed from top to bottom. Every cupboard, every corner had to be cleaned, in order to remove all possible breadcrumbs or other chametz (leavened bread). The geese were stuffed with feed twice daily to be ready for the holiday. The beets were cleaned and put into wooden barrels to ferment for the borscht we ate almost every day. It was delicious the way it was prepared with beaten eggs. I just loved to come home on the day before Passover. The whole street smelled of the aroma which drifted from each Jewish home on that day. Mother made some *teperto* (the skin of the goose cut into small pieces and fried, till all the fat came out) with fried onions served on top of mashed potatoes and cold borscht. We had that for lunch. On the stove, the chicken soup was cooking and other mouth-watering dishes for the Seder that we were to eat that evening. It was a celebration. The table was set beautifully with white linen and the best dishes and glasses. Sweet red wine was served that evening and the next, even to the children. The candles were lit by Mother and the platter was filled with the traditional herbs, roasted egg, a lamb bone, bitter herbs and of course matzo, and charoset (chopped apple, nuts and wine).

Every year, Father used to read the Haggadah and we had to be quiet for hours and participate in reciting the blessings over each food on the Seder plate. We had a chance, to drink wine; I think that was the best part, as far as we were concerned. All prayers were said in Hebrew, which we did not understand, but we accepted it as a prayer, so we did not ever question the necessity or the meaning of the Hebrew words. We knew the story of Passover and the liberation of our ancestors who were enslaved in

Egypt, and we knew that the reason for the Seder was to commemorate their lives in slavery and never to forget our past.

In 1944, Passover was celebrated in a different mood. We felt that new history was being made once again for the Jewish people. We were very quiet all evening, we anticipated something but did not know what. We sure found out real soon. All Jews were notified that they would be relocated right after Passover, and each family would be allowed to carry thirty kilograms of their belongings with them. A few families were exempt; and they were left at home for the time being. Yachet Neni and her family were one of them, because her son was working for the government owned "Karpathian Electric Company," and he was needed.

Ghettos

I am wondering how the sky can be so clear and the sun shine so brightly when there is so much tragedy and unhappiness going on. On this day we are marching toward the unknown future, a long line of Jewish families with a few kilograms of personal belongings and some food. Some carry it on their backs, others in their hands. We are told that we are being relocated, taken to work.

As I look around at these old men and women, my heart is breaking. They are crying like lost children, bewildered and scared. We are surrounded by armed guards, one to every few helpless Jews, so we would not run away. The truth is that there is no place to go. It all seemed like a horrible nightmare or as if I were watching a play or a movie. It sure did not seem as if it were happening to us - to me.

We had been forced to wear the yellow Star of David, since before Passover, and now, just after the holidays, we were being taken from our homes. A couple of days before, all Jewish families had received their orders in writing. They were full of threatening and intimidating commands, warning us not to hide any of our valuables, not to give them to our neighbors, not to take them with us, just to leave everything in the house. We were told that the reason for that was, so that we could find everything when we came home. What a farce! It went on and on: Any person who dares to disobey will be severely punished. They also gave us the exact time and place to assemble.

Some of our gentile neighbors turned out to be informers for the Hungarian Fascists, and they did not hesitate to report every move a Jew made. No wonder everyone was so scared. In spite of all that, some of our neighbors still remained kind and helpful. A couple of ladies came in to express their concern and sympathy and they offered to hide some of our belongings. My mother told them to take what they wanted, but cautioned them to be careful so we would not all be punished by the authorities. They came back after dark, and one woman took our sewing machine, another took all the yardage goods we still had in the house. I do not even remember the rest. It just did not make any difference any more.

As we were marching, the police sergeant whom we had befriended earlier, while our father was imprisoned also turned out to be our guard. He walked up to us and very softly offered to hide Herczi and myself if we would stay behind. Both of us answered him practically at the same time. We told him that wherever the rest of our family went we would go with them, and we thanked him very much.

After a long and exhausting walk, we reached the old brick factory. It was a large parcel of property with open stalls, where finished bricks used to be stored. Now all the bricks were gone and in their place were people, lots of people from all the nearby villages. There was no more room left for any of us in the stalls. It was left up to each individual family now to fabricate a shelter for themselves. Poor Father, he wasn't handy at all, and since we were all girls in the family, it seemed almost hopeless for us to put together something before dark. Nevertheless, we went to hoard together whatever kind of scraps we could find, and as we were doing it, we ran into some of the boys we knew, and they offered to help us. Before long we had put together a small tent-like shelter. It was barely large enough for all of us to sleep on the floor.

One boy gave me a package, saying take it this is good. I took it to my mom and opened the package. It contained a slice of cured smoked pork. I looked at mother and asked what should we do with it? She said keep it, we may need it for nourishment for your little sisters.

How can I describe the life in the Ghetto other than as complete degradation and surrender? There was nothing to do there except walk around in circles and trying not to think, just accept life as it is and not to make waves. I went for long walks by myself, however it felt as if my soul were absent from my body.

I felt that I was, in a way responsible for my family, since I was the oldest of the children, but I did not think that I could handle the burden. I went to the kitchen to ask for more food and tried to get out, to bring something in, but I could not accomplish anything. We had to rely on the thin soup they gave us. After the war we found out that some neighbors had sent us food, but it was stolen, and we never received it.

The trouble was also that my mother who had always been the strong one in our family seemed to be giving up. She was very depressed and always kept close to us, repeating to herself over and over, "As long as we are together, I'm all right, but as soon as any one of you is taken from me, my life is worthless." How could I have reassured her, when I felt no hope in my heart either? But somehow the time had come when we had to leave.

After six weeks in the ghetto, we ran almost completely out of food, so we had hardly anything to take with us, but someone gave us a couple cans of sardines, I do not remember who gave them to us.

Rumors were spreading, that we were being ordered to work on farms and that was the reason the soldiers came, picked out certain groups of people and told them to be ready to leave in the morning. We believed those rumors because we needed something to cling to. We knew that eventually all of us would be taken away and there was nothing we could do about it. Soon our turn came. Some people were crying, others felt relief at getting out of that terrible place and hoped for the best. When the time came for us to leave it was raining, and it was a sad, sad day.

May 1944 - Leaving the Ghetto

The morning of our departure from the ghetto was a dismal day; dark clouds were rolling in and it looked as if it would start raining any minute. We had to be ready to walk to the trains and we were lined up with everything we owned.

Oh, those terrible uniforms, or rather the people wearing them! They were mean and did not hesitate to use their rifle butts. Everyone was scared enough already, and when the soldiers started to shout obscene words to drive us into the waiting box cars like cattle, they seemed to enjoy every minute of our misery. We all carried our meager belongings. My father had a briefcase filled with prayer books, his prayer shawl and the phylacteries that he used in his daily prayer.

I had on three or four dresses under my coat and felt very clumsy, but everyone tried to take extra clothes in this manner for protection against the cold weather. And so we were ready for the journey into the unknown. I cannot get my father out of my mind. His legs were hurting very much, he had a hard time keeping up with everyone, but he really tried.

When we came closer to the box cars, we were shoved against the walls of the wagons; we had to move real fast to avoid being hit by the guards. We were pushed into the box cars with our packages. As we climbed up it seemed already full to capacity, but they still kept pushing more and more people in, until there was standing room only.

It took some time before the doors were locked and the train started to move, but once in motion it picked up speed and we were on our way to meet our destiny, still believing that we were being taken to work.

By now it was raining outside and dripping into the box car. Soon people had to go to the bathroom. Something had to be improvised in the semi-darkness. There were no windows; the only light came in through the narrow openings between the planks. A blanket and a bucket were donated for the cause by some of our fellow passengers. When someone had to go, two persons had to assist by holding the blanket to shield the user of the bucket. In no time, the stench was unbearable, and constant complaints were heard, but there was nothing anyone could do. One cannot rebel against nature.

The train stopped at different places to refuel or whatever and as we were able to peek through the spaces between the planks, occasionally we could see some faces which belonged to the employees of the railroad company. Every face was very readable indeed. Some showed gladness, others deep sadness. I was sure that those workers knew more about our future than we did, and it reflected on their faces.

Somewhere from the front box cars we heard a baby's cry. Then we heard a woman's voice, I assumed it was the mother, begging for a cup of water for the baby. The guards started to shout at her to be quiet and keep the child quiet. One second the baby was still crying and the next we heard shots fired, followed by terrifying screams, and then quiet again.

Everyone was pretty scared by now. We had no idea of what route we were traveling or how much longer we would have to endure this misery, before we arrived. The conditions were getting from bad to worse by the minute; it was only the first day, but we all had problems accepting the situation as it was. Since there were about 80 people and baggage, there was no room to stretch out, we were just too close to each other and as the night was rapidly approaching, people became very irritable.

As I mentioned before, we did not have much food left. My little sister Iren asked me to open the sardines and I told her to eat whatever else we had first and save the canned food for later. As it happened we never did open those sardines and I lived to regret this decision all my life. At the time there was no way of knowing how long this journey would last.

Somehow we slept off and on from sheer exhaustion. Morning came but it did not bring any changes. It was still ugly outside and a lot worse inside the box car. As I looked at my parents and sisters, my heart went out to them. They looked as lost and helpless as I felt. I needed someone, an adult to reassure and comfort me; instead once again I felt a certain responsibility because I was the oldest daughter. I kept talking to my mother and father and told them not to worry. I told them that Herczi and I would work hard and we would be together on weekends. My mother must have felt our destiny, because she kept repeating these words; "If any one of you are taken from me I'm as good as dead." I kept reminding her that we had been told that we were going to work. I think that I believed that, because I needed something to believe in.

The majority of people seemed to be in a trance-like condition, bewildered and quiet. Perhaps some of them had an idea of what was awaiting us, but no one talked about it. I guess they could not accept it as a real possibility. The second day came to pass and somehow so did the third one. On the fourth day the train came to a stop.

Part II: Auschwitz-Birkenau

Auschwitz-Birkenau 1944

"ARBEIT MACHT FREI"

("WORK MAKES YOU FREE")

After 4 Days of being locked up in that filthy, smelly, overcrowded box car, a woman from inside called out: "Are we hearing music? Yes, we are being welcomed to our new home." She answered herself. Rumors started to spread immediately about how we will be working here and would stay together. Unfortunately these rumors did not have a chance to circulate long.

Suddenly the gates to the box car were opened. The sunlight nearly blinded me. There was a big commotion. Music was indeed playing somewhere. But before we had a chance to see what was going on, we heard and saw a lot of German S.S. soldiers with rifles, barking obscenities in German at us. They were calling us the most vulgar names while shouting at us to get out fast, without our packages. Everyone tried to get down as fast as they were able.

As I mentioned before, my father's leg was very sore, so it was harder for him to get down than for us; he reached back for his briefcase which contained his sidur (prayer book), Tallit (prayer shawl), and his teffilin (religious objects he used every morning and evening at prayer time). Almost immediately I saw a German S.S. Soldier come over and start hitting my father on his head, over and over with his rifle butt until my father collapsed on the ground all covered with blood.

The Nazi murderer just glanced at a couple of prisoners dressed in white and blue stripped clothes. The two of them immediately ran toward us each grabbing a foot of my father, and dragged him toward a nearby truck and threw his lifeless body into the back of it. I watched as Father's bloody head bounced up and down with each step. I screamed in German "You just killed my father, why?" The German SS murderer lifted his rifle butt over my head and shouted at me "You want to go with him?"

I got scared and ran away crying, trying to find my mom and sisters. I did not tell them about Father. That was the last time I ever saw my father. That experience left me emotionally numb. I had just witnessed the killing of my father. I went through the motions, did what I was told to do. Somehow everything seemed as if it were happening to someone else and I was floating in midair, just looking on.

Renee   Hajnal   Iren   Herczi   Lili

**Photo of "Hungarian Jews arriving at Auschwitz" page 17 of the Auschwitz Album;
A Book Based Upon an Album Discovered by a Concentration Camp Survivor Lili Jacob.
Compare the faces with the family photo on page 24 of this book.**

In the meantime we were pushed on and told to stand in rows, five abreast. My mother and the four of us formed a complete row. We started to walk forward. The shouting never stopped. I can still hear them using bullhorns to warn us constantly against taking our valuables with us. By that time, we did not have anything, so we ourselves had nothing to worry about, but lots of other people threw cash and jewelry into the gutter.

A few yards ahead was a good looking German officer with a smile on his face. I found out later that he was the infamous Dr. Mengele. He was waving his hand left and right in rhythm. We could not see what he was doing until we got closer. Mother cried out "If any of you would be taken away from me, I am as good as dead."

We were now close enough to Dr. Mengele for me to observe him making his selections with his hand. The very young and the older people went one way, and young adults and teenagers the other way. Mother cried out "They are taking you away from me. I can't stand it!"

How could I have consoled her? I do not think I had any hope anymore either, but I repeated the rumor over and over that we would see each other on weekends. I even advised my sister Renee to pull herself down, to make herself look smaller, so she could stay with Mother and Iren. I thought it would be easier for Mother, if an older child would also be with her. I just couldn't let go of the hope and the thought that we would see each other from time to time. We didn't even have a chance to say goodbye. We went our separate ways. That was the last time I saw any of them.

I will never cease to wonder if Dr. Mengele would have sent my sister Renee with Herczi and myself if I had not given her that ill advice. Would she still be alive today? Well, at the time I meant well, but for the rest of my life I have had to live with that doubt in my heart.

While all this was going on, someone pushed a loaf of bread under my arm. I was not even aware of having it on me. Once again we were standing in line this time with two sisters from Uzhorod and their cousin who had also been our neighbor and friend.

From behind the bushes a man in the same striped outfit I had seen earlier, tried to attract my attention. He pointed to the bread and asked for it. I asked him if he had a knife; I wanted to give him half of it. He was trying to tell us that everything would be taken away from us in the building, but we thought that he was crazy. He produced a small makeshift knife, but as I started to cut the bread for him, an S.S. soldier came out, and the poor man ran away. I felt terrible after that. Not only he did not get the bread, but he lost his knife also. Later on I realized the value of owning a gadget like that.

We were standing in the same place for a long time, until an S.S. officer came out and told us to start walking into the building. As we came closer, I noticed some stairs in front of a wide door. They arranged it so that only one or two rows were admitted at one time, and we could not see anybody exit the building, so we did not know what was in store for us.

Soon we were let in, and when I walked, in I saw tons of hair on the floor in different colors. I could not figure out where all that hair came from, I could not think about it too long, because of the commotion that was going on. I saw about 5 or 6 S.S. soldiers standing around talking, laughing and shouting at us to take off all our clothes. I was waiting for them to leave before I started to undress, I could not do it in front of the men.

Then several female S.S. helpers started shouting at us to hurry up. They started to tear off our coats and dresses until we were standing there naked. We were only allowed to keep our shoes. Those girls were Polish Jewish girls, and we were very angry at them, but they were only doing their job. I asked one of them, "Why was she throwing my clean clothes on the dirty floor and how will I find them?" She just pushed me into a chair and said you will get other sterilized clothes. At that point I was very scared; she was coming toward me with something shiny in her hand and reached for my head. I had beautiful long hair and she started to shave it. I screamed what are you doing? I tried to push her away from me, but another girl came and held me down. My beautiful long hair was blended in with the other piles of hair on the floor.

Now the S.S. men and women were all around us, driving us toward a door. We were terribly embarrassed, but to them we did not even exist as young girls. Herczi came in after me; we looked at each other and started to cry. What did they do to us? We looked so ugly without our hair; we could hardly recognize each other. There were no mirrors to see ourselves, but looking at each other we could imagine how ugly they had made us look. We did not have too much time to dwell over it, as I looked up at the ceiling I saw showerheads and the cold water started to stream at us. We started to enjoy the refreshing shower after being locked in that smelly dirty box car for four days. At the time we did not understand how lucky we were to get the water from those faucets. Our families before and after us got the gas from those same faucets.

After the shower they made us stand outdoors, naked, for hours. At a distance we saw some men go by from time to time and just hoped that we were invisible to them. We were waiting there until late afternoon, when finally we were taken through a door and given some clothes. I got a very short skirt and a short sleeved top, no underwear or stockings. I was freezing, but nobody cared. We all looked like a bunch of crazy people who had just escaped from an asylum. By now we were also very hungry, since we had not eaten all day.

While we were getting dressed in the hall, I noticed piles and piles of objects, and each pile was being sorted by at least four or five women. I saw hundreds of eyeglasses in a pile; the children's were being separated from the adult glasses. Then I saw hair ribbons, clips, combs and all kinds of clothes - men's, women's and children's. The most puzzling pile was a pile of dentures. Why had they been discarded? How could the old people eat without them? Or maybe they had been given better ones, or maybe the dentures were there for repair. Hm... How stupid! Even if someone would have told us the truth at that moment, who would have believed it?

Later I found out that that place was referred to as *Canada*. There the incoming baggage and clothes of all the people that undressed for the gassing or, if lucky, for the showers, were being kept and sorted out. Lots of jewelry and other valuable items were stolen by the S.S. officers.

The Germans helped us maintain the make-believe with yet another action. All of us were given postcards with printed messages which said: "We arrived safely." It did not say where; we had to sign them and mail them somewhere. I mailed one to my boyfriend in the forced-labor camp Bor, in Serbia. (After the war, I found out from the same boy that my boyfriend had been shot to death in Bor.) He had received the card and they all had tried to figure out what it meant.

It was late in the afternoon when we were introduced to the first of many "*Zählappells*" (lining up for roll call.) We were told to line up five to a row to stand motionless for hours to be counted several times by different groups of Germans. After they were satisfied that each group had come up with the same results, we were ordered to march forward.

We marched past many blocks. There were barracks on each side of the streets and in front of them two or three large barrels of some horrible looking mush. I thought that now we would really start working here, because the food for the animals had already been prepared, and we would have to feed them.

At that point, one of the gates to the barrack in front of us opened and a bunch of gypsies ran out shouting at us, "You came to take our place here, why don't you go back and leave us alone." Of course we had no idea what they were talking about. They still had their long hair and wore well-fitting dresses. This *lager* (camp) was called the *B-lager*. We were led to another section adjacent to *B-lager* which was called the *C-lager*, and that was to be the one for us. The barracks were arranged in numerical order. Our group had to stop in front of barrack 28, and as we were waiting there again, I noticed a mirrored reflection in a small window with a lot of bald people. I just kept looking. At first, I tried to look for myself, but I couldn't recognize myself. I started to nod my head in different directions to establish which one of the bald monkeys I was.

Before I had a chance to react to my discovery, the gate opened and a young well dressed woman with long hair came to receive us from the Germans. She was the "*Blockaelteste*," (block supervisor, her name was Edith and she was a Slovak Jewish girl who had been in Auschwitz since 1938. Edith was promoted to do the dirty job for the Germans, and earned some extra privileges) She ordered us to come into the barrack and assigned bunks for us, five to each slab, two blankets for each bed. I really do not know what to call those things. There were five layers to each, they were all put together from boards and 25 women had to sleep on those bunk beds. Edith informed us that she was in charge of our block, and she had about six helpers "*Stubendienst*" (block orderlies) and we would have to do whatever they told us, or else...Everyone started to cry and carry on, running to the gate to try to escape. She stopped us immediately with a cruel laugh and shouted at us: "Do you think that you have something to complain about? I was here doing your dirty work for years, while you were still sitting by the fireplace eating delicious roasted geese." She told us that, when she was taken to Auschwitz-Birkenau, there was nothing but mud here, and she had to build these barracks for us. When we heard that she was actually one of us, and yet acted so mean, we figured: "What can we expect from the Nazis?" And again we tried to attack the gates. This time she did not try to stop us as before, but she said, "Do you want to end up like the rest of your family?" At this point she opened the gate herself and said, "Look, there are your families burning!" When we looked up, the sky was bright red, and the air smelled of burning flesh. This time we knew that she was telling us the truth.

We cried the rest of the night, and forgot about the hunger we had felt earlier. The mush in the barrels was for us, but we could not eat it anyhow; it really wasn't fit for human consumption.

When Herczi and I sat down on our assigned bed we found that we had been put together with a friend of mine and her mother. Ever since I had known her, she had always been sick, and she looked old in comparison to my mother. My friend had had to do all the housework at home, because of her mother's ill health, and yet her mother was with us. I do not think that I was jealous, but I was wondering whether my mother could not have come with us and survived, but the choice wasn't mine anyhow. I could not accept her death. She spoke beautiful German and she was a very intelligent lady, she would find a way to survive. I was looking for her everywhere we went for the rest of my stay in that camp.

I did not sleep all night, the tears were just rolling down my face, my heart was breaking quietly. I never knew before that a person had so many tears to shed. The morning came soon enough. All the *stubendiensts* were up to help the *blockälteste* to keep order. They had the authority to order us around or even beat us to their hearts desire. It was still dark outside when they started to shout for us to wake up and get ready for a *zählappell*.

The Nazis were smart; they appointed prisoners to help them do the dirty work. They saw that after a period of mistreatment and starvation, any *Häftling* (prisoner) as they called us, for a little favor like extra bread, more and better food, and authority, became a willing tool for them. Some of the *kapos* and *stubendiensts* and also *blockälteste* were meaner to us than the Nazis might have been. Though I cannot say, that all of them were the same.

Now back to the crude awakening in the concentration camp, Auschwitz-Birkenau. After we got up, we were led to the latrine. I had no idea what it meant, but we found out fast. There was a long trench and something that looked like a narrow bench in front of it.

On this bench you sat at your own risk and did your eliminations. One had to be very careful not to lose ones balance and fall in; that trench was deep and foul-smelling. Some of the women even had the nerve to ask for toilet paper. First, our guards were outraged and then they started to laugh as if they had just heard the funniest joke. There was no paper for us, we did not have any underwear, and the morning was very cold. No water to get washed, no time either.

The *stubendiensts* were shouting their orders to us to line up fast, hitting anyone within reach. After that, we learned to hurry up, to avoid her whip. We were lined up and waiting to be counted, but for a long time nobody came. It was daylight already and we were still waiting. Some of us had to go to the bathroom but we were not allowed to move. Finally the *blockälteste* came out and looked at us with utter disgust. We were unable to understand how she could hate us so much, when until yesterday she had not even known that we existed. After more shouting, *"Los, Los"* which we later figured out meant "hurry-hurry" and a few slaps across the face we were standing straight enough for her to count us, and half an hour later the S.S. women came with the vicious German shepherds and counted us again. Apparently the count balanced out, because they told us to line up for coffee.

Our First Breakfast in Camp

Six girls were selected from our group to fetch the coffee from the kitchen. While they were gone, the rest of us had a chance to go to the latrine. I was looking for some water to wash my face, but the faucets did not work; I could only get a few drops.

Soon we were in line for the coffee, or rather just something called that, it was some brownish water but it was hot, so it hit the spot because we were freezing. They did not have enough cups for all of us, so we had to wait until the first group finished, and only then did we get to drink.

I do not think they had any plans for us the first day, because we were allowed to stay in and around the barracks as they were referred to, the blocks. As I looked over the high fence to the neighboring *lager*, I saw complete families together, with children and old people, and as I listened to their conversations I heard them talking in Czech. I found out that they had been brought from *Theresienstadt* two weeks earlier. They had left their homes many months before, some even years before and had stayed in *Theresienstadt* with many other families, but gradually they had been taken away from there. They had no idea what was awaiting them here.

At that moment I heard the *blockälteste* come out and she saw that I was talking to the people over the fence. She told me that if she ever caught me doing it again, she would beat the heck out of me and that I had better stay away from the fence. She threw a rag against the fence, and it burned immediately. She said: "This will happen to you if you get close enough to touch the wire fence." By next morning as we looked over the fence, the people were gone. The *lager* was completely empty. The smell of burning flesh was in the air constantly. That could have given me an idea of what to believe, but I know now, that if I had believed the obvious, then I would not be here to write about it today.

Somehow the day passed and we were given a small piece of moldy, dry black bread and a small slice of liver sausage. We ate it up all at quickly, for once not thinking of tomorrow. We had hardly finished the bread, when we heard the stubendiensts shouting, *"Alle antreten, los for Zählappell."* ("Everyone line up for roll call! Hurry up!") Again the same thing, straighten out the lines or get hit. Standing in line for hours, until the S.S. women came and counted us over a few times. Finally they were satisfied and let us go.

Now it was dinner time; again six women were chosen to get the food. It was dark already when they returned and, as the doors were opened, we had a chance to glance out. The sky was still a vivid red. Later we found out that Hungarian Jews were brought in every day, and 20,000 of them were burned daily.

The view caused a lot of commotion again. Even though we did not want to believe what the *blockälteste* had told us the day before, the red sky still disturbed everybody. It took a few slaps and threats to quiet us, but eventually we all settled down. The food distribution went pretty smoothly, this time everyone had a separate dish and we each got a little watery soup, which tasted like dishwater, but it was hot. We all cried a lot, but very quietly.

I felt like someone from another world, just looking on the mass of people like puppets just milling around and letting our captors pull the strings to control every move. These feelings followed me through my stay in Auschwitz.

We were told to go to sleep after eating the soup, but who could sleep? Once we were fitted into the cot, it was very hard to get out of it unless all five of us got out. The same was true when we had to turn. The boards were very hard, and it hurt our bones to sleep in one position too long. Especially my friend's mother suffered a lot, as I said before she was not well. She would wake us up frequently and ask us please to turn, because we were packed so tightly that she could not move by herself and neither could any of us.

I was thinking all the time about our situation; nothing made much sense. Why did God let us go through all this degradation? I was a religious girl, who had completed four years of schooling in a very good religious school. I knew more about Judaism as a young girl than I know now.

We had just celebrated Passover and recited the story of our enslaved ancestors and the way God led them out of Egypt into freedom by showing Moses the way. We had read about the miracles, the plagues that were inflicted upon Pharaoh and his people. The Jews were free, never to be slaves again. Would history repeat itself now? We certainly were in worse shape now than our ancestors had ever been. Or at least that is how I felt. Would any Jew survive to write our history? Would we stay alive to bear witness? Would any of us survive?

The next morning the same thing happened, but we had to stay a lot longer in line, before we were dismissed. Some of us did not make it to the latrine. The cold morning without proper clothing and underwear brought on some bladder problems, and some of us could not hold back after such a long time, so they let go. The first day it was not noticed by any of our guards, but a couple of days later the *blockälteste* saw one lady urinating on the street. She jumped her and beat her savagely for it. As the days passed, this became a big problem for many girls. It was easy to get chilled and suffer a bladder infection as a result, and to loose control. There were no antibiotics to cure the illness, and no doctors.

Our duties were to keep the block and its surroundings clean. We were given some white powder that smelled very strongly of ammonia. I could not stand that smell; it made me nauseous all the time.

Each day we saw some new people coming in to the *lager,* and they kept coming steadily. We wanted to know where they were coming from. They would ask us if we had seen their relatives, who had been taken away two or three days earlier. The Germans did not seem to run out of Jews. I heard the train whistle every day and saw the transports coming in. The *B-lager* was again occupied. The newcomers were taken there, the gypsies disappeared. Now one day drifted into the other. I knew that there was a holiday following Passover, called Shavuot, and I mentally kept track of the dates.

After the first day or so, we became totally dependent on the food we were being given. It tasted horrible and it looked awful, but it meant survival, so we ate it. I noticed that something had been added to it. I did not know what, until I found out that it was a drug that kept us from menstruating. All the time we were in the *lager,* the only girls who had regular periods were the ones that worked in the kitchen, and that was because they did not eat the same food as we did. That was when I found out that the Germans were feeding us some supplement. I do not know what else they were putting into our food, but it brought about a change in people.

Every day someone's bread was stolen. I started to understand the *kapos* and the *blockälteste* and others that were holding on to some miserable jobs, who were to gain some privileges in the *lager.* Everyone became quarrelsome and increasingly selfish, while I was still living in my dream world. I do not know how, but somehow I kept myself dissociated from this place at least for awhile. My sister was making fun of me all the time, because I kept talking about going home some day and kept insisting that my mother would return home also. She told me off all the time and called me crazy, but maybe that thought kept me going.

One night I woke up and felt that somebody was pulling off our blanket and covering us with a completely wet one. I sat up and saw that my friend's mother had taken away our dry blanket to cover her daughter with it, and was spreading the wet one over Herczi and myself. It was raining heavily and the roof was leaking over the part of the bed where my friend was sleeping. I started to complain about it and told her she was wrong. Just because she was more fortunate than my mother and because she was here, she should not abuse us. "My mother wouldn't do it to your daughter," I said I do not know whether she was ashamed, but she became nasty; I'll never forget it. I do not even want to repeat what she said.

As I said before, this terrible situation was affecting most of us. Some girls actually risked their lives for some additional food and resorted to stealing. As it happened they got away with it most of the time and they had extra food, which I could not provide for Herczi and me.

One morning, as we were standing for *zählappell*, someone whispered something to her neighbor and the *blockälteste* heard it. As a result we were all punished, after the German officer, had counted us and left. Our *blockälteste* told us that she would teach us to obey her when she orders us to be quiet. She made us kneel down on the cold, frozen ground, and left us there for an hour and a half. I felt sorry for my friend's mother; she really suffered. The cold did not help her arthritis. The tears were flowing from her eyes and also from her daughter's. I really felt the pain with them. We were all sore and stiff after the punishment.

No sooner were we released, when we heard the staff talking very excitedly among themselves. We overheard the word "*selection,*" but it did not mean anything to us yet. Then it all started again with their shouting, "*Alles antreten, los, los!!*" over and over, which meant that we had to line up again. We did not know the reason for it, but soon there came the S.S. soldiers led by Dr. Mengele, whom we had seen at the gate the first day. We had to go to him one at a time and he squeezed everyone's arm and again the right/left separation started. Quite a few of us had a sister or mother with us and now that we saw what he was doing, everyone was scared, including myself.

By now we realized that he was selecting out the weaker group for the gas chambers. When our line was getting closer, I pushed Herczi in front of me and decided to go to the same side with her somehow. He sent Herczi to the side of the strong ones, so I flexed my muscles, and he sent me to the same side.

It so happened that the Germans were only working on our nerves with this torture. We were the ones to move immediately out of the barrack we had stayed in, while the rest of the women remained there. My friend and her mother remained in the *C-lager* and we were taken to the *B-Lager*.

First, we had to again go through the same procedure as we had upon our arrival at Auschwitz, only by now we knew that we could either get a nice, refreshing shower or gas to finish us off. Our hair was shaved again, and we were taken to the showers.

I lucked out this time. I got a dress that almost reached my ankles. We did not have to wait as long as the first time to get our clothes. The Germans must have felt that our dehumanization was nearly complete, and so they did not pay too much attention to that aspect.

In the *B-Lager* we met *blockälteste* Olga a freckle faced young woman. She wore a pair of nice-looking boots and held a stick in her hand, which she used frequently. All she said when we arrived was, "Be quiet". A line had to be formed for the bread distribution, and she meant "quiet." As soon as someone whispered, she was ready to jump her and beat the heck out of the person.

By now we had to choose our partners to stand in line with, very unobtrusively, so *Blockälteste* Olga would not notice, with the hope that we would be able to share a cot. Sometimes Olga separated the girls, almost purposely because she saw that they wanted to stay together. Now she was taking, or rather pointing to, five people at a time and shouting the ever popular 'los, los' to hurry. There was no place for anybody to go but they were always in a hurry.

In front of me was a mother with her three daughters and a niece; they hoped to get one cot, but Olga was getting close to the line and the mother, Mrs. Paktorovic, turned away to talk or whisper to someone behind us. I sensed that Olga would separate her from her family, if she continued talking, so I whispered to her to go back, or else her daughters would be placed without her. To my bad luck, just at that moment, Olga turned back and saw me talking. She could not hear me, but she came over to me, screaming her head off, shouting all kinds of obscene words, and she hit me right below the chin. I thought my head would fly off. The bread flew to one side, the sausage to another and I to the floor.

Everyone became very quiet and scared. Someone picked up my bread and sausage and cried with me silently. We got a cot together with a friend and neighbor from home and her two cousins. At that point I made up my mind to stay out of Olga's way as much as possible. I was a good girl; I never made any waves and just existed.

One afternoon after returning from working (breaking small rocks with a tiny hammer into an almost powder-like consistency) Olga had us line up; we had no idea what for, but we found out. A few privileged prisoners came over with something that looked like a fountain pen in their hands, and each of us had to come up and stretch out our left arm. The pen wasn't a pen at all; it was a needle with special ink in it. We felt a sharp pain caused by repeated needle pricks. We were being tattooed, marked for life now. We each had the letter A, a dash, and five numbers tattooed on our arms. My numbers are A-10946.

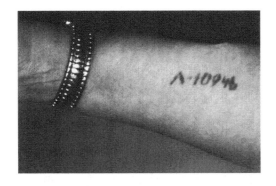

The next day my arm was red and swollen; it looked like an infection. There was not much any of us could do, just wait for it to run its course. It was sore, but somehow it cleared up in a few days. There was no doctor and no medicine. From this time on we lost our identity, we were only numbers.

While still at home, I had managed to memorize my brother Leonard's address in Detroit. I tried to maintain it in my memory, so that some day when we were free, I would be able to contact him. I scratched the address into everything I was standing or sitting near, even when I was standing at *zählappell*. Only there I had to cover it up fast, so no one would catch me doing it. My brother was the only free person in my family, so I felt that it was essential that I have a way to get in touch with him when all this was over.

I found it very comforting that one of the two sisters whose name was Edith was older than myself. She had been married before she was brought to the *lager* and her husband was taken to the forced labor camp. The other sister's name was Etta and the fifth girl's name was Bella. Edith was very protective of Etta and poor Bella felt left out. She always cried that she had nobody. I told her that here we all should be sisters, but it really was not so.

Our life did not change at all except that Olga grew meaner and meaner every day. Hardly a few hours went by that she would not kick and beat someone for no reason at all. One day we were standing at zählappell, when a woman could not stand up any more and just sat down for a minute. Olga saw it, and promptly came over and started to shout at her to stand up. She told her that after the zählappell she would teach her a lesson she would never forget. Sure enough as soon as the Germans had left, she started to beat the old lady, kicked her and ordered us not to move or we would be next. At that point a young girl jumped out of the line and started to shout at Olga to leave her mother alone or she would kill her. She really did not have a chance. Olga was strong as a horse, and we were all weak. The stubendienst grabbed the girl and she was reported to the Germans. Soon both women were taken away and I never saw them again.

Meanwhile Edith advised us not to eat our bread all at once. Instead we should save some for the next day. Because we were always hungry, she said that this way we would teach ourselves discipline. We listened, and it worked for awhile, until one day we heard that someone's bread had been stolen. Herczi said, "I will eat my bread before someone else will." But the next day, when she was starved, I gave her some of mine, so neither one of us had enough. That day we were given some ugly-looking and terrible-smelling cheese with the bread. I had never had that stuff before; I guess none of the other people had either. As hungry as everyone was, nobody would eat that cheese. I guess I was hungrier and more willing to take a chance than the others, so I ate a piece.

It was very salty and since we were not getting any salty food at all, it tasted good. This time I could eat all I wanted; there was plenty of it. I ate a lot that night, and I slept well on a full stomach. The cheese was given to us a few more times, and slowly the others started to eat it also. Now Herczi was eating it, too, though before she had made plenty of fun of me, when only I ate it. Sometimes she would laugh and mock me and talk about me with Edith. That upset me very much, but I became passive and took a lot of abuse from her. She was throwing at me the fact that I was too chicken to go out at night and steal some extra food for us. I just did not know how to go about it.

Some girls ran out at night and came back with all kinds of goodies, but I just would not dare. My sister held that against me. One evening I heard that the kitchen was getting truck loads of squash and some girls were planning to go out and steal some only there it was called "to organize," not "to steal". I decided to try it also. By then my shoes were gone and had been replaced by wooden shoes. There was snow on the ground, and as I was running to grab some of those melons or squash, all of a sudden the light went on and I had to run so as not to be caught. In the process, I lost one of my wooden shoes, so I was again the subject of ridicule. It proved that I could not do anything. Most of the time, this depressed me very much.

It was early yet for such cold weather, and it felt especially cold to us, because we had no decent clothing. Here and there some people would save their portions of bread and trade them for a jacket or whatever they could, but at the time of selections, it was taken from them.

Now it seemed that we had those torturous selections very often. Most of the time, those who were taken from us were never seen again. Sometimes we were just separated for no other reason than simply to cause us anxiety. I cannot even describe the disoriented feelings we were experiencing at such times.

The Day We Were Separated From Our Friends In Camp

The next selection was tragic for us. Herczi and I were left together, but Edith, Etta and Bella were separated from us. Bella was looking at me from the other side and crying bitter tears. Her face haunted me for a long time afterwards. We had become closer than my sister and I. I later heard that she did not survive.

It was hard to get adjusted to the separation and we were constantly thinking and talking about the girls. In the few months we had really grown close. Now we had to join three other girls, and we were all taken to a building where the S.S. made us wait for an eternity.

Finally five S.S. women with three large vicious-looking German shepherds came out and shouted at us to come to attention. They took us into one part of that large building and handed us over to another woman whom we assumed to be a prisoner, only one of the privileged ones *(kapo)*.

She was dressed well and her hair was at shoulder length. She showed us our place of work, *The Weberei* (Weaving room.)There were some large looms and some other girls were making something out of some strings.

The *kapo* ordered one of the girls to show us how to weave, but first we had to cut the strings from a large piece of thin rubber and use them like yarn. I do not know what the purpose of this work was or if they used the product for anything, but it was very hard to work with that material. We had to work there for a few weeks, before we were transferred to another room.

Now we had a Polish *kapo*, she was somewhat milder at first than the others and spoke more softly, but, as we gradually found out, it was all a cover-up. In this room there were mounds of all kinds of beautiful satin bedspreads, damask tablecloths, expensive brocade draperies and other rich household items.

She pointed to a table with chairs around it and told us to sit down on the chairs, in front of every chair there was a nail hammered into the table and a pair of scissors. She told us to cut all those materials into thin ribbons, and we had to obey her, but it almost hurt us to do so. When we had a whole bunch of ribbons cut, we had to take three long ribbons and three equally long rubber strings, make a knot and hook it on the nail. Then we had to braid all those strands together as we would someone's hair. We were given a quota, of so many meters per day.

When the length of the ribbons or the rubber strings, came to an end, we had to braid some more strings with it to continue in a smooth manner. Keep braiding and rolling it into a ball. We tried, but we could not figure out, what those braids might be used for; maybe to clean the machine guns or something like it. Some days, some girls were able to exceed their share of the meters required per day, but I was somehow very slow with it and could barely make the quota.

Our *kapo* with her soft whining voice was always threatening us. She told us that the Germans would use a hose and let the water run on those who did not complete the daily quota, until they froze to death. I was very scared and worked as fast as I could. All the time I worked there, once was I able to make more than I needed to and I got a coupon for it. I was able to buy a cigarette for it. I was hoping to trade it for some food, but as luck would have it there were no takers. I could hardly get rid of it, but finally I traded it in for a small jar of mustard.

I saw some girls make aprons from stolen pieces of material we worked with and trade them for food. I decided to try to do the same thing. I finished the apron. It took me a long time to sew it by hand, but in the morning I got up very early, before the *zählappell* and went toward the kitchen, very proud of my accomplishment. I could taste the extra food I was going to get for my pretty apron.

As I walked into the kitchen all the girls gave me a look as if to say: "What is she doing here?" When I showed them my apron, they said that it was pretty, but they had too many of them already and they did not need any more. I did not even have time to say anything. All I know is that someone pushed me down on a sack of potatoes and someone else pushed a potato and a knife in my hand and whispered: "Peel it."

I started to do just that and at the same time the door opened and four S.S. men walked in looking around. I felt as small as any one of those potatoes. After a short time they walked out and the girls pulled me up, gave me about four large sugar beets, sent me back to the barracks and told me not to come back any more. What an experience! We ate up the vegetables in no time. It was good because it was something extra that we did not get very much of or very often.

Somehow the days seemed to melt one into the other. By now we had been told several stories about our *kapo's* life. She had lost her little girl; she had been in camp for four years already; she could not speak too loudly, because her lungs were injured when the Germans beat her. We were wondering how she could exist, but this was her story when she was mad at us, which was pretty often.

Every day we were awakened very early in the morning. It was still dark when we had to assemble for *zählappell* and remain standing until those hated Germans came to count us. Sometimes it took many hours more than other times and we were shivering from the cold and from malnutrition.

The high electric fences surrounded us; there was no escape, but they still had to torture us with those roll calls twice daily. Heaven help us if we moved. If one person disobeyed the *blockälteste* by any voluntary or involuntary movement, the whole block had to kneel on the cold ground until it was time to go to work. We would not even get our hot black water.

At work, the same things were being done day after day. Each time I picked up a tablecloth or spread I tried to imagine the people that had used it. Where did they come from and what kind of homes did they have. It was just a game to keep my mind occupied. The days went by and we were allowed to talk only when the *kapo* left the room for a few minutes.

Yom Kippur

A few months later, the lady I mentioned before with the three daughters, Mrs. Paktorovic, said to us: "Girls, the Yom Kippur holiday is approaching. Maybe we could start saving up some extra work every day so that on that day we could just pretend to work and at the end of the day still have our quota." Everybody was in favor of it, and we did as she suggested. The Day of Atonement arrived, and as starved as we were we even made arrangements with the *blockälteste* to save us our bread portion until the evening. She graciously agreed. We were determined to fast all day.

The bundles of work were hidden under the uncut material, and I thought we were doing our duty, to God and to the miserable Germans. Only we did not count on being discovered by the *kapo.*

I do not know where she came from, but suddenly she was at the table, reaching under the cloths in front of the girl sitting next to me, and she found the bundle. She started to beat the girl on the head over and over until she could hardly breathe. But that was not enough for her; she reached again and found the bundle in front of the girl next to the first one, and the beating started all over again. I knew that I would be next. I just hoped that by the time she would be done with me, she would lose her strength and that way at least Herczi might be spared. Sure enough, she started on me and kept beating my poor head harder and longer than the others, until I was bleeding. When she saw the blood, she stopped, as if she had just come to her senses. Luckily, Herczi was spared.

This incident left me with a lot of bitterness in my heart. I could not understand why God was punishing me so much, why He did not just let me die like the others. It made me doubt any purpose in my religion and my faith in God. After that day, I was getting headaches all the time and to this day I still suffer from headaches.

After that experience, I gave up on life. Many times in the evening I went out walking by myself, and the thought came to me to just throw myself against the fence, and it would be all over. At those times my mother's face appeared in front of my eyes, and I started to believe that it was worth holding on to life; that we would all be home together some day. I think that this thought helped me to survive life in the camps.

One day, while I was on one of those walks, I was so lost in thought that I did not even hear the bullhorn announcing the orders to stay off the street. I just kept walking, until someone grabbed me by the arm and pulled me into a barrack. It was an older lady and she started to shout at me, asking me if I was crazy or what. But when she saw how sad and depressed I was she soon calmed down and asked me if I was hungry. She did not even wait for my answer, but told me to sit down and gave me a pot half full of thick soup and a spoon, and she said: "Eat." I did not need much encouragement. I was always hungry, but after I ate part of the soup, I asked her if I could take the rest of it to my sister. She said, "Sure," but made me promise to bring back the pot the next evening.

When I came back the next evening, thanking her for the soup, she told me to come every evening to pick up some soup. I did not know what to say, but I was very grateful to her. No one ever gave me anything for nothing. I returned for the soup, and it kept me going. I was able to save up my bread and trade it for a pair of shoes. It took a whole week's allotment, but it was worth it; those wooden shoes from Holland were impossible to wear. They hurt my feet and in the winter they were slippery, like sleds.

At least now I was able to provide something extra and delicious to Herczi also. We both enjoyed the soup tremendously. I found out that the name of my mentor was Hannah, like my mother's. I almost believed that Mother sent her to help me go on. She came from a small Hungarian village. What a wonderful person! She saved my life. God bless her.

At that time a large group of prisoners were brought into the camp. They practically took over the road I heard them speak Russian. They were loud and used their hands a lot while talking big and strong, warmly dressed women. I still had the Holland wooden shoes it was dangerous to walk in them on the frozen ground as we were walking home from work they walked by me and gave me a shove. I was sliding all over the street on the ice and I do not know how I made it to the barrack that night.

Trying to Stay Away From the Hospital

We were working in the *weberei* for a long time. We felt somewhat secure in the belief that we would not be taken away while we worked there. It was very cold and I got sick, probably with a high fever, because I was so dizzy that I could hardly walk straight. I felt very sick and would not go to the hospital, because we never knew what night the S.S. might come with their big truck to pick up all the sick ones and take them to the gas chamber. We had seen it happen many times, even to patients with only a few pimples on their bellies.

Every Sunday morning we had to lift our clothes and expose our abdomen to the S.S. women for them to check us for any skin disease, and if anyone had a pimple on her belly, she was ordered to be hospitalized. We tried to avoid it by keeping as clean as possible, getting up in the middle of the night and washing ourselves with drops of water that we could get in a washroom. It took us forever.

In time my health improved, but we kept up with the washing regularly. I am still thankful to Edith for that, because she was the one who got us used to this schedule and it may have saved our lives.

One night when we were sneaking out to one of those dripping faucets, it was very cold outside and we rushed as much as we could, so we could be finished fast, when, all of a sudden, someone tapped me on my bare shoulder, and when I looked up there stood a tall S.S. man with his whip. I thought he would kill us all, right then and there, but to our surprise, he complemented us saying "Keep on doing what you are doing. It is good for you to clean yourselves." We continued to wash. We had acquired a piece of soap in exchange for bread, but it was like a rock and had that awful smell of plain soap, but we used it anyway.

Selections, Selections

Meanwhile the selections continued every day in different sections of the block. We could see the line-up for selection every day on our way to and from work. Sometimes I saw girls I knew being taken away. By now all we cared about was surviving one day at a time. This is one aspect of life in the camp that I did not like: we had lost our true personality. Most of us gave in to the feeling of wanting to survive at all costs. Obviously we all wanted to survive at that point, but I really tried not to do anything that would harm any other prisoner in any way. Of that I am proud.

It started to snow, and I was freezing. Winter came again and it did not find us in any better situation than it had left us the year before. Occasionally some men were allowed into the camp to haul the snow away. The only times that we saw any males since we had come here, was when they were sent over to repair something. Some women got all excited, put on a scarf and pinched their faces until they were red, and they sneaked out of the barrack and later came back with lots of goodies. Most were slightly older than we were, more sophisticated and also more experienced.

Even though it was very cold, I used to walk a bit every day after work, just to keep active. I cannot imagine now how I could stand it without warm clothing. I guess I had become acclimatized. As a young girl at home I always ran around without a jacket in the winter time but only as far as across the street to buy something in the store.

By now we were again living on bread and an occasional thin slice of sausage, hot brown water in the morning, and hot watery soup in the evening. Hannah, who had given me the good thick soup that came from the bottom of the kettle, was gone; she had been deported. So far, there were no rumors about our fate, as to how long we would stay here or whether we would be taken somewhere else. No one ever knew the destination of those transports or whether one would be relocated or taken straight to the gas chamber and crematorium.

One day, as I was on the latrine, I saw a little girl that looked like my younger sister Iren (we nicknamed her Pipike.) I called her by that name but she did not answer or look my way. She kept talking to the Polish women in fluent Polish. She was a *schreiberin*; I do not know why they were called by that name. They weren't scribes, the S.S. women or men used them to take messages from one station to the other, and rumor had it that those poor children were abused by them.

It took me a long time to settle down after this incident. It still puzzled me, and I thought that maybe it was my little sister, and that she had learned to speak Polish by spending a lot of time with the Polish prisoners. Deep down I knew that I was daydreaming, but I grabbed onto anything that would maintain my will to just go on.

Most of the time I did not even know what day it was, and so the days were slipping away. One day we were informed at the *weberei* where we still worked that it was December 31st and the S.S. women were planning with the *blockälteste* to make a party on New Year's Day. Everybody who had any talent could perform in front of them, besides we would have some better food that day, and no work. Well that sounded great. It seemed that we were lucky on the night of December 31st.

We had just finished with the *zählappell* and were ready to go for our food, when the wind started to blow, and by the time the barrels of food were brought into the barrack, the wind had intensified to such an extent that it was blowing away whatever happened to be in its path. For a while it was shaking our barrack so strongly that I thought it would collapse any moment. No sooner did it seem as if it would quiet down a bit, than the snow started coming down in the largest flakes I ever saw. In no time at all everything was covered in white, by morning we had about 10 inches of snow on the ground.

As much as we dreaded it, we still had to go out for *zählappell* while it was still dark. After the counting we came in and waited for our bread, but it did not come. We could not figure out what was going on and there was no one to ask. We were told to be quiet. Of course the rumors started right away: We are going to receive an extra-special lunch, because it was the New Year.

On the first of January 1945, at about 9 or 10 in the morning, we were sitting on our beds. It had been a while since we had seen any of our *stubendiensts* or the *blockälteste*. No one knew what was going on. Everyone was waiting very quietly without knowing for what. There was an eerie atmosphere around us. Again we were full of anticipation and anxiety at the same time.

Soon enough, an announcement came on the loud speaker: "Everybody out! A transport is being formed." Well that spelled selections for us and gas chambers. We were advising each other not to go out, just to hide in the barrack as long as we could, and maybe the Germans would have enough people from the other barracks and they would leave us alone.

No such luck. Our *blockälteste* practically flew in and started to order us out. When no one moved she told us that it was up to us. If we wanted to be shot down by the S.S., then we should stay. One way or another we were being evacuated from Birkenau. What we did not know was that the Russian Army was getting too close for their comfort.

The S.S. entered with rifles and started to shoot in the air, shouting, "Alles raus!" (everybody out) and the hated, "Los-los!" with obscene names for us. Needless to say, we were scared and started to run out. In no time they had us lined up in fives and after counting us a few times, we were led to the place where we had first come in. They shaved our heads again, and after that, we were taken to the bath, or would it perhaps be the gas house?

Apparently we were still lucky, because we got the water and not the gas. After the shower we got some rags to put on and an extra large piece of bread with a very good slice of sausage, sausage larger than the ones we had had before. Now we were crowded into a Box car once more. We hardly knew any of the women who were with us in that car. Closest to us, were two sisters from Budapest, with whom we made friends in no time. The younger girl looked very young and not at all well, the older one was a loud and domineering person. Most of the others were Polish.

Most of us ate most of our food, and we were thirsty, but there was nothing to drink. So far we had not stopped even once. The train was going quite fast, and we couldn't see too much through the slits in the box car, but we could tell that we were riding through some beautiful country.

After a while, the train came to a stop to take on water. It was sad, but all the time we were on the train, most of the Polish group was at the front of the car, the rest was occupied by the Hungarians, and Herczi and I were in the middle. At this stop the S.S. opened the gate, gave us a bucket of water and closed the gate very quickly. I had no idea what part of which country we were in. The water was grabbed away by the Polish group, and they would not share it with the rest of us. The young Hungarian girl looked very ill and feverish and was asking for water. Those Polish women were so full of hatred toward the Hungarians that they simply ignored her pleas.

When I could not take it anymore, I spoke to them in Czech and told them: "You should be ashamed of yourselves! How much better are you than the S.S.? They at least gave us the water!" I showed them the young girl's feverish face, and asked them: "How can you refuse her the water? It is as much ours as yours." They understood me and were shocked to hear a Slavic language from us. They handed over the bucket and apologized to me. So we all had water. After that, the tension seemed to ease between us, and everybody was somewhat friendlier.

I do not know how long the trip lasted. I fell asleep from time to time. Some of the time we were talking and speculating about our destination, and after that we talked about our favorite subject: food and recipes. We were always fantasizing about food and how it is the most important thing in our lives. I even promised myself that, if I ever got to own a whole loaf of bread by myself, I would not use a knife. Instead, just tear it apart, as I ate it all.

I did not know how long we had been in that smelly car, but eventually the train stopped. We had arrived at our destination. When they opened the gates, I saw the sign: "Bergen-Belsen."

Bergen Belsen Konzentrationslager (Concentration Camp)

What a hell-hole! People all over, wall to wall, except there were no walls, just people lying on the ground on some dirty straw. We were shown a few feet of ground and were told that this was our new home. Some straw was thrown toward us, but before it hit the ground it was grabbed by other prisoners who had been there before us. They said they needed it and had more right to it than we; they were also stronger than we were. We pulled some of the straw back, but it was not enough to even line the ground beneath the two of us.

I felt weak from all the traveling and not having had anything to eat. Soon an S.S. man came and told us to go and get the soup which was to be our dinner for the day. Six girls went to bring the barrels to us and after a while came back with a little watery soup on the bottom of the barrel. The stronger ones had won again. A group attacked the girls and took our soup. Everyone was very upset, but there was not a thing that we could do. All these bad things were being done to us, and it was frustrating. This was a very disorganized camp.

By this time I was in sheer agony. I must have been to the latrine more times than I can say. I had a bladder infection and I was hurting so much that even the food or the lack of it did not bother me. This camp was so dirty and sloppy that I was afraid to stay there. I thought a lot about what to do. The next morning I came up with an idea and told Herczi and the two sisters I mentioned earlier, "Let us keep our eyes open and as soon as we see a selection going on we should stand in line." I really did not think that anything could be much worse than this. We all agreed to it. Sure enough, a couple of days later, we were all four of us together when we saw the line-up, it wasn't very long. It was odd to run to be in a selection, when all the other times we had tried to hide from it.

As before, I pushed Herczi ahead of me, so that I could finagle to go the same way as she went. Just a bit ahead of us, a young German in civilian clothing was doing the selection, looking over the girls and sending them to the left or to the right. Nobody knew which the good side was, we just wanted to get out of Bergen-Belsen.

Soon it was our turn to come before the man who was doing the selection. He looked at Herczi and sent her to one side and looked at me and sent me to the other, except I did not go. I tried to run after Herczi but he insisted that I go to the other side, but at that point I shouted at him, "Bitte, meine Schwester." (Please, my sister.) He heard me and called me back and told me to go with my sister. He was a decent human being, even if he was a German.

Now we were all four of us together, being taken toward a new life, still not knowing what was ahead of us, but glad to get out of that place. This time we traveled in a large covered truck. It was not long before we arrived at a new location. I do not think we were ever told its name.

We were taken to a large yard with a long building. We were told that this is the place where we would work, but first we would clean up and eat. In the next building it was heaven: A large room lined with bunk beds, each large enough to sleep two people, and we each received a blanket. Before we had a chance to get over our shock, another person brought clothes for everybody and showed us the showers. A German man gave a speech, telling us about how this was different and it would stay that way; we would always have food and clothes as long as we took care of everything. I am afraid all this kindness came a bit too late. We did not behave like human beings anymore. Everybody dashed out to the shower all at once, like animals. No restraint; everyone wanted to go in first. Somehow we all had our turn at the showers and put on clean clothes. That in itself made me feel like a lucky girl. After that they fed us real food. The food was being brought in from a restaurant in the city, three meals a day. They informed us that we would start working the next day and there would be two shifts. One in the day time and one at night, and the shifts would be rotated weekly.

We were very happy and more at peace than we could imagine possible in captivity. We slept really well that night. I felt much better, the bladder infection did not hurt anymore and I was ready to tackle life under these improved circumstances.

The next morning after breakfast we were briefed about our work schedule. Herczi and I got the day shift, and after the meeting, we were taken to work. Herczi was put on the assembly line and I was led to a drill press. A foreman showed me how to make holes in a round piece of metal. I have no idea what it was used for, but that was my job. I caught on pretty fast. Anybody could have done it, but it would also have been easy to drill holes in one's hand if one were not careful operating the drill press.

For a concentration camp this was wonderful. We were off on Sundays, and free to do anything within the area. No one could leave the premises. We were provided with a replacement of clothes, and they tried to give us pep talks. The ones who appreciated what was done for us were happy and content to stay there till the war would end.

Even so, there were some trouble makers who stole or relieved themselves on the lawn. That could not be tolerated. We all had to accept the scolding because nobody would tell who the guilty ones were. I did not even know.

I was given an old black sweater to wear, and we did not have any stockings, but since my feet were cold all the time, I decided to do something about it. I ripped the sweater and rolled the wool into balls, borrowed a knife and I cut out five needles from some scrap wood I found lying around.

When my next shift ended, I started to knit knee high socks from the wool. I do not remember how long it took, but before I had used up all the wool, I completed two pairs of beautiful, warm socks. Herczi and I both enjoyed them until we were free to go home.

One day as I was working on my job, I broke the drill. I do not know how it happened. This was a scary experience, because it could have been taken for sabotage. The other girls were upset. What would happen to all of us now? Well, I figured it happened to me; therefore I am the one who has to take the responsibility. Everyone was terrified as they watched me go in to the foreman.

When I approached the door to the foreman's office, I almost fainted. I knocked, and the foreman came out and looked at me as I asked for permission to speak to him. He could tell how scared I was and prompted me to tell him what was wrong.

When finally it came out of me, he smiled and said in German: *"Ist das alles?"* ("Is that all?") He took out a new drill bit, gave it to me and asked if I needed his help to replace the broken one. He did not wait for me to answer, but came with me and showed me how to do it. What a relief!

Unfortunately, this situation did not last. The next morning as we went to work, I saw about five cars filled with high ranking S.S. officers driving at the compound. This gave rise to speculations among us. The truth was that none of us had any idea of what was going on. We found out soon enough.

Before we even entered the factory, the foreman came out and told us that there would be no work today and that we should go back to the barracks and stay there. While we were waiting, we were served lunch and about five hours later the man who did the selection in Bergen-Belsen came in. He looked sad as if it hurt him to tell us that we had to leave. The factory was being relocated, but we could not go along.

He told us that we would be fed before leaving and we would have to wait for the trucks to take us to our new destination. He wished us good luck and he hoped that we would reach our homes safely. It was nice of him to say that, but it did not penetrate. Still this was the only place where we were treated as human beings, while incarcerated. Again, what we did not know was that the Russian or American soldiers were closing in. This was some time in February, 1945. By now I was 21 years old, but felt like a scared child.

We were very quiet just waiting for the next move. I had hoped that we could stay here till the end of the war. I was very disappointed and scared. Again we became the hopeless, helpless bunch without a place to stay.

I walked around the house we had lived in for about six weeks, for the first time under humane conditions, since we had been taken from our homes. This yard was very nice and clean, the trees were bare now except for the evergreens that were growing there. The factory was empty and quiet now. Soon the large trucks arrived, and it was time to leave.

Again Facing the Unknown

I saw the men that were running the factory looking out the window of the big house, and I had the feeling that they were sorry to see us leave. They probably assumed that we would be killed. As I was climbing into the truck, I looked back towards the big house and waved goodbye. I saw their hands waving back to me.

While riding in the truck, no one cared enough to look up and see what direction they were taking us. We were a very subdued bunch. It did not take too long before the trucks pulled up before a large old, two- story building. I had no idea what it had been used for before, or where it was located, but now it looked as though it would be housing us for a while.

The large double doors opened, and two women came out. They were talking to the truck drivers for a few minutes, and then told us to get off the truck fast and go into the house.

We did what they told us to do. In the large room there were a few long tables and just a few chairs. It seemed that the people occupying the house were a mixture of German criminals, prostitutes and others. The labels on their clothing were different. Each symbol represented the crimes for which they were in camp.

All this time I knew that in Budapest a Jew could survive by obtaining gentile papers, like a birth certificate, a new Hungarian-sounding name and a lot of good luck.

When I saw Jewish women there with long hair and fairly nice clothes, I wondered where they came from. Then I found out that they had been caught in Budapest and brought directly to this camp. That was the reason they had not lost their hair as we had.

We were given some soup, and after we ate it, one of the women distributed some blankets to each of us, took us to the back of the house and designated certain areas on the floor for us to sleep on.

The next morning at zählappell time, we looked around and did not see anybody from our part of the country. After the homey place we had come from, this was again something to get used to. Every part of my body was aching, since there was no meat on my bones. The hard floor did not help. I did not think that there was any specific job to be done by us, it just depended on the leader's mood what work they made us do.

I was living, or rather existing, one day at a time. One afternoon we were taken for a walk in the forest by our leaders, two women who I thought loved each other. They would always walk arm in arm, while singing German songs. They sounded pretty good.

The next morning was very cold and windy, and we were sent out to work with a few of the criminals in charge. We were taken to a steep hill, and they told us to form a human chain, starting at the bottom of the hill and all the way to the top. It had rained all night, and the ground was muddy and slippery; it was hard to keep one's balance, but we managed. Now she pointed to a large pile of heavy rocks and told us to throw one at a time to the next person, until all the rocks had been taken down. By now they all had the whip ready to strike any minute. One looked meaner than the other, as if they really had it in for us. I cannot say that we were very coordinated, the rocks were slippery because they were wet, and they kept slipping out of our hands, sometimes landing on our feet, and, boy! That really hurt. Besides, we got hit by the whip once or twice. The names those outcasts were calling us cannot be mentioned in polite society. It was terrible.

Finally, after several hours of drudgery, the pile of rocks was now at the bottom of the hill. We were relieved that we could now go in and get warmed up a little; we were all numb and could not control our fingers very well. Of course, we did not have any gloves, and it started to rain again and the wind picked up. I guess they were cold also, because they let us quit working, but told us that the next day we would go out again and work some more. We did not look forward to it, but we were hopeful that their mood would change and they would find something easier for us to do. Some older people (by that I mean those in the early thirties) found it much harder; some were also sick.

Food was scarce and irregular. When I looked around this time I saw a lot of new faces, a new, small transport must have come in. Some of the newcomers were beautiful. There were two sisters from Budapest, both had gorgeous shiny black hair, they had just been reported to the Germans and brought to this place immediately.

The younger one was supposed to be pregnant and she was getting very gentle treatment because of it. The *blockälteste* brought her special goodies and called her "little mama." She did not have to go out to work, and even her sister got off so she could watch over her.

I lost track of time here, maybe more because of the deep depression I was experiencing than for any other reason. Somehow, when I had been in *Auschwitz-Birkenau*, I could picture myself, or rather ourselves, living through the war, but here, everything seemed hopeless. The days blended into nights, and I felt like a zombie. The *kapo's* whip hit me more than once and the stick always seemed to find a home on my poor head. I was dragging myself, could not concentrate, and moved slowly.

I heard the rain at night, it was heavy and it always seemed to be followed by a strong wind. I felt that in the morning we would be taken to do the same nasty job, and, sure enough, right after the *zählappell* we had to line up, and those same criminals took us out to the same hill where we had worked before. Now we had to do the same thing as before, except in reverse. That day the whips were dancing and screams heard, and people collapsed everywhere. When I saw how they were picked up and tossed to the side like unfortunate bundles rolling down the hill, I think I came to my senses. I snapped out of this lethargic state of mind and, as though I was revitalized instantly, I was able to function better and thus avoid the whip more successfully.

The day went by. I do not know how many times we managed to relocate the rocks, but the time had come to go back to the house. We all received a small piece of bread and a slice of sausage. The *zählappells*, the never ending line-ups were still going on twice daily. Before we were dismissed, the *blockälteste* told us that in the morning we would receive some warmer clothing, possibly coats. That sounded great, since we were all freezing to death. It was good news.

In the meantime, we were still together with the two sisters we had met on the train going to Bergen-Belsen, the older one's name was Lili and younger one was called *Alizka*. I felt sorry for *her*. She was a few years younger than the rest of us, and fragile, but she was surviving. She was always fantasizing about food and paprika potatoes in particular.

Came the morning after *zählappell*. Large bundles of all kinds of coats, sweaters and other clothing were piled in the room, and as we were walking through, each was given a coat or sweater. I received a large checkered coat and Herczi also. This was great. We wrapped ourselves and as soon as we could, went to wash our bodies wherever we could find water. We still believed that by trying to keep clean, we could stay healthy.

As soon as we had drunk our hot black 'coffee,' we had to line up again. Two of the criminals brought in a large can of black paint and a brush and we were curiously waiting to see what would happen now.

We didn't have to wait long this time. They instructed us to line up with our backs toward them. Now that made everyone nervous and we panicked. The *blockälteste* came over and asked what the matter was. I do not know why, but she had a kinder way of dealing with us. She explained that our coats had to be marked, and so they proceeded to paint large letters of K and L across our backs which described us as prisoners of the *Konzentrationslager* (Concentration Camp). We really didn't need it. One look at our thin, worn-out bodies told the story.

I do not know how long we had been at this place, when somehow the little pregnant lady was not pregnant any more. There was a lot of commotion made by the *blockälteste* and her partner, shouting at the sisters, calling them liars. Apparently she never had been pregnant, but saw an easy way of making her life better and went for it, and for a while it worked. Now all the privileges were taken from them, but I never found out what their punishment was, because the next day a messenger came and we were told that we had to leave right away.

Rumors started to circulate, someone said that we should stay behind because maybe the war was coming to an end and we were being evacuated. That was really happening, but we were not sure, and not one person among us was of leadership quality, and so we all lined up for the horse blanket and piece of bread that each of us was given. What we did not know was that this was the start of the infamous death march.

'The Death March'

I lost track of time completely and did not know what month or day it was. The group of approximately twelve hundred women started out walking. I did not know what direction we were taking, just followed the crowd. We were picked up by a group of S.S. men and women, each carrying a rifle and a pistol, and we were always surrounded by them. The first day, we stopped somewhere and were given some hot soup, and a large barn to sleep in on top of the hay.

In the morning we had to continue the walk. The S.S. were pushing us ahead and they threatened us and urged us to walk faster. Already after the first day, some people had blisters on their feet, and it was hard for them to walk. I thanked my lucky stars that in Auschwitz, I had had a chance to barter a piece of bread for a pair of shoes. Now at least my feet were comfortable.

As we passed towns and villages, I read the signs, the names of the places, but they were all unfamiliar to me. As the days passed I became more and more exhausted and disillusioned. I did not know it at the time, but this was not the worst of it yet.

We walked through some pretty towns and villages; now and then we received something to eat, but not regularly. Sometimes a day went by without any food, and the S.S. had a harder time to find a place for us to sleep.

One day it was pouring all day, our blankets were soaked and so were our jackets. This time of the year the rain and wind were unpredictable. Once it started, it did not know when to stop.

Walking became harder and harder for more than one reason. The wet clothes were heavy to drag around and we were very weak from starvation. As the weeks went by, we lost a lot of people. Some got sick and could not continue so they were taken out of the line, and the S.S. soldier who remained with them, always came back shortly afterwards and joined the march by himself.

The S.S. could not find any place for us to sleep, the weather turned freezing cold, and we were informed that we would have to sleep out in a field on the frozen ground. I put one blanket on the ground, and the other one we used to cover ourselves. I do not know what I was hoping for, because both of those blankets were soaking wet in no time, and the top blanket was frozen. Miraculously, we fell asleep almost instantly, or maybe it was a bigger miracle that we woke up in the morning.

I was totally numb. My body felt as if paralyzed, but we were forced to move on. I do not even know when and how we became infested with lice. They were literally eating us alive, and everybody was covered with them. We had no combs. Our hair started to grow, and we had no way to wash it. Our condition deteriorated more and more day by day. I was so hungry that I was scraping under the ice for some grass that remained from the fall days, and ate it. Soon other girls tried to do the same thing, when the S.S. woman blew her whistle and shouted at us: "Do not eat the grass, you stupid girls! You will get diarrhea." She did not seem to care that we were dying of starvation, but she did not want us to eat the grass.

As we were getting ready to leave, I saw another transport group of men in striped uniforms. This was a pathetically emaciated group, we felt terribly sorry for them, we were sure that they were being taken to the crematoriums. The Germans referred to them as *Muselmen*. As we could not see ourselves, we did not realize that we did not look any better.

That day we came to a city and people were crowding around to look at us and were staring at us and laughing. One fat German took a piece of dry bread, threw it at us and, laughing loudly, enjoyed the sight of us, as everyone jumped for the bread and fought to keep it. Soon the bread was all over the ground, mashed into crumbs, and no one had any of it. Apparently that was the whole purpose of it, and the fellow could not stop laughing. Boy, how I hated him. They all knew that we were Jews and if they did not, the big K-L painted on our backs would certainly let them know.

Somehow we went further, and we came to a farm. The S.S. man went in to ask the farmer to let us sleep in the barn and give us something to eat. We were left outside waiting; some of the girls walked away and found a large tub filled with steaming boiled potatoes. They motioned to the rest of us to come. We emptied the tub in no time. It was the best meal we had had in a long, long time.

The farmer came out after telling the S.S. that he did not have anything to give us, because another transport had stopped there earlier and he had given them all he had. He noticed the empty tub and almost fainted. He shouted; "what am I going to feed the pigs now that these animals have eaten their food?" He chased us away fast, threatening to get his rifle, if we did not leave. We left. That night we slept in a barn on another farm.

We barely kept walking. As we were passing the signposts we noticed that the signs were familiar. Had we seen that same sign yesterday or maybe a week ago? All of a sudden we heard the ugly-sounding siren, it did not mean much to us, we just did not care, but the S.S. tried to scatter us off the street. We ran; everybody in a different direction. Herczi and I just kept running and we found ourselves in a field of broccoli surrounded by trees. We pulled out a few broccoli plants and started to eat them while waiting for the S.S. to call us back. Everything was very quiet and peaceful. All of a sudden we felt very much alone. We went back to the place we had started to run away from, but there was no one there. The transport had left without us. At first we were happy to be free. We saw a group of people standing by a house discussing the air raid, and went up to them and asked for help in German, but they just turned away from us and walked into the house.

We went further and a few little German Hitler youths started to follow us, throwing stones at us, spitting at us and calling us all kinds of names. So, now we could have our freedom, but we did not know what to do with it. Whomever we asked did not want to help us. We did not know where we were; it was scary. So after long deliberation and discussion we shamefacedly decided to follow the transport and join our group again. If only we would have known how close we were to Czechoslovakia, it would have made a world of difference.

No one had even noticed our absence, so we did not have to explain anything to the S.S., and the other girls were glad to see us. Some of them had thought that we were foolish to return once we had escaped, but when I explained the situation, they saw it differently also.

Soon we stopped at another field; it must have been April by now. The weather was a little milder. We stopped at a lake, with clean water, surrounded by large trees. We did not need any encouragement, took off our few clothes and went into the water to wash ourselves. We didn't have any soap or clean clothing, but it was refreshing, and we felt cleaner than before. There were some weeds growing on that field. I remembered those sour-tasting wild leaves from home. We started to eat them, and that was our dinner. We spent the night in that field.

Next morning, as we started our walk again, I noticed that the same signs came up very often now. I figured that we must be going around in circles and those circles were getting smaller and smaller. That night they herded us into a dark, closed-in barn. My sister Herczi found some kind of squash, we ate it and she became very ill from it. She vomited and soon felt better.

The barn was semi dark and looked like a dungeon I noticed a small opening at the bottom of one wall, we were so skinny that I was sure we would fit through the opening. I asked Herczi to go out with me to beg for some food, but she didn't feel up to it. I tried that opening, but it would bring me out in the front of the guard station. Facing the back of the building there was a very narrow window. It would have been too small even for a very young child. I teamed up with another little girl and slipped through the narrow opening with ease, and we went to look for some food.

We came to a row of nice houses and knocked on the first door. A lady came to the door and just motioned to us with her hand to go away. As she opened the door slightly I saw a group of S.S. soldiers eating and drinking around the table. We ran from there fast.

We knocked on the next door. A man came out and we asked him for some food; he invited us in and asked us to sit down. The family must have just come out of church and were finishing lunch. Now we knew it was Sunday. The lady apologized for not having any meat left, but she gave us some mashed potatoes and gravy with bread. We assured her that it was plenty and we greatly appreciated it. They just watched us eat and had tears in their eyes. They asked us some questions about the whereabouts of our families, and when we told them that everyone had been killed in Auschwitz, they were really crying and the lady asked her husband: "What can we expect to happen to us now that we are losing the war?" That was the first time I heard anything about what was going on on the battlefields. No wonder the circle was always getting smaller; we were being surrounded, by whom, the Russians or the Americans? We did not know.

I told them about my sister and asked them if it would be all right with them if I took my bread back to her. The lady of the house even gave me a little more, and I hid it in my dress.

We came out feeling a lot better. Now we had to try to make it back to the window and sneak back in. We had hardly taken a few steps, when a big fat man and with him an equally fat boy appeared in front of us from nowhere and promptly whistled to the S.S. soldiers and shouted, "Here are a couple more!" By then we were running toward the gate anyway. As we were coming closer I was sure they would kill us. By then I was so full of bitterness that I did not even care anymore. They gave us a good beating and searched us, but by some miracle they did not find the bread, and I was able to give it to Herczi. It strikes me as funny that both of the times that men did us wrong during the Death March, they were fat and ugly.

Now we were back in the barn after my poor head had suffered some tremendous blows. At least we did not have to climb through the window, which would have been quite a job, being much too high up from the ground.

On the road I always tried to attach myself to older women, and we often discussed what we would like to do, if and when we came home. We all had different ideas and cravings.

The only problem was that these women had less of a chance to survive, because somehow they kept contracting some diseases or other problems previously unknown to me. Their legs turned blue and became very swollen, and they seemed to know that this was the end for them. Sure enough it was. I lost my dear friends one by one, and we just had to leave them behind wherever it happened. Later we heard shots and after another group came and buried them in mass graves where ever they could. I suffered each time we lost someone. Finally, I decided not to make close contact with anyone. I did not want to be hurt over and over. Every day our group was shrinking more and more.

Not Much Hope Left

Now the S.S. did not pay too much attention to us; we did not eat but neither did they. The farmers refused to give them anything. Our march still continued, only now we were walking in a pretty tight circle. Mostly we slept outside somewhere and ate grass, or sometimes we raided some fields. We were like locusts. I felt sorry for the farmers, when they came out and saw that there was nothing left of their crops. We were just trying to survive.

One night we stopped somewhere and slept in a barn. Someone luckier than we were; had stopped there before us, and had eaten some potatoes and left the peels. What a luxury! We fell on those peels and ate them from the dirty straw, no matter that they were a week or so old!

By next morning more people died there. Apparently, others died before us. They tried to keep us away, but we saw the mass graves in which they had buried who knows how many people at one time. We still did not know what part of Germany we were in. The civilians we overheard were talking German. More and more frequently we saw other prisoners, mostly in striped uniforms. We waved to each other, shouted a few questions, inquiring about where they came from, and they did the same. By now it was obvious that the S.S. did not know what to do with us. They were supposed to take us to *Terezienstadt* to finish all of us off, but they ran out of time. The war was ending.

I looked around and noticed that there were very few of us left. When we first started out, I looked behind us and saw a long line. Now, I could even count the rows; there were hardly more than fifty rows that would be only 250 people out of the 1,200 we started with.

I did not think that we would survive; the lice were biting us, sucking out what precious little blood we had left. Our hair was full of lice, as well as our clothes; everywhere I looked people were scratching and looking for lice in their clothing. The more we killed the more we found. It was a terrible situation; just to watch us must have been disgusting. We could not help ourselves.

Run Run

We were walking through a beautiful forest. A wide, paved road was cut through the middle of it, and on both sides the big trees swayed in the breeze. On the ground, moss and gorgeous white flowers were growing everywhere. Now I knew that spring had arrived.

It was a sunny day, and we were dragging ourselves, still lined up five to each row. We were aware of the S.S. soldiers not paying too much attention to us anymore; they were gathered behind us holding a heated discussion about something.

Suddenly, they shouted at us; "Run, run! Go anyplace, just get lost!" Their behavior scared us. I thought that, as in a cowboy movie, they wanted to shoot us while we were running. I just stood there, until they started to hit us with rifle butts. I did not know that the reason they were letting us go was that they wanted to escape without us. Now we all ran for our lives into the forest and tried to get in deeper and deeper. We still did not realize that the war could be over; our minds did not work properly. Everyone seemed to disappear in small groups.

I do not know how long we were walking in the forest, nor did I know our location. I found myself and Herczi together with ten or twelve women, and I did not know where the others were.

Soon we came to a clearing, and not far ahead there was a house and some other buildings; then we saw animals. It was a farm. A man came out, and I asked him in German where we were. He told us that, "This was the *Sudeten area.*" I had learned about the place in school, so I knew that we were actually in Czechoslovakia. I spoke to him in Czech and he replied, so I asked him for something to eat. It so happened that of the twelve women, only Herczi and I spoke Czech. He told me that, when Hitler had taken over the *Sudeten area,* he had remained there and lived on his farm. We received some milk and potatoes to eat which tasted delicious. He said that he did not have anything else. We were lucky that he did not offer us some rich, fatty meat, because we would surely have died from it. After we finished the food, the other girls asked us to be their interpreters and ask the man for jobs for all of us, just for food. We asked him, but he informed us that the war was over and we could go home. The Germans had lost the war.

I remember we were just sitting there looking at him, as if we did not understand what he was saying. He was shocked when I told him that we did not know. I could see that he could hardly wait for us to leave. Herczi and I decided to start out toward home, and the two Hungarian sisters, Lili and Alizka from Budapest, decided to join us.

Lili had a big mouth and was very bossy, while little Alizka was a sickly little thing. It was a miracle that she survived, but she had a strong will to make it.

We were free now! I could not believe it; we did not even know how to act as free people. The Germans were fleeing with some of their belongings in small wagons; we were still humble toward them as before. Oddly enough we did not encounter any military. As we came to the end of the town, after some distance we saw a house and a nice yard, and since it was getting late and we were very tired we went up to it, knocked on the door to ask if we could sleep someplace. To our surprise it was empty and open, so we walked in. It looked as if someone had left in a big hurry.

We walked through the house and made sure that there was room for all of us to sleep, but mainly we were interested in food. We came to the kitchen and found it stocked with everything we needed. I cooked paprika potatoes, so little Alizka was happy, and we made a soup. That was enough. We ate well that night and soon we were ready to go to sleep. Someone was knocking on the door, and that startled us. When we opened the door, we saw three very distinguished looking men standing there, asking us who we were and what we were doing there? We told them and, thinking back now, they must have known it as soon as they saw us. They told us that sometimes it can be dangerous to enter an abandoned house as we did, because the Germans could have set up some explosive material inside before they left. These men spoke Czech to us. We were told to go to sleep for the night, but in the morning we would have to leave. One man said that he would come over in the morning and help us get in touch with an organization that took care of survivors. Before they left, they showed us how to lock the door, and we went to sleep.

The next morning the men came back with a couple of people from a hospital. We were taken to a hospital; we were questioned, photographed and tested for different things, but first we got to take a nice hot bath. We were given clean night gowns and a nice clean bed for each of us. We stayed there for a few days and got all kinds of treatments, and we felt a lot better and stronger.

After we were released from the hospital, we were taken to a sanatorium. There they also treated us very nicely; we had to rest a lot and they fed us oatmeal and milk three times daily.

After a while we became restless and demanding. We were tired of the same food and wanted some meat. They tried to explain to us that any heavy food would make us very sick, maybe even kill us, after what we had been through, and they kept feeding us oatmeal.

Later we did find out that after the war lots of people died of stomach typhus, and that it was because of the food they were eating. We had to face the fact that our severely dehydrated bodies could not take a normal diet yet. The Czech people were very compassionate and generous toward the survivors. As I think back, I am grateful for everything they did for us. We spent about two weeks in this sanatorium, and then we were released. It was time to think about going home and see who of our family had come back. I was still hoping that my mother would come home.

(USHMM, photo # 24707)

"Major Frank Ankner with the 5th Infantry Division, Medical Battalion, takes the pulse of a female Jewish survivor of a death march at an American military field hospital in Volary, Czechoslovakia." This photograph is an example ofhow thin and emaciated Lili and Herczi were when they survived the death march. They each weighed about 35 kilograms (70 pounds) at the end of the death march.

Going Home

Everything seemed to be my responsibility again. I never asked for any of it, but I was pushed into it by the loud-mouthed Lili. At each railroad station, I had to go in to the big boss and request some travel vouchers for the four of us. We were at the mercy of the people in the office, and there were some who would rather have seen us all dead than going home now and needing their help. Anti-Semitism still very much existed, even in Czechoslovakia, but the majority of Czech people were very helpful in aiding the survivors without asking where we had come from originally.

Our transportation home was free, most of the time. However, as time went by it was getting harder and harder to get travel vouchers for the railroad, since most parts of the rails were bombed out and there had to be detours by whatever means we could find.

Finally Lili's harassments and insinuations were getting to me, and I told the sisters to attach themselves to another group that was actually going their way and we would do the same, because I just did not feel assertive enough by myself to get us to our destination. She started to complain and accuse me of abandoning them in a strange country. Her quiet little sister told her to be quiet and said that she did not blame me, because not too many people could stand her constant bickering.

Traveling Homewards

It was a long wait for the next train, and when it came, it was full already, but it looked as if we lucked out this time. I heard someone shouting my name, and when I looked up, I saw our neighbor Iren Moškovic motioning to us to come up and join her group. These were all older people who were more resourceful, so I felt that this was our chance to make sure we would get home soon. We said a quick goodbye to the sisters and climbed up on the train. They also climbed up, but into another compartment, and so we were on our way, but we never saw each other after that.

I felt a lot safer now that Iren took us under her protection. She had held a position in the camp, and it was evident that she had had enough to eat. She was as fat as she had been at home, and we were skin and bones and still had lice. There was no place to get rid of them.

Sometimes we were without any means of transportation for a few days, and then we just loafed around trying to figure out the next move. On those days we were on our own as far as our food was concerned. We still had to beg for it and offer to work for food. We did not know any other way. We still existed on scraps only.

The next day some Russian soldiers came by, drunk like pigs. I was scared of them, but Iren saw a way out as soon as she spotted them. They had a horse and wagon with them, and Iren wanted them to take us to the next available train station.

She had owned a tavern before we were taken away from our homes, and she was quick to recognize a real drunk. Iren knew that she was safe in offering anything to the "Rusky," because he would pass out soon. It was quite an education to Herczi and me to watch her play up to the man in his drunken stupor; she hugged him and cajoled him, until he gave her the wagon, before he passed out.

At that time we were somewhere in the middle part of Czechoslovakia. We still had a long way to go. Some survivors, if they were strong enough and bitter enough, would go into homes that had been German-occupied during the war, and if the Germans were still there, they would take things from them. That was true mainly while we were still in the Sudeten area. They then had valuable items to trade with the locals for useful objects. I was not smart enough or brave enough to do it. I did not even want anything at that point, just to get home. Later it would have come in handy, but all I had on my mind was getting home as fast as possible. My thought was that Mother had survived and surely would be there, waiting for us. I nourished that fantasy all through the time I was in the camps.

That was my reason for living and I did not stop anywhere for material help that was being offered to the concentration camp survivors from time to time. Consequently, I was not registered as a survivor anywhere. A short while later I found myself regretting this very much.

Iren made sure that Herczi and I were on the wagon before we left in a big hurry. We did not stop until we reached the nearest station. There we left the wagon and boarded the train. When the conductor came to check for tickets, we of course, did not have, any but he asked us if we have any proof that we had been in the camps. All we had was the tattoo on our arms, but that was enough.

The train took us somewhere through the Slovak territory, and from that point there were no connections at all. As we walked around the street, I really do not remember what town we were in, but we saw a lot of survivors. Here I received another very painful shock. As I said before, when we saw some new faces, we always asked where they were coming from. I met a young man, and we started talking, and he told me that he came from a place called Bor in Serbia.

I told him that my boyfriend was there and asked him if by chance he knew him the expression on his face told me that he had some bad news for me. I found out that my boyfriend had been shot in that God forsaken Bor. (Bor was an extended forced labor camp, where the men from other camps were deposited to await final termination. We had heard bad reports from there, even before we were taken away.) Now I really felt alone. I cried a lot. That did not change anything; I just had another heart ache to contend with. It made me very angry, bitter, and full of hate.

The rest of the way home we either had to walk, which we did most of the time, or get a ride somehow on some wagon. Again I felt completely removed from reality, just floating along helplessly and almost hopelessly.

Since the time in the hospital back in the *Sudeten* area, at least our clothes were fairly clean, no lice in them, but our hair was still loaded with them. Now we had come to the end of June 1945, and we were finally getting close to home. At the rate we were progressing, it probably would take us another ten days or so. I started to feel very anxious about going back to our house. Deep down I knew that none of my family was coming back. After all, I had seen them being taken to the gas chambers, and I had seen the sky afterward. I still tried to convince myself to push toward home as fast as we were able to.

Now we were almost home, tomorrow we would be in our own home. Will Mom be there to welcome us? As in the fantasy I built, believing that she'll survive? How much of our home had remained the same? Were any of our belongings left inside? Tomorrow we would find out.

Part III: 1945 — Time for Adjustment

We Arrived in Uzhorod

The Carpathian portion (Podcarpatsky Rus) of Czechoslovakia where Uzhorod was located, was now being occupied by the Russians. Under the Russians it was now called Uzgorod. After World War II, this portion of Czechoslovakia was actually taken away and annexed by the Russians as part of the USSR (Union of Soviet Socialist Republics), while the remaining portion of Czechoslovakia became a satellite country of the USSR. Today, with the dissolution of the USSR, this portion is now a part of the Ukraine.

Chronologically, I was an adult, but emotionally I felt like a frightened little girl, as we were walking through our town. We came to the crossroad where we used to play a lot as children. Our neighbors came over and welcomed us home, asked us about our parents and sisters, but when we told them, they were sad and felt sorry for us. By then I was very anxious to get home, because Mother was waiting.

We walked through the gate to our house; Mother was not there, everything had changed. Herczi knocked on our door it did not open, but someone shouted, "get out of here. This is not your home anymore it's my house now." The yard was covered with green grass, which we had never had, because of our barnyard animals. Herczi fell down on the grass and started to cry, and I joined her. All our feelings were poured out right there.

I thought, why did we survive? We cannot go into our own home; we were without help and hope. But when I looked up I saw *our non-Jewish neighbor Mariska neni* running toward us with tears in her eyes. She came over, and hugged us and said "come to my house, I'll take care of you." God must have sent her, just as I was losing every hope, she offered her home to us, we did not know what to say; we just followed her. First she fed us, then she gave us hot water and a basin to wash up and we washed our hair thoroughly, but the lice didn't come out. We informed her of our situation concerning the lice, and she gave me a comb and some newspaper to comb them out onto the paper. Afterwards, we burned the whole thing. It was an ugly and disgusting business, and it took us some time to get rid of the lice, and even after that the eggs settled in our hair and would not budge. Eventually we got them all out.

That first day that we were home, a young man with whom we had been friends before we were taken away, came over to visit us, and when he left, he shook hands with me and left me with a thousand kronen. I did not know what to say, but he told me to take it and use it. He would not miss it, and he was glad that we were home. We gave the money to Mariska neni and told her that she should keep it for taking care of us.

We recuperated a few more days and then we tried to get into our house. The people who were occupying our house told us that they would not move out and that this was now their home.

I found out that there was a man handling such cases and we got his address and went to see him. We walked into his office, but when he saw two skinny, helpless kids, he told us we would be better off living in the city than in the outskirts by ourselves, and he gave us a key to an apartment in the middle of town.

We went to see it. It was a mess. In the middle of the kitchen someone had dumped a load of sand. Is this why we survived? One disappointment after another, I was so depressed; nothing was going right for us. The boys we knew from before told us that most places were in bad condition, and they offered to help us clean it up. They could not help us get back any of our parent's belongings, so we lost everything because there was nobody strong enough and forceful enough to fight for us.

It took us days to get the apartment cleaned up but finally we could move in. Some old neighbor gave us a Hollywood bed, but it had a large hole in the middle. We set it up in the front room and covered it with a blanket. I slept on it every night. Even so, some time went by before we were able to relax and call the apartment our home. By now Herczi and I adopted another orphan girl who had been left alone; she moved in with us and shared our meager supplies.

Slowly our friends brought us some odds and ends and we set up house. One day our neighbor brought back my sewing machine, and so I was able to do some alterations to supplement the food we obtained at a kitchen set up for survivors and funded by American Jews.

I was no longer surrounded by electric high wires, but what the Hitler era had done to my mind and heart left its traces for a long while to come. Eventually I recovered and if I had had the determination then that I have today, I would have gotten back every stitch of my parent's belongings.

My Feelings of Insecurity

In the beginning, we were often invited for dinner at the home of different gentile families, who had been friends of our parents. We were served food that we had not eaten for a long time. One evening we were invited to three families and we accepted all three dinners and ate everything so we would not miss anything. I do not understand how we managed that as far as the timing was concerned. It did not take too long before we got tremendously overweight, not only us but almost all the survivors in the neighborhood.

Soon the boys and girls started to go out to dances and to dinners; for me it was too soon after we had come home. I could not understand how they could forget so fast. I did not realize it at the time, but this was their way of being able to cope with life and face the future. I was unable to accept it. I cried a lot, worked and ate some more. My sewing did not go too well either as I never liked it; I just was not good at it. I did not make enough money to sustain us; we did not have anyone to turn to except the American soup kitchen that was set up for the survivors. But I was always hungry, and one meal just was not enough for me. One day I approached the man who was in charge of the whole operation and asked him for more food. He refused me, even after I told him that I went home hungry each night. Everyone knew that he had pocketed plenty of funds that had been sent to feed us.

Farmer's Market

Usually on Thursdays the farmers brought in their goods to sell. A certain street was designated for their display and people came from all over town to shop. I went there every week also, mostly to look, because I could not afford to buy very much. Sometimes, I was able to buy a cup of butter and some tomatoes, green peppers, and a large loaf of bread to supplement our meals.

On one of those Thursdays I bought some cabbage, onions, rice and tomatoes for stuffed cabbage. Of course I did not have money for meat, but I remembered that my mother used to make stuffed cabbage without meat. She did this only on a holiday when we were not supposed to eat meat.

I came home all excited, thinking that Herczi would cook the meal the next day. I approached her as soon as she came home, but she did not say anything. The next morning she told me that she could not cook without wood. All we had was a broken-down cabinet that was left in the apartment, and we slowly used it as firewood for cooking. Cooking with that dried wood was hard; it flared up and went out, unless you kept adding more wood continually. We had to sit there and watch it; otherwise we would have to start all over.

I had to finish some alterations because the customer was planning to pick it up after dark. As it was Friday, I had to clean up the place, because I did not work on the Saturday Sabbath. Well, my dear sister got mad and threw down everything and in less than two minutes she was out of the house. I was angry, but I had to do what I had to do.

It was easy to get angry those days. My body seemed to be the home of hate, anger and bitterness, and it did not make me a very nice person. So I finished the dress and cooked the cabbage which turned out very well and I also cleaned the house. As it was getting dark, I lit the candles for the Shabbat and was on my way out to meet a man who had asked me for a date.

Just as I was walking toward the door, it opened and Herczi appeared in the doorway with two "bodyguards." The two young men resembled each other. One was walking with a cane, to show off I suppose. As far as I could see, there was nothing wrong with his legs. They both wore hats and high boots, which were in style at the time. They were handsome fellows. I had never seen either one of them before.

I was angry at my sister and let her know why, right in front of them. They must have felt sorry for Herczi, that the poor baby had to live with someone like me, but they did not know my side of the story. I watched from the corner of my eye as one of the fellows was easing himself toward the bed with the covered hole, and with the cane in front of him he sat down exactly in the hole. His legs flew up in the air. It was the most comical sight I had seen in a long time. I could not stop laughing as I walked out of the apartment. (Who knew at that point that this same person would someday be my husband?)

My date had arrived, we went out for a bite, but mostly he wanted to talk me into staying in Uzhorod and not leaving because he "had plans for us". I had known him since before the camps, but I never thought he was right for me. In fact, I was beginning to think about leaving because I was also feeling uncomfortable with the Russian occupation of Uzhorod.

Will I Ever Feel Normal?

Since I was eating mostly the wrong kind of food, I became heavy and felt ugly. I still had lots of problems, including the remnants of the lice infestation. Those terrible little white eggs were sticking to every hair on my head like glue. I tried to pull them off, but most of the time the hair came with it. My hair was perhaps two inches long and it grew very slowly. It took a while until it was long enough for me to cut those unsightly nits out.

It was close to my birthday October 1945. As time went on, I became more and more introverted. I used the excuse that I did not have any time to make friends, but the truth was that I was not emotionally ready for it. Most of my days were spent in tears. It was so easy to cry, and I had plenty of reason for it that's for sure. While I was working, I had to be careful not to stain the fabric with my tears.

90

My Dad's Orchard

One beautiful sunny afternoon I decided to go home to our garden and pick some of the great-tasting fruit of the trees that my father had planted. They were just getting ripe. I walked over to one of the trees and started to pick some of the delicious plums and put them neatly into my basket, tears running down my face as I realized where I was and reminded myself that now I was but a stranger on our own property. While struggling with my emotions, I heard someone shouting at me to leave her fruit alone. I looked up and saw the old woman we called "Bobics neni". My parents had been friendly with the whole Bobics family all their lives, and now she was chasing me away from the property that she knew, was rightfully mine. I got so angry that I grabbed a large chunk of dried out mud and threw it toward her, shouting: "If you don't get out of here, I'll kill you." She ran out of the yard and I never saw her again. I do not think that I would have harmed the old woman, but at that point I just filled up my basket and never went back there again.

Shortly after that episode, I decided to leave my home town just as soon as I could. Rumors were spreading about the Russian's plan to close the border, which would make it impossible for people to get out. I did not want to wait for that to happen and be stuck in a Russian occupied territory.

Shortly afterwards, a couple of friends came back from Czechoslovakia and told us that in the Sudetenland, survivors were being given homes that had been occupied by Germans during the war. I saw an opportunity for us to start life all over again.

Herczi and I talked over the possibility of leaving Uzhorod. We decided to go to the Sudetenland. The little girl we had taken in wanted to stay in Uzhorod, so she moved out. Herczi left with our friends and I stayed behind to sell whatever few things I had, like the sewing machine, some material and such. When I was done I was suppose to follow them to Podmokly.

About two weeks prior to our decision to leave, a friend named Sam, had left some parcels in our apartment. I had finished selling our belongings; however, I could not leave because of Sam's parcels. Sam returned two or three days later with big plans: He wanted to marry me. Well, I almost fell over. Then he showed me the contents of the boxes, and I told him to get out. "What kind of person are you?" I asked.

The boxes were filled with money, and he let me take the risk of being caught with it. In those days one had to deal on the black market to earn that much money, and if somehow that money would have been found in my apartment, the Russians would have sent me to Siberia, probably never to come back again. He was full of apologies, but it did not make any difference. He did offer to take me to Podmokly, where my sister was living and waiting for me. I accepted, thinking that he owed me that much. I had no feelings toward him. Unfortunately for him, he took it as an encouragement and told everybody that we were engaged.

Soon I found out when we were to leave, and I started to prepare for the long journey. I did not have much to take with me, but when all was packed, I had a large bundle to carry. I did not have any suitcases, so everything was crammed into a pillow case. I had many spools of thread in assorted colors and was thinking that I might be able to do some alterations in my new home, so the threads and other leftovers would come in handy. {As it happened I never used any of the things I took with me.} Anyway I was ready to leave, and to tell the truth, I had no idea what might come next, but I had no regrets whatsoever at leaving the town I had been born and raised in. It did not feel like home any more.

I Left My Home Town for Good

On the morning of our departure, four more people came with us and I found out that we were all going together to a little town called Kapos. There someone would put us up for a couple of days, before we would take the train to Prague. Since everyone had to take care of their own packages, I was sorry now for bringing so much junk, but it was too late to do anything about it. The others were afraid that the large bundle would attract too much attention, when the guards came to check the passengers.

They were right. When we arrived at the check point and the Russian guards came up, my bundle was the first thing they noticed. They wanted to know to whom it belonged. I had to say it was mine and tried to explain that I had nothing important in it. I offered to open it for them to see, but they just took me off the train, bundle and all. The others told me to take the next train to Kapos. The guard said, laughing "If they will let you go at all." Now I was really scared.

It was getting dark, and I had no idea where this guard was taking me, but we were walking toward a building. When we entered, I saw some other people there also waiting, and I was told to sit down. Soon another guard came over and told me to bring my stuff and follow him. I walked to a desk where a young man greeted me in a very friendly manner. I looked at him and all I saw was his thick bleached hair and I must have been staring at him; I had never seen a man with bleach-blond hair before. He smiled at me and asked: "Don't you recognize me?" As I looked up, it came to me. His mother used to come into my parents' house on Saturdays to light the fire, since it was against our religion to strike a match on the Shabbat.

I remembered his mother bringing along a couple of kids when she came to add wood to keep the fire going. My parents paid her for it, and she needed the money, so she was happy to come every couple of hours to make sure that the fire did not go out. He was one of her sons, and that is why he knew me. It was lucky for me. He told me to relax and asked me if I wanted something to eat or drink, but I did not want anything. He informed me first that there would not be any transportation out of that place until the next morning. He took me into his office with my bundle. I have to admit that I was afraid of him. He was the person in charge there, and the others listened to whatever he said. He asked me what was in the bundle and I told him that the best way I could answer would be to open the bundle and show it to him. I did that and he asked me if he could have some thread for his mother. I said, "Take what you want," and he took two spools and thanked me for them. At that point he explained something to me that by then I had figured out by myself. Lots of people were dealing on the black market, and when the guards saw my bundle, they were sure of finding in it cigarettes or other items to be smuggled. He asked me, "What are you going to do with all those remnants and threads?"

I had to make up a story about taking it to an old lady to help her out because she was doing alterations. After that, we talked about the past. He told me that, when he was old enough, he had joined the Russian army, and now he was a border officer, got pretty good pay and was able to support his mother. He asked me about my parents and sisters and when I told him that they had been killed, he had tears in his eyes.

Finally it was time to go to the train station, and he came with me and carried my stuff. We said good-bye, and he helped me get on the train. I never saw him after that. The whole episode could have ended a lot worse, so I thanked God for everything. (God was in my life again and still is.)

The train ride was short. Apparently the guard station was not very far from my destination for that day. I was very upset about the whole episode. I did not know where I was going. I felt so alone. When I got off the train, two young men came up to me and told me that my friend had sent them to take me to the house where everyone was waiting to get started on our journey. Kapos was a small town. I remembered having been there before. My father had been raised in Doboruska a nearby village and my aunt and uncle and cousins had lived there until they were taken to the concentration camps. When I was a little girl I visited my relatives, and once they took me to Kapos. It did not impress me too much. I also had known a few young men that came from there.

When we arrived, someone gave us something to eat and when I told them that I had been up all night, a woman took me to a room with a day bed. She told me to lie down and try to sleep. I must have fallen asleep immediately, when the lady came in to wake me up, I only had time to wash up a little, before we had to leave for the station to take the train. This time my bundle was no problem. I noticed lots of people carrying even bigger bundles. The Czechs were not as strict as the Russians. Lots of survivors were on the train. Like us, they tried to escape from Russia in time. Some people remained there, to regret it later on.

I do not remember how long the train ride from Kapos to Prague took, but I know that I had a lot of time to think things over. Also the scenery was very beautiful and constantly changing. As I looked out the window and the train passed one town after the other, I wished that I could remember more of what I had learned or was supposed to have learned in my geography class. It would have been more fun if I could have identified the beautiful places we passed.

After a long and tiresome ride we finally arrived in Prague. We got off the train. As for Sam, my "protector," I had ignored him along the way, because he was so grouchy. Every time someone just looked at me, he was ready to jump out of his skin. I did not like that at all, and I told him so, but it did not help.

Sam also told me that the Czech government was giving homes that had been occupied by Germans during the war, back to Jewish Czechoslovakian survivors. Czechoslovakia was the only nation that made the Germans leave their homes with no more than 30 kilograms of goods, and leave all the rest of their belongings behind. That was what the Germans had done to us. Sam's brother had already been given a home in Prague.

Maticka Praha (Mother Prague)

Well, Sam's brother had a gorgeous home in the best section of Prague, and Sam offered to take me there for the night. As it was getting dark already, I thought that it would be a good idea and I said, "Fine!" His brother's family was very nice to me; they gave me a nice room and a good dinner. I was so exhausted that I asked to be excused and went to sleep. Before I fell asleep, I heard him tell them about his plans to marry me.

When I woke up the next morning, it was beautiful outside, and I wanted to look around a bit in Prague. I had been there only once before at the age of five, when my parents wanted to immigrate to America. I surely did not remember much from that trip, except the *"HORKE PARKY"*- Hot Dogs that were being sold on the streets all over Prague. Not any more, as everything required coupons. All food was rationed.

Prague was and still is a beautiful old city. I loved it there but stayed only a couple of days. I sent a telegram to my brother, Leonard in Detroit. By then I was anxious to get to Podmokly, where Herczi was living and waiting for me.

Lili, Herczi and Laczi's brothers Mike and Andy in Podmokly. Laczi was Lili's boyfriend who was killed in a forced labor camp in Bor, Serbia.

We left Prague the next morning, and it took only a few hours to get to Podmokly by train. I soon found the nice apartment where Herczi had obtained a room for us. It was in my boyfriend Laczi's (who was murdered by the Nazi's in the forced labor camp at Bor) brother Miklos's apartment. His younger brother Andy and an old aunt of theirs (who was also a camp survivor,) lived there. There was plenty room for all of us.

I was happy to see that the two boys had survived, and it was good to see my sister also. I had missed her a lot. We stayed up late that night to catch up on all that had happened since we had seen each other last.

Sam had come with me to Podmokly and also told everyone there that we were engaged. He talked about his plans to marry me and how we would someday buy a ranch with horses and he would teach me to ride. The more time I had to spend with him, the more annoyed I got. We were taken out for meals, but I don't mean that anyone paid for any of our meals. They just had to provide some coupons for food, as everything was rationed and we had not received any ration books yet. We were able to buy bread, dumplings and gravy without coupons, so I ate those most of the time, until I found out where to apply for ration stamps for meat tickets, one kilogram a month.

I kept telling Sam that I did not want to marry him, but I'm not sure that he believed me. I told him that I did not love him, but whatever I said did not seem to penetrate. After a few days Sam finally went back to Prague, alone.

Problems-Problems

Again the days and weeks seemed to just disappear, and one day I read in the papers that several people had been arrested for loitering without proper identification. Now I was scared because I did not have any papers to prove my identity, and without papers I could not get a work permit and therefore no job. I did not know where to turn. A week later Sam came back, and I told him about my dilemma. The answer he gave was that if I married him, my problems would be over. Well, I was not that desperate yet, but I had to find a way soon, because people were being turned over to the Russians and taken away by them. Since I came from Uzhorod, which belonged to Russia at that time, I did not want to get on their list.

Sam told me that he knew somebody in Prague who could help me. In the morning, we took the train to Prague and from the station we went to a hotel where lots of survivors lived. A friend he knew from his home town lived there also. Sam was sure that this man could acquire an I.D. for me. As we came to the hotel, there were three men sitting on a bench. One of them was the young man that Herczi had brought home once, who had fallen into the hole in the living room sofa. Sam did not stop or introduce me to them, but just pushed me past them. We went straight to the room where the person we had come to see stayed, but he was not there. What a disappointment!

Sam did not know where else to look for his friend, so he said that we were out of luck and would have to come back some other time. As we passed by the bench where the boys had been sitting earlier, there were only two of them now. The one that I knew from before said something about my shoes needing to be repaired, but at that point I could not afford it. This really made me angry, and I said to him, "Not everybody knows how to use the black market." I immediately regretted my snappy answer, which came out with a lot of anger.

When he saw that his remark had hurt me, he followed me to apologize and to ask what my problem was and why did we need to talk to the person we had come to see. Well, I told him about my papers and he said, "That's no problem. My cousin works for an organization that supplies I.D.'s for survivors." I was very interested in what he was telling me and asked him if he could take me there. He made a phone call and found out that she was not working that day. He told me if I came back some other day he would take me to see her. We settled on a specific day the following week and he gave me an address where I could meet him.

The Wild Goose Chase for My ID

I went back to Podmokly, full of hope and thanking God for helping me meet this fellow and felt that now my problems would be solved. The day arrived when I was to go back to Prague to meet him. I found the address he had given me, and I met a couple who lived there by the name of Gluck Kalman and family, but Mrs. Gluck told me that she hadn't seen Javor (that was the nickname of the person I had been looking for) for days and she had no idea where he could be. I could not understand how someone could behave this way. To me, someone's word still meant something. If I promised something, I kept my word. He had made me come all the way to Prague on a wild goose chase. I became very disillusioned by that experience.

I spent lots of time alone in the house In Podmokly. I did not feel like going out too much, and it really wasn't even safe. I did not want to end up back in Russia. One day I was walking home from somewhere and I passed by a window which had a sign "Attorney at work." I thought maybe he could help me, so I went in and asked for him. He came out of his office, asked me in and inquired what he could do for me. He was a very nice gentleman. He gave me some good advice about getting the necessary papers, to prove my Czech Citizenship. He asked me to write to someone that had lived in our city before the war and might remember me, like a teacher of mine or someone who was holding some kind of position in our city and could verify my place of birth. Meanwhile he wrote a letter for me that would serve as my temporary I.D. provided I brought in somebody to sign it who knew me from home. So now at least I felt fairly safe.

A few days later I ran into someone I knew, and he told me that a teacher that had lived not far from us had sent him the letter he needed because he was applying for the renewal of his citizenship. He gave me the teacher's name and address. I remembered him very well. I wrote him a nice letter telling him who I was and explained my situation. I told him that I had not been his pupil, but we had lived very close to his house. I informed him of what I needed and asked him if he could help me. A couple of days later I received his letter. He was very nice; he wanted to know what had happened to my parents and sisters. He said that he remembered my whole family quite well. He sent me a very strong document signed and notarized and we corresponded for a while. This paper was useful to me even later, when we were trying to get passports to come to the United States.

Can Ones Destiny Be Forced?

One day I met a girl on the street whom I knew quite well, and she told me that Javor had come to Podmokly and she had talked to him earlier. I remembered that this was the fellow who had lured me to Prague and had not kept the appointment. I still wanted to know what had happened that time. I asked her to tell him that I wanted to talk to him.

He came over in a big hurry. Maybe it took him an hour or so before he knocked on our door. I was busy changing the beds, the linen was white and fresh and he came in and just stared. I could not help thinking; who knows when the last time was he had slept in a clean, white bed?

Javor after the camps in 1945.

I looked at him; he was so handsome, tall, dark and slim. (He looked like the man of my dreams.) I asked him if he remembered me, he said he did. He also remembered our first meeting at the apartment in Uzhorod and the bed in the living room, with the large hole. He asked me to go for a walk, and we talked about ourselves a lot and got acquainted. I felt very comfortable being with him. I am not sure if the issue of the reason I asked him to come over ever came up even. He kissed me warmly when we parted and asked if he could come over again. My answer was yes and we saw each other often.

Now that my papers were in order, a big burden was eliminated, and I could go on looking for a job in Podmokly, but since there were a lot of people coming up every day from the Carpathian area, jobs were scarce.

Javor became a regular in our house and as time went on we developed a friendship. I did not realize that other people knew Javor as a womanizer and probably were talking behind my back. At this point our whole relationship was very innocent. He never even suggested anything other than a kiss and a hug. I was comfortable with him and gradually I began to enjoy his company.

Sam also appeared every now and then. Each time he urged me to make up my mind and marry him. Each time I told him that it would never happen, because I did not love him. He insisted that I would learn to love him eventually.

The next time he came, I decided that I did not want him to bother me any longer and told him that I was in love with Javor and would marry him on the spot if he asked me. Sam actually started to cry. I felt sorry for him, but I had never led him on, so I thought it was better to end it right now.

Javor took me out to dances, but he himself did not dance, except the "czardas", which is a Hungarian dance, which I did not like. But I always could dance with his friends or mine, and it was fun.

By this time I was impatiently waiting for an answer from my brother. It had been some time since I had sent the telegram, to inform him that Herczi and I survived. I was so sure that I had memorized the right address, but by now I started to have doubts. There was no need to worry, because a couple of days later I received a telegram back from my uncle Morris in which he said that he was very happy to hear that at least we two were alive, and he informed us that he was forwarding my telegram to my brother Leonard *(nickname Loli)* in Germany, since he was in service there and he would come to visit us. He sent our address to him in Germany.

Suddenly my mind went crazy. I started to cry and wondered: What is my brother doing in Germany? Is he in a camp there? All kinds of stupid things came to mind. How could he end up in Germany when he was in America? I kept on crying until someone came and took the telegram out of my hands and read it over out loud. Don't you see? He is in the United States Army and he is stationed in Germany. Soon I calmed down and felt pretty silly. I had never thought it through in the first place. I had let my emotions carry me away and made a fool of myself.

After that, there was nothing to do but wait. I knew that Leonard would come sooner or later. I was very anxious to find out what he would say about Javor. I knew that Herczi was not happy that I was so serious about him. She kept saying that she could not understand what I saw in him, since we did not have anything in common. Herczi had a pretty big mouth in those days, At times she was even nasty, but I mostly ignored her.

The days went by quickly; I still did not have a job. I did not have much money to spend. The few kronen I had from selling some of the items in Uzhorod would have been fine, but just then the currency was changed in Czechoslovakia, and we had to turn our money in or lose it for sure. The 10,000 kronen I had, were devalued by some percentage. I was given 3,000 cash and 4,000 had to be deposited in the bank. I suppose that this was done so as to control the black marketers somewhat. One had to prove where the money came from, and there was a limit of how much money could be changed. The deposited amount or rather part of it could be withdrawn for some of the following reasons: Marriage, childbirth, or death. Otherwise you could not touch it.

By now I saw Javor every day. We had become emotionally involved with each other. He told me about his feelings of responsibility toward his brother Bernie and youngest sister Gityu-Ilona. They were still in Uzhorod, and he wanted to go after them and bring them over the border. I could see his dilemma. He hated to leave me, and yet he had to go and bring back the "little orphans," as he referred to them.

Javor when we were dating in Podmokly (1945).

A few days went by. We talked a lot. He told me a great deal about his life as a youngster and I must say, it sounded quite eventful. Finally the day came when he had to leave. We said good-bye. I was pretty sad about his departure; at that point I was not sure whether he would come back or not, because it became harder and harder to cross the border. I missed him a great deal. I truly loved him.

About this time I met a young man who came from a village near Uzhorod. Now he lived in a resort town called Tisa. The Czech authorities had given him a large home completely furnished, which came with a tailoring shop equipped with sewing machines and all other items necessary to run it. His name was Morris Herskovic and he was looking for some workers. He said that he and his two younger brothers lived and worked together and asked if I and another girl named Rose would be interested in working for him. He had a room for each of us. I wanted to work and Rose wanted to join me. Tisa was a beautiful place to live in. I have lots of nice memories of that place. Morris' brothers were very nice young men, but very shy. Morris was a bit silly, but a good person.

I worked in Tisa for a few weeks; my nightmares about the beating by the Kapo on Yom Kippur, my arrival to Bergen Belsen, sick with a bladder infection; tortured me. The Death March and the other horrors kept occurring and made me very miserable. I cried and screamed and someone had to wake me every time. I tried to learn to live with those episodes. I went out dancing now and then and enjoyed myself as much as I could. I got a couple of post cards from Javor to let me know that he was all right.

The Changes That Came About

After spending about six weeks in Tisa, I decided to take some time off from work and visit my friends and my sister in Podmokly. As soon as I stepped off the train, a friend came to inform me that Swartz Patyu, a man I was friends with from my home town was looking for me. I liked him; he had helped us a lot when we first came home from the camps. I was told where he was staying and I went to look for him. We were happy to see each other. Then he told me that the real reason for his coming up from Slovensko was to warn me. He had heard that Javor was going to marry me, so he came to talk me out of it. He told me that Javor was not right for me, because he was a skirt chaser. He had had a lot of women and he would cheat on me and I would suffer a lot.

He kept talking to me for about an hour or more, bringing up reasons why I should back out. Finally, when he saw that he was getting nowhere, he said, "I never dared to ask you to marry me, because you were so independent and I didn't think that you wanted to get married at all." By then I told him that I loved Javor, and it was too late, I just hoped that he would come back safely.

After that I visited with my sister and some friends, and then it was time to take the train back. The train ride was pleasant. I always met some interesting people going my way. After I arrived at the Libouchec train station, a long walk was ahead of me to get to Tisa. The country-side was very beautiful at any season. The paved road was bordered by colorful trees, and the effect was breathtaking. Still it was a steep, long climb. By now I was getting used to it, and actually I always enjoyed that hill. Sometimes somebody would stop me to ask for directions and at the same time would give me a ride in their car. That was exciting; because there were not that many privately owned cars.

When I reached Tisa, it was still early, and since I did not feel like going home, I stopped at the restaurant to have a bite. As I sat down, a young man I used to dance with came up to me and asked if he could sit with me and have his meal at my table. I had no objections; it was lonely to sit alone, and he was very pleasant. We were talking about different things and before we parted, he invited me to the next dance.

The Big Party Bash

One day the two younger Herskovic boys approached me, to ask my opinion about throwing a party for their brother's birthday and wanted to know if I would help them. I praised them for the beautiful thought and told them that of course, I would be happy to help. I was very lonely. I missed Javor so much, and the truth was that I was wondering if he would be coming back. I was not sure at all, and at times I was nagged by doubts.

We were busy preparing all kinds of food for the party; this occupied my thoughts, at least for the time being and that was good. The party was to take place on the following day, which was Saturday, and lots of people were invited. We cooked and baked and decorated the house. The boys did most of the work, but we helped.

Around noon we had finished the party preparations, when there was a knock on the door. Otto, one of the boys, answered the knock, and I heard a voice that I had been hoping to hear for some time now. It was Javor asking for me. Otto brought him in. His shirt was all wet, for he had come up the hill on a bicycle. I was flattered and happy to see him, and asked; "Where are the kids?" Javor said that; "He was unable to find Gityu and Bernie because they had already left Uzhorod on their way to Prague." The boys arranged for him to wash up, and he was given a clean shirt and something to eat. They invited him to stay, since there were several rooms available in the house. I thought that it was really nice of them, and I told them so.

Being Friday we quit working early. Javor and I left for a while. We walked all over the countryside and talked about his trip. Javor told me that he missed me, and that he was happy to be back with me. By the time we returned it was getting dark and Javor needed a shower and get some rest, so he retired early in the guest room. I returned to help the others finish the party preparations. After that, everyone went to sleep.

The next morning after breakfast we straightened out the kitchen. Javor said that he wanted to go out to talk to the people of the village and see what was going on in Tisa. Around noon, when Javor came back, everything was ready for the party, and about an hour later the guests started to arrive. When the people from the village came in, they greeted Javor as if they had known him for a long time. They met and talked, and he learned about life in the village. They encouraged him to stay and get involved in a business. The party was coming along very well; everyone seemed to have a good time.

The next morning we had a beautiful day. The sky was a bright blue and the sun was warm. We walked around the lake in Tisa, and talked to the people around us. There were picnic tables set up for some families. Other families were playing musical instruments and singing. It seemed as if the whole world was gloriously at peace. Everybody was very friendly toward us and we enjoyed the time spent with them. On our walk home, Javor told me that he was leaving the next day to see about finding someone in Podmokly to start a business in Tisa. He said he had someone in mind and would talk to him about it and be back in a couple of days.

Another Proposal?

I was sad to hear that Javor was leaving again, but the fact that he was thinking about starting a business here was encouraging. I knew that he had strong feelings toward me; I could see it in his eyes and feel it from his touch when he hugged me and that was comforting. I was in love with him by then, but would not let him know until I was sure of his feelings. He left the next day and I missed him.

After Javor left, my boss Morris told me that he wanted to talk to me. I figured that he would probably fire me now, but when he started to talk he seemed to be very ill at ease and was actually stammering. I got worried and asked him if he was all right? He said yes, but he had to tell me something. He slowly calmed down and told me that he had loved me ever since he met me, and now that Javor left, he hoped that he might have a chance to convince me to marry him. I told him that I loved Javor and I could not even think of marrying anyone else.

The poor man started to cry and told me that he must have waited too long to ask me, but he was very shy and could not bring himself to tell me about his feelings before. Now he felt that his delay was the reason he lost his chances with me. I slowly started to explain to him that there never was any chance, because when I had first met him, I was already in love with Javor. I told him not to be so hard on himself and to start going out with girls. The more I talked to him, the more worked up he became. He behaved almost like a child about to throw a tantrum. I asked him if he wanted me to quit working for him right now. He jumped up and said, "No, I would like you to stay." After this incident I did not feel very comfortable with this situation, but I was not sure what to do next.

The day Javor left, a very uncomfortable time began for me. My boss started to harass me, knowing that I was alone. I did not like the way he insinuated that I liked Javor better than him, only because Javor must be more experienced in sex than he was. At that point he made me sick and I wanted to leave immediately, but his brothers came to me and started to apologize for Morris, saying: "He gets that way every now and then. There must be something wrong with him. Don't pay any attention to what he is saying and stay at least until Javor gets back."

So I gave in. After that episode I avoided him. It was easy because I spent very little time in the house.

The Spy

That evening the young man, I had seen in the restaurant came to ask me to the dance and I was very happy to go with him. We had a real good time. I loved to dance, and he was a very good dancer. We stayed out until midnight. When he escorted me home and we said goodbye at the door, I felt somehow as if someone was watching me. As soon as I walked through the door, I saw Morris standing there in the dark. I turned on the light, and he had an ugly smirk on his face saying: "You sure stayed out late with him. What do you think he has that I do not have? You go out with him, but you refuse even to talk to me." I could not resist flinging an answer at him as I walked toward my room: "He has common sense which you don't seem to have."

Javor's Proposal

Javor came back the next day with an old friend of his whom he called Alex or Shloyme in Yiddish. We met in the hotel restaurant, and they told me about a delicatessen business that they were thinking of taking over and starting to operate right away. Javor also told me that he had made arrangements to move into a nice house on the hill, but close to the highway. I was flabbergasted. I did not know what to say. All this was just too fast for me.

Javor and Alex's Delicatessen in Tisa.

The next day Javor took me to see the store and the house to which he already had the key. A German couple and their daughter still lived downstairs, and we told them that the upstairs apartment would be enough for us. The building in which the store was located had spacious living quarters, and the plan was that Alex would bring his sister and Javor would bring his brother Bernie and sister Gityu, from Prague to live there with them.

I went down to Podmokly and told Herczi my good news. She thought that I was crazy for thinking about marrying Javor. She said: "You have nothing in common. It is all a physical attraction, and you'll be sorry." We parted on that sour note. Of course, no matter what she said, for me there was no one else but Javor.

When I got to Libouchec by train the bus had just arrived and I took it up to Tisa, where I was met by Javor. He asked me to walk with him. As he wanted to talk to me about something very important. We were walking and talking for at least a half hour. He talked a lot but did not say anything important, just everyday small talk.

Finally it started to rain lightly, and then he told me about some of the girls he had known and had had sex with before the concentration camps. Also there was a little girl named Viola whom he had liked very much, but since her father was of Polish descent, the Germans deported them together with other families. Quite a few of them were taken to Poland and were shot over a rock quarry. After they fell in, they were covered with dirt by a bulldozer. It was a terrible way to go, but this method was quite common in those days. It kept the S.S. busy and many Polish gentiles were very happy to lend a hand killing Jews. I think that the reason he brought this up was that at one time he cared very much for little Viola and he wanted me to share his grief.

Now the rain started to come down heavily, and I suggested that we had better go in. When we walked into the house, it was nice and cozy. Everyone was at home, as if waiting for something. Gityu was holding something in her hand and asked: "Javor, now?" and Javor motioned to her: "Not yet." I could not figure out what she wanted. She did not give up, but kept asking the same question. Finally I had enough of it and asked Javor what was going on. He explained to me that he had planned to ask me outside to marry him, but he did not get around to it, so he was asking me now. Everyone was looking at me, waiting for my answer. When I said "Yes," Gityu smashed the object she had been holding in her hand all this time. It was a beautiful porcelain plate. It broke into many pieces and they all shouted; "Mazal Tov and we were engaged. Lots of hugging and kissing welcomed me into the family and I was very happy.

After the war Javor found some of the jewelry his family hid before they were taken away. All were divided between the brothers and sisters. Javor kept a diamond engagement ring. It belonged to one of his sisters. I was honored with that ring. It made me very happy.

I was anxious to share my happiness with someone and decided to go to Podmokly again, and tell my sister. From there, I went to see my friend Lilly Weinberg, and we talked for a long time. She said, "You have to listen to your heart." She knew how I felt about Javor and she was very happy for me. Even some years later, she told me that my eyes sparkled whenever I talked about him, and she could tell that there was true love between us. I talked to a few other friends and told them about our engagement. I think they were expecting this to happen. My friends seemed to be happy for me. In those days all kinds of marriages took place. Most of them would have never happened in normal times. We all needed to be loved and love somebody.

Now that we were committed to each other, the thought of our wedding kept us occupied. We chose January 15, 1946 for our wedding date. In the meantime, the store had been opened and was doing quite well. I asked Javor if he wanted me to keep kosher since we had both been brought up in a kosher household. He said no, and I was not strongly in favor of it either. I came home from the camps with a different feeling toward religion. It did not make any difference to me. He said no, so that was good enough for me. Cooking did not come easy to me. I had never cooked at home; I did not even know how to cook eggs. I thought that if I cooked them long enough, they would become soft-boiled, but the shell never got soft.

Preparation for the Wedding

We took the bus to Libouchec and from there the train to Podmokly. This was a day we had to spend running errands. We went to see the rabbi about the wedding and made arrangements for him to come up to Tisa on the 15th of January to officiate at our wedding.

Now that this was taken care of, I had to think about a gown. As there were not any ready made dresses available and everything had to be custom made. Well that was too expensive, so I decided on renting and went to look for one. I found a nice long gown and ordered it for the day before the wedding.

Since the rabbi told us that he would get the license for us, thank God we did not have to worry about that, but we had to go for blood tests and wait for the results, to make sure that we did not have any diseases that we could pass on to each other. They gave us an all-clear certificate and we were done for the day.

We still had a couple of hours to spare, and we spent the time visiting friends. We also stopped by to see my sister. After, we rushed to the train station, and got to

Libouchec just in time for the last bus to Tisa. By the time we got home it was pretty late, so Gityu fixed up a bed for me in their house and I slept over.

In the morning I went back to the Herskovic house where I still had my room and we agreed that I would stay there and work until my wedding. Morris opened the door for me and when I saw a smirk on his face, I just walked past him and started to work. I could hardly wait to get out of there, but I had to be patient.

Gityu and Alex's sister Faygu offered to cook and bake, and they invited some other friends to help. We sent out invitations to all our friends and relatives. January 15 was coming close and the girls were baking lots of goodies and cooking stuffed cabbage and lots of other dishes. Since the weather was very cold, we did not have problems keeping the food from spoiling.

It was necessary to have two couples lead us under the Chuppah (Canopy) during our wedding ceremony. Javor invited his brother Herman and his wife Helen to represent his side of the family. I invited Miki and Bozsi Klein, who were distant relatives of mine that I had earlier met in Podmokly. It had to be a married couple, and they were the only ones I knew. The designated couples had to bring the *Challahs* (the braided egg bread) to the wedding. I remember that Javor also invited his cousins Edith and Harry. Thus we had three *Challahs*. Of course he made a joke that we had three couples instead of two, and everyone, accept me was laughing about it for a long time after the wedding. I felt it was very embarrassing.

Finally on Saturday, January 14th the guests started to arrive from all over. I did not even know most of them. I guess they slept all over the place and pitched in to help with the final preparations.

The Big Wedding Day

On the night of January 14, I did not sleep well, it seemed to me as if I had tried to summon my lost family and ask their spirits to be present on my wedding. I missed them so much I cried all night. Sunday morning, my big day had arrived. I put on my gown and somebody fixed my hair. In those days, I did not need any make-up, not even lipstick. A large chair was brought up from somewhere into one of the rooms and I was supposed to sit there until the rabbi arrived and actually was ready to marry us. According to our religious custom, the bride and groom were supposed to fast on the day of the wedding and after the ceremony eat together as husband and wife.

It was a long day, but people came in to visit with me, and it was fun until Herczi, Miklos and Andy (they were Laczi's, my late boyfriend's brothers) arrived. Miklos had wanted to marry me, and he had been quite serious about it. When they came in and saw me all prepared for the ceremony, they all started to cry and ran out of the room. I do not even remember if I saw them again that day at all.

In the afternoon the last guests arrived. They were telling us how hard it was to get on the sleigh, since we had sent only one down, and that was for the rabbi. All others were supposed to provide their own transportation. Well, everyone had arrived except the rabbi. We thought that maybe he had missed the train and he would come with the next one, but it was getting late and he still did not come. I guess it was decided by someone that, since the rabbi was not coming, Herman, Javor's brother would do the honors of performing the ceremony. I was still upstairs and getting very impatient by now.

Finally someone came up to tell me that it was time to go down for the ceremony. I was jittery, because I did not know what to expect. Someone freshened up my hairdo and straightened out my dress, and I was about ready to go down.

Two women were holding my arms, one was Helen and the other one my new cousin Bozsi. They led me under the Chuppah, where Javor was already standing, and we circled around him seven times, as Jewish custom prescribes. We all stopped moving, the ladies stepped aside and the ceremony began. I was in a daze, unaware that all this was not worth anything, as far as being legally wed to Javor, since Herman did not have the authority to do it.

After the "I do's" were said, the focus was, of course, on us. The guests congratulated us and we were taken to a separate table and were served some delicious chicken soup just for the two of us. To me it tasted like heaven since I had not eaten all day. I had fasted, but Javor told me later that he had eaten. When we finished the soup, we joined the rest of the family and guests and ate with them the rest of the goodies.

A good band had been hired, and all night long they played beautiful songs, and we danced a lot. I enjoyed my wedding, I had a great time. In the big commotion none of us thought about a photographer and no one was hired. Consequently we have no wedding pictures at all. That is a shame.

Javor and Lili after the wedding.

Well, like everything else, this had to come to a conclusion also. Some people stayed there and found a corner to spend the night. It was too late to do anything else and it was still snowing outside. There was no place to go. Javor and I went to our new apartment, thinking of finally being alone. When we came to our house, we saw the lights on and could not figure out how anybody could have gotten in but, sure enough, when we stepped into the apartment, we saw that all the beds were occupied by the out-of-town relatives and friends, and there was no place for us. There was a small cot in the kitchen and we took that. We sat up the rest of the night talking and telling ourselves that we would have the rest of our life to make up for this night. Neither of us even thought of going to the hotel that was not very far from us. When I think back I cannot believe how unsophisticated I was. I had to fight off Javor all night because I was a romantic, and this was not my idea of what a wedding night should be.

Somehow the rest of the night went by, and it was morning. I wished to be miles away from that place, but I was there and faced the sneering faces of the guests. I guessed that they were feeling a little bit guilty for pulling a dirty and selfish trick on us. Someone suggested that breakfast should be eaten at the place of the wedding since there must be a lot of leftovers there. So they got dressed in no time and were out of the house. Soon after, Javor wanted to join the party and I got whisked along.

We came to the store and went up to the apartment and there were almost all the people from last night, eating and still partying. I hardly knew most of those people and I was still in a daze. I just went along with everything without giving it a thought. I always wanted to be close to Javor and did whatever he wanted me to do.

Around mid-morning, the sun came out and Tisa was radiantly beautiful. Nobody felt like leaving, but when one o'clock approached, the time the bus was to leave for Libouchec to meet the train, they got ready to go. Only a handful of close relatives stayed over for another couple of days, and there was plenty of room for them above the store.

New Beginning

I moved my few belongings into my new home, and truly, I did not even know where to start my duties as a new housewife. I did not know how to cook or bake. I did not even know how to keep the house clean. I found myself cleaning all day long, and yet the house was never tidy. We had a good-sized kitchen, and on the same floor, there was a small pantry, which was being used by the German couple that still lived downstairs. In the bedroom there were two twin beds and a stove, a dresser and a night stand.

It was decided that Gityu and Bernie would live with us, and soon they moved in. In the kitchen there was a large brick oven. One could sit on top of it and keep warm in the winter, and there was a table with chairs, and a sewing machine, also a cot resembling a Hollywood bed. Gityu was to sleep in the kitchen on the cot and Bernie occupied the twin bed next to us where Javor and I slept. I objected to this arrangement as I was a shy person and it was very embarrassing to me. I told Javor how I felt and we had our first argument, because he did not see anything wrong in Bernie sleeping next to us. After all, he was his brother, not a stranger. No matter what I said after that, it did not help.

This was a bad beginning in my married life and it left an impression for the rest of my life. After that there were lots of episodes that I did not like, but when I said something, it was dismissed as nonsense. I felt as if my needs were secondary to those of Javor's brothers and sisters, and I was hurt more times than I want to describe. I do not want to hurt anyone's feelings, since it happened such a long time ago, but the memories are still alive, even if they are suppressed.

I did have lots of good times with the kids. Gityu was a good girl, and if I asked her to help me she was willing, only I did not ask very often. She showed me easier ways to change the bed and to do ironing. I liked Bernie too. They both were so close that I felt that I could not penetrate the circle. They were happy to be together, went to dances, and I felt left out. I tried to find my own friends, and slowly it came about. Javor and I met a lot of people walking and talking on outings like picnics on weekends by the beautiful lake. Usually the whole community came out. There was always music, played by some local group and folk dancing.

One morning I woke to a beautiful sunshiny day, I got dressed and felt real good, ready for anything. At that moment there was a knock on the door, and a man from the telephone company came to install a phone for us, which Javor had arranged. That was a big deal there. Now, I would not feel so isolated when I was by myself.

That same day I received a call from my brother Leonard. He told me that he was in Podmokly and had come to see us. I told him that I would be in Podmokly as soon as I could and that I would bring him back to Tisa with me. I would meet him in the apartment where Herczi lived.

I called Javor to tell him that I was going to Podmokly and told him of my good news. He said: "Wait for me. I'll be right home and we'll go together." I was extremely happy. Javor was home in 10 minutes, cleaned up, changed and we were on our way. We caught the bus going down just in time, and as soon as we came down, the train was ready to leave. Everything worked out beautifully. Leonard arrived exactly 6 days after our wedding. Oh, it was a big pleasure to see him after so many years. As we were looking at each other, the tears flooded our eyes and we were both thinking of our families, how we wished they could be with us.

He looked so sharp in his officer's dress uniform! Mother would be so happy seeing how handsome her little Kaddishel looked. I was so proud of him! Everybody envied us. It felt good to walk through Podmokly with him. We also had a lot to talk about, but very little time, because he had to go back in a week.

He came to Tisa with us and he could not get over the beauty he saw there. The snow-peaked mountains looked so picturesque as we were approaching Tisa, and the sky was clear and everybody on the bus was very friendly. An American officer was not an everyday occurrence in Tisa and our fellow passengers felt very good about traveling with us. The people in the town were talking about it the next day, when we showed Leonard the town and introduced him to the merchants and to our friends.

We stopped at one of the farmers' houses and Javor bought a large smoked ham that I knew Leonard would like. We brought it home and Javor hung it up on the window in the kitchen. Leonard wanted to taste it right away and Javor cut him a big piece. He said he never ate such good ham, and from then on he just kept going to the window and slicing his own. We were happy to see him enjoying it so much.

Leonard apologized for not bringing us any wedding gift. He had six cartons of cigarettes left, and he gave them to us. He saw that for American cigarettes we could get lots of things that money could not buy, and he gave me 6,000 kronen. I told him that that was a very generous wedding present. I thanked him and put the money away to buy a pair of boots for myself, because mine needed to be replaced in time for the rainy season.

Leonard in his U.S. Army uniform with friend Andy in Tisa.

I noticed that my brother was tapping his foot quite often, so I asked him for the reason. I found out that his feet were freezing in those beautiful shoes, and he was trying to move his feet to maintain circulation. Those thin leather shoes were not suitable for our cold weather. I asked him if he wanted to get some warmer shoes, but he said no, since he would go back soon and on the base he would have all kinds of shoes.

The next day we went down to Podmokly, to see the rabbi and find out why he had never shown up at the wedding. At the same time we wanted to pick up the Marriage Certificate. Leonard came with us, and only then did we find out that we were not even legally married. The rabbi had sent his associate, and when he arrived in Libouchec, he saw the sled with the horse. He went toward it, but by the time he got there all the other guests were already seated, and they left without the rabbi. The sled had been sent down to pick up the rabbi, but came back without him. The rabbi's associate decided to take the next train back to Podmokly, because the weather was so bad. There was a blizzard, and he was not willing to walk up to Tisa.

In Podmokly, the rabbi himself performed the ceremony, once more "officially" right then and there, and Leonard was our witness; he signed the certificate, and we took it home with us. Leonard spent most of his visit with us. We took him down to Podmokly, because he wanted to stay with Herczi a couple of days. Once, as we were walking together on the street, I heard Herczi making fun of me and I also heard Leonard reprimand her. I was walking a little ahead of them, but I could hear what was said. It hurt me a lot that she always seemed to be so much against me.

The Sad Departure

The next morning Leonard went back to Germany, but before he left, he told Javor and me that, if we wanted to go to America, he would try to make arrangements in Prague at the American consulate. At that point, I was happy to finally have a home and a bed again so I did not want to give it up, after having slept on the floor, or on wooden planks for so long, he seemed to understand that. He told us that we would probably have to go to Germany and stay in a camp for the time being. I did not want to hear about going back to a German camp. It unnerved me. He said, "Okay, I will try to come back again soon." But I didn't see him until we arrived in America 3 years later..

The house seemed empty now, but pretty soon we were so occupied that we could not even think about that very much. It seemed to become a pattern in our life to live from moment to moment. Enjoy everything while it was still there, because, in an instant, everything could change.

A few hours after Leonard had left, Javor came home with a terrible toothache. It was so intense that he was rolling under the table in agony. I asked Gityu and Bernie what we should do about it. I said, "Let's go to the dentist." But he started to holler that he did not want to go, because he was afraid the dentist would pull his tooth. Finally, with a lot of talk, I convinced him that it was better to have it pulled than to suffer from it.

We knew of a dentist in Decin near Podmokly, and we went there by bus, and within one and a half hours we were at the dentist's office. I had the hardest time with Javor until we got there. The dentist took one look in his mouth and told us, "The tooth has to come out." It took me two hours to talk him into letting the dentist pull the tooth.

When it was all over, the dentist told us to stop at our doctor's office in about two hours and ask him to pull the gauze out. He could not do it himself, because his office was closing in half an hour, and he really packed it tight so that it would not bleed. Javor began to feel a lot better. The local anesthesia numbed his mouth and he did not feel any pain. We visited our friends Miksa and Lilly Weinberger, stayed for a while and then we went to Dr. Havas and asked him pull out the gauze.

Dr. Havas had practiced medicine in my home town before his family was murdered in Auschwitz. He had since opened up an office in Podmokley, and became our doctor. He had met Javor in the concentration camp and had saved his life, when he was hospitalized in Auschwitz. Doctor Havas knew that the Germans were coming to empty the hospital and to take all the patients to the gas and crematorium and he arranged for Javor to get out of the hospital in time.

Dr. Havas pulled out a couple of pieces of the gauze, and did not see any more, so he wrote a prescription for some pain killer in case it hurt too much, and sent us home. By the time we came home the anesthesia had worn off and Javor was hurting. Luckily we had bought the medicine on the way home, and so I was able to give him a pill, and he slept all night through.

In the morning, he woke up again with pain. He took another pill and went to work, by the time he came home for lunch his face was quite swollen. And there was some bleeding. By the next morning, the swelling went up to his eyes, and he could hardly see. His face looked blue, and that scared us. He was standing in front of the mirror, checking his tooth cavity, and since I was so much shorter than he, I was able to see inside his mouth when he opened it and I saw a white thread hanging from the cavity. I told him about it and asked him to keep his mouth open, and I would try to pull it out. Sure enough, I grabbed hold of the thread and very gently started to pull it down, and a piece of the gauze appeared and slowly came out. Javor said that it felt as if something was coming out of his eye. After that he healed quickly. But he really could have developed blood poisoning and, even have died from that.

By now I had been married for six weeks and could not understand why I was not pregnant yet. About two months before our wedding I finally got my period, so I felt like a healthy woman again. I believed that if a boy touches you once, you can get a baby in nine months. I wanted a baby so badly, but Javor really did not. He kept saying that we had plenty time to start a family. I stopped every time I saw a baby and asked the mother if I could play with it.

It was March by the time I had missed my period, and that was the sign to me that my wish was coming true. Javor was very upset when I told him. This hurt me a lot. He was talking about taking me to the doctor to get rid of the pregnancy. I started to cry, and he walked away. I decided that, no matter what, I would keep my precious baby. He took me to the doctor, and when I was alone with him in the examination room, I told him that I wanted the baby.

Pregnancy-Hurray

Doctor Havas said to me, "Don't worry, you will keep the baby." He told Javor that he had given me a shot to induce a miscarriage, but that it doesn't work all of the time. He did not tell him that he put water into the syringe. So, nothing happened and I continued with my pregnancy. I could hardly wait for the time the baby would be ready to be born. I had a very bad pregnancy, with morning sickness every day, all day.

One day our friend, the police captain, came over and wanted to speak to us. We invited him for some ham and sausages, and we always had good home-made bread. After he finished eating, he said: "I'm really not supposed to talk about this, but you are such dear friends of mine that I feel that you should know about what happened today. Some Russian officers came to my office and asked if there were any Jews from the Carpathians living here, and he wanted to see the books to make sure that all people living in Tisa are "registered."

Luckily in those days, having learned from past experiences, when we were asked what our religion was, we answered, that we did not have any. He said that this saved us from being rounded up and taken to the jail in Prague and eventually to Russia.

Javor and I had a lot to think about now. We decided to write to Leonard immediately and ask him for an affidavit to immigrate to America. He sent us one shortly. We went to Prague to register, but we received a very high quota number, which would mean a wait of three years. We had to apply all our energy to get together the necessary information and releases for our trip. Each time we turned in a requested document, they wanted something more.

As I mentioned earlier, I was sick all the time through my pregnancy. I was not gaining any weight. I did not eat well, since I always threw up my food soon after I swallowed it. The doctor and others told me that this should only last the first three months and then I would be all right. It was not that way at all. I was in the fourth month and started to feel the baby, and yet I was still very sick. I hardly ate anything. I lost weight. I remember a very embarrassing day when I had to go somewhere by bus. I had eaten a piece of chocolate before I left, and I threw up on the bus. That chocolate was all over, and my new coat was a big mess. The bus driver kept giving me some newspapers to wipe myself off and when the bus stopped, I cleaned it up as best I could, but I know that the bus driver was not very happy. My pregnancy hardly showed, so everybody probably thought that I was drunk. It was disgusting.

All in all, I had a hard nine months. Lots of things happened around that time. Herczi, Miklos and Andy decided to run away to Germany to a D.P. (Displaced Persons) camp, because rumors were circulating that from there it would be easier to go to America. They hardly said good-bye. Shortly after that, a young man named Ernie Mittelman, who was born and raised about ten kilometers away from where Javor's family lived, and he liked Blanka, (Javor's sister) very much came to us looking for her, but she was in Italy on her way to Israel. So he asked Gityu if she would like to go with him to Germany. They would get married and go to America as soon as possible. Bernie decided to go with them also and asked us to come, but I was not in any condition to undertake an adventure of that kind. The next morning they left, and we all parted in tears.

Meanwhile I was quite unhappy, because things did not work out very well for me. Being always sick did not help, and I felt neglected by Javor. To this day I do not know for sure if he was cheating on me, but I was very jealous and lonely. I never saw him with anyone, and he always came home to me.

We had a lot of company from time to time. Javor's uncle Andor from Lucenec used to come up. He was a funny guy; everybody liked him. He loved gourmet cooking, and he himself was an excellent cook. The fancy meals he prepared were always delicious, but he used up a month's worth of coupons for two meals. In those days, one had to have coupons for food, especially for meat. He also knew how to make cognac, for which he used up all the eggs allotted for a month, but by that time I had enough American cigarettes for barter, and it was easy to replace most of the ingredients.

Herman and Helen, Javor's older brother and sister-in-law also came up to visit every now and then. Herman seemed to criticize me a lot. It really bothered him that we did not keep a kosher house.

His cousin Bill (Palagyi Bela) also came up very often and ate meals with us. He asked me why I did not cover the table with a tablecloth when I served the food. I told him that I wanted to but that Javor always discouraged me from using tablecloths on the table. I never could understand why, but if I insisted, we always ended up in an argument over it. Bill said: "When I get married, in my house the table will be covered with a clean white table cloth." I told him to talk to his cousin. (Poor Bill, when he got married, he did not even get dinner on the table every day).

One day the German lady from downstairs brought up a delicious *kuchen* (coffee cake) that she had just baked and told me to taste it, and if I liked it she would teach me how to make it. We sure liked it, and I was very anxious to learn how to make it. I bought all the needed ingredients to make the cake, and the next day the lady came up, and with her help I made my first delicious cake. I was so proud to serve it! Everybody loved it; the cake was really good. After that I made it every week, always with some different filling. She also showed me how to make *Buchticky* (baked dumplings) from the same dough. I needed and wanted to learn new things.

The Lost House Key

One evening I was waiting for Javor to come home for dinner, but he was quite late. As time went on, it got to be eleven o'clock, and I felt tired and worried. I could not imagine what could have happened to him. I was very cold; it had been snowing all day, and I was in about the eighth month of pregnancy, so I decided to go to bed. I cried a lot, but eventually I fell asleep. I was awakened by a lot of noise, and when I went to the window to investigate where the noise was coming from, I looked down and saw Javor throwing snow balls at my window to wake me up. When he saw me, he called out to me; "Come down and open the door, because I lost my key." I looked at the clock and with a shock I saw that it was past 2 a.m. I saw that he was drunk, and it made me very angry and hurt. I told him to go back to where he had been until now. He replied, "I can't. They closed the bar." I reached through the window and said," Here!" and dropped the key. There was a large pile of snow under the window, and he was not very steady, so he missed the key and it fell and got lost in the snow. I closed the window and went to bed. I could not sleep, but I was too upset to give in to him. In the meantime, it got quiet. I did not hear anything from Javor, so I figured that he had left.

In the morning I got up, dressed and went down to see what had happened. Maybe I could find the key. We had a wood shed on the property and there was some straw in there. I noticed that the door was slightly ajar, so I went over and from the impression in the straw; I saw that Javor had spent the night in there. As I was leaving, I noticed something shiny in the straw. I bent down and saw that it was Javor's gold pocket watch, which had belonged to his father. I picked it up, brought it into the house and put it away. He came home at lunchtime to eat. I did not talk to him. I saw that he was searching for something, went outside to the woodshed and came back. I did not say anything to him, I knew that he was looking for the watch, but I thought that he deserved a little punishment for what he had put me through. He kept on telling me about the previous night and how, on his way home, the policeman had called him in for a drink, and then came a second, third, and so on. He forgot about the time. I did not answer him. He went back to work. In the evening, he came home on time, his dinner was ready for him, but I kept up the silent treatment.

I hardly ate anything, everything came up anyway. On about the third day he asked me how much longer I wanted to punish him. I felt bad about the whole thing anyway, so I pulled out the watch and gave it to him. We made up, and life went on. I found the key in the spring, when the snow melted.

New Friends

I befriended a Polish lady, who was about my age. Her tall blond husband was Czech. His name was Jan and hers was Anna. She was expecting about the same time I was. The only difference was that she was well, not sick like me. She told me that her mother had been a cook in a Jewish home, and she taught me to prepare lots of dishes.

Unfortunately they were only visiting. The husband had come to see about a job, and they had to go back to Prague. Anna promised to come back after the birth of the baby. I had the feeling that it was just as hard for her to leave as it was for me to see her leave. In a short time, we had become close friends, and I missed her a lot.

Around that time, I received a letter from Herczi. She was in America, in Detroit, living with our uncle Morris and Aunt Cecilia and family. I was very happy to hear from her. She wrote about her life in America and that she was working in a chocolate factory. She also told me that she had sent a package to us it arrived shortly. One of the benefits of living in a small town where one knows everyone was that the postmaster brought us the parcel himself and waived the inspection. He saved us the money we would have had to pay for duty. Herczi sent me the most beautiful dresses I had ever seen. When we went to a party, I was the best dressed woman there. Lots of people came to me and asked when I had traveled to Paris. When they saw my blank look, they looked embarrassed and said, "We only wanted to know where you bought your dress."

The package also contained a few pounds of chocolate which we enjoyed for months. From then on we corresponded with Herczi regularly. I could not get over the way she changed. Herczi was very happy about the baby and wanted me to write about everything I felt during my pregnancy.

Sometimes, in the afternoons, I would walk over to the store to see Javor and Schloime (Alex), our partner, stay until closing, and then walk home together. By now I was in my ninth month of pregnancy and I met the midwife who was to deliver my baby when the time came. I bought a few items for the baby. In those days, babies were wrapped and tied in a special kind of pillow to keep their spine straight. I bought a beautiful embroidered one and kept practicing how to wrap and tie in a make-believe baby. Javor thought I was crazy.

My Surviving Cousin

One day I received a letter from my cousin Mariska from Doboruska. She told me that she had come back by herself. Her parents and all her brothers and sisters had been killed in Auschwitz, and she joined up with a man and his family - two sisters and a brother. They all came home, but they were not very nice people. My cousin was brought up in small village, she had been very sheltered. Her mother had not even wanted to let her come to visit us; she was always afraid that something was going to happen to her.

Once, as a young girl, I went to Doboruska for a visit and convinced my aunt to let Mariska come with me to our house. I was about sixteen years old and could not understand the strict discipline to which my aunt subjected her daughter. She told me that she would let her come if I made her a dress like the one I had made for myself. I agreed, and Mariska came with me. I made the dress for her with my mother's help. I took her to the dance that Sunday afternoon. She didn't really know how to dance, but I taught her a few steps, and she learned fast. I introduced her to my friends, and every time I saw her sitting down, I asked another friend to ask her to dance. All in all she had a great time, but being as insecure as she still is, even today, she just insisted that she was a burden to me, but she said that she had had a very good time and thanked me for taking her.

She wrote that the man she had joined up with told her that he loved her and asked her to marry him. Poor thing, she was so alone that she agreed to the proposal. As soon as they were married, his whole family moved into her house and took over completely. She told me that she was quite intimidated by them. They made her sign the house over to her husband. I guess she did just that, because they threw her out of the house and took it from her. I asked her what she wanted me to do, although I could not have done much, since I was expecting my baby any day.

In the next letter she asked if she could come up to Tisa and live with us. Javor told me to write to her to come right away. Her letter did not sound good at all. She was with us about a week before I started to go into labor. I was glad to see her, and when she asked us not to talk about her past, we respected her wishes and never mentioned it.

Mariska was really a great help to me, but she had a hard time learning Czech. In her village only Hungarian was spoken. We tried to teach her some words and sentences, but it went very slowly. We invited some young men for company, but she would not talk. She was always afraid that they would laugh at her. After a while we stopped interfering.

Finally my time had come, and I started to have labor pains. When they became more intense, like every 10 minutes, I asked Javor to get the midwife, because I would not know what to do if the baby came. Javor rode down on his bicycle and brought her back in no time. She checked me and said that I had a long way to go; the baby had not slipped down yet. I told her about the pain I was feeling, but she said it would take time. I was suffering and she was drinking coffee. The hours went by, and still - nothing happened. The pain had started in the morning, and now it was dark already and still, no baby. She was checking me all the time and just shook her head. I asked her if it might not be a good idea to call in the doctor, but I guess that would have hurt her ego, and she said that when the time came she could handle it.

It was the next morning, and the pain was getting to be unbearable. She said, "I can feel the baby now." The water broke, but she could not pull the baby out. She still encouraged me to push hard at each contraction but nothing happened. I was feeling very weak by now. Javor came home from work, and I told him not to listen to the midwife. "Just go and get the doctor, I can't take it anymore."

I think Javor got scared, and in less than 10 minutes the doctor was there, and less than 5 minutes later, a beautiful baby boy was born. The midwife was peeved, but the doctor told her she should have called him a long time ago. It was not necessary to let the mother suffer for 36 hours. He went on explaining that the baby was approaching with the width of his head, and he had to move him a bit. He brought the instruments and was ready to use them if he had to, but he did not need any of them. It merely took some rearrangement of the baby's head.

Our Little Miracle

The baby was born December 24, 1946. I was a mess, sore all over. I was torn, and no one ever did anything to sew me up as is commonly done after a hard childbirth. I did not know anything about those things. I only found out later.

The midwife cleaned off the baby. The doctor cleaned me and pretty soon they brought the baby to me to feed. That was the most precious and most beautiful experience in the world. It was worth all the suffering. Mariska brought me some nice hot soup that I really enjoyed, since I had not eaten anything for days; they had only given me liquids.

Prior to the birth of my baby, I wrote to Herczi and asked her about a nice American name, and she wrote back that at the time she was going out with a boy named Irving. I guess she must have been in love with him, because she raved about the name Irving and how beautiful the pronunciation sounded. So I decided to name the baby Irving for his American name and Jiricek for his Czechoslovakian name. I always called him Jiricku or Jirka.

At first I was afraid to touch the baby. A nurse came in to show me how to bathe him, and I remember her saying, "Don't worry, he won't break."

In time I learned how to enjoy my baby. I loved to dress him up in different outfits, and I bathed him often. He was such a joy, a good baby and beautiful. I received packages from America with all kinds of baby clothes. My aunt Johanna sent us beautiful things for Jiricek; he was the best dressed baby.

Lili, Javor and Jirka in front of their home in Tisa.

Lili and Jirka in front of their home in Tisa.

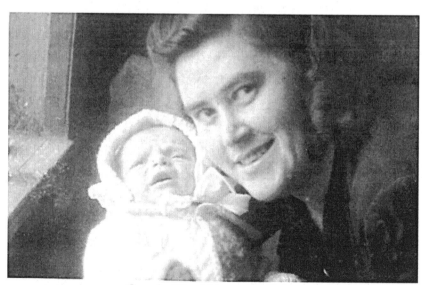

Cousin Marishka with Jirka.

We always had lots of company from Podmokly. When Willy and Lida Lebovic (they were friends from my hometown) came to visit us, Willy took lots of photographs of the baby. Cousin Mariska was a great help, and she was very happy to find a home with us.

As time went by, Jirka was growing into a toddler and we had a lot of fun with him. Every afternoon I took him for walks in the stroller. We walked on the road, and on each side of us were forests. All I had to do was to just break off a small branch from the blueberry bush and give it to Jirka, and he picked the berries and ate them. For a baby, he was very clean and neat; he never messed himself up with the berries. The baby always came first with me. Sometimes that caused some problems, because I never wanted to go anywhere, if I had to leave him at home.

On top of a hill there was a famous Czechoslovakian restaurant, where we had our dinner quite often. The food was excellent. When Javor's cousin Magda came to visit us from *Usti Nad Labem,* a town not too far from Tisa, she asked us to have dinner there. On weekends they had entertainment and dancing. Since it was Saturday, this was a good day to go there.

Lili and Jirka (almost 2 years old).

I dressed up Jirka; he looked like a little prince. He was almost two years old and very friendly, talking to everybody. Magda loved him. We all dressed up and went out for a good time. Since Javor knew the owner and the whole crew, it was no problem to get a good table. We were seated and the owner brought out some good wine. It was quite pleasant. We talked and danced and visited with the other guests. We knew almost everybody there. The food was brought and as always it was delicious. Jirka finished eating before we did and walked away from the table. I looked up and saw him sitting on a lady's lap, two tables from ours, talking. I figured that it was fine, and I went on finishing my dinner.

It seemed like only minutes had passed when I heard a muffled cry. I looked up, but I didn't see Jirka anywhere, I ran toward the sound and the owner was running at the same time, screaming, "Oh, my God! I left the cellar door open just now!"

By then it seemed as if everybody was running toward the cellar. I saw Jirka at the bottom of the long staircase. I felt my heart in my throat. I ran down the steps, and the owner was following me. We were both very scared. When I reached my baby, he was trying to sit up. I touched his body to see if he had hurt himself, but he didn't complain of pain. I grabbed him in my arms and took him upstairs. His face and his clothes were dirty, but other than that he seemed to be all right. Just the same, we took him to the doctor. He examined my little boy from head to toe, and he said that everything was all right; he was not hurt. He seemed to be very happy, and so were we. I thanked God for being so good to us. Wow that was a close one. After that episode I always stayed close to him.

I was corresponding with all my uncles and aunts, but the most precious letters came from my aunt Johanna, Uncle Adolf's wife in the Bronx. In every letter she sent a two-dollar bill. It was a lot of money. We received some care packages from the other uncles and cousins also, so we had more delicacies than other people in the neighborhood.

Since most of the letters were from Aunt Johanna, they were written in English. The problem was, I did not know English, so I found a man named Janosek who did. I invited him over for (American) coffee, and he very happily translated the letters and wrote answers for me in English. We had an electric coffee pot, and I made some fresh coffee and was just ready to serve it with some home-made cake. Little Jiricek was walking around us having a good time, when our German shepherd who was always lying under the stove heard a noise from outside. She jumped up pulling the electric cord from the coffee maker, which I had left unwittingly hanging down and the whole pot of coffee came down and spilled. The baby started to scream. It had spilled all over his legs. We got terribly scared. Javor jumped on his bike and ran down to the doctor's house. He came back with something that looked like aluminum foil, but it was lined with some kind of medication. We wrapped the child's legs in it and kept it on for about half an hour. All the pain was gone, there were no blisters or discolorations left. We felt very lucky. Janosek was happy to see that Jirka was O.K. and told us he would come back some other time.

A couple of days later, Janosek came back and wrote down the whole episode in the letter to my aunt. I also noticed an announcement in the newspaper that came out about that time. It said that anybody could receive up to six hundred cigarettes from America, duty free. That sounded fantastic. I thought that my aunt could save herself some money, if she would send cigarettes instead of the two-dollar bill that she was enclosing in each letter. Janosek wrote this also in the letter. From then on we received six hundred Pall Malls every month. The next letter from aunt Johanna was written in Hungarian. The dear lady had written it with the help of a dictionary. It was precious. I wish I would have saved it. I owed a lot to her; she made our life much easier.

Javor, Lili and Jirka walking in the woods in Tisa.

Life Is Full of Surprises

By now Mariska with Javor's help, had met a widower who came from a village close to where Javor came from. He was quite a few years older, but she decided to go with him to live in Decin, and they got married. We did not see her too often after that, but I was happy to know that she had somebody to take care of her, since by then we were working on our papers to go to America.

I didn't feel good leaving her alone, and we could not take her with us. She seemed to be very happy with her husband; he was an honest hard working man who would never hurt her. Later they had a baby boy, and they lived a nice family life and enjoyed baby Milan they took him everywhere they went.

It seemed to us that we had already collected a ton of papers pertaining to our emigration, but we still needed a lot more. Each time they called us to the consulate, we sweated it out, because we never knew what would be the next demand. Once we were told that Javor needed a release from the Military Department, since he was only 32 years old at the time and still eligible to serve in the Army. It looked bad, lots of other people we talked to had tried and could not get the release. I was the one who had to get all the documents, because Javor could not leave the store. The Military Department was located in another town, and that meant a long ride by train. It seemed so hopeless, but I had to try. In those days I smoked and a cigarette had to be in my mouth or in my hand all the time. I had plenty of American Pall Malls, which used to be a favorite in Czechoslovakia. There were a couple of packs in my purse all the time.

The situation in the country was deteriorating, and I had to gather all the documents needed without delay. Almost daily the communists were after us to join their party. We were offered all kinds of benefits. Once they wanted to give us a large textile store, filled with fabric, if we would just sign up. I kept telling them that we wanted to go to America to be with my family. We knew that America would never let communists immigrate.

We had to get everything the consulate required from us immediately. So it came about that I found myself sitting on the train going toward a city I had never been to before. As I had started out early, I was in the city (I have forgotten its name) before lunchtime. I was scared while walking toward the office I had been told to go to, and for some reason I hoped to talk to a male officer rather than a female. I could not explain why, and I still cannot. I got my wish and I had to face a very morose man. When I greeted him with my best smile, he asked me to state my business, so I told him why I had come. As soon as I said the word "release," I could see the refusal on his face. He said: "Your husband will not be released from the military, until he reaches his 40th or 45th birthday, and why would you want to leave Czechoslovakia anyway? Don't you like it here?"

Now I had to use my brain and be very careful with my answer. Everything might depend on it. I opened my purse and took out a pack of cigarettes. I asked him if I might smoke in his office, and when he said yes, I started ever so slowly to open the pack. His eyes followed every movement. Finally, after I pulled out a cigarette, I asked him if he would like one. His eyes lit up. He took one, offered a light to me, and lit his own. I started to tell him, that all of my family had been wiped out by Hitler. I said that I was not comfortable being here by myself. I wanted to be with my brother and sister, and they were living in America. While I was telling him all that, my arm reached out toward him with the package and I asked him if he would like to have the rest. He very eagerly accepted them and as we were parting, he said: "As for the release, I will try to get it for you and mail it to you possibly sometime next week." I thanked him for seeing me. He thanked me for the cigarettes, and I left his office. I did not think that I had accomplished what I had come for.

I boarded the train back to Libouchec, from there took the bus to Tisa, and arrived, completely exhausted and discouraged. I did not really think that the man would keep his promise, but when I related to Javor what had happened, he was sure that he would send the document to us. To my big surprise, a few days later a large envelope arrived at our address, and there was the coveted piece of paper. It only took one package of Pall Mall cigarettes.

Sometime in November 1948, we received the confirmation from the American Consulate that the permission to immigrate had been granted. We had to be ready to leave by the end of December.

The preparation for the big move took place immediately. We invited our friends to come and see what they would like to buy from us, and they were very grateful and envious. The ladies of course were mostly interested in my dresses from America. Herczi had written to me not to bring those back. I did not have to price anything. I got higher offers for them than I would have dared to ask. We sold all our household goods, and some we gave away.

We had a beautiful German Shepherd dog with papers to prove her pedigree status. I was terribly afraid of her. Her name was Adina, very aristocratic sounding. A man bought her from us with a promise to never abuse or mistreat her. We were hoping for a good home for her, since we could not take her with us.

Two days later Adina came back and when I opened the door and went out, she ran to me with such a joy that I felt like a traitor. I was scared to even pat her. Then I saw the man who had taken her, coming up the walkway and he grabbed the dog and wanted to hit her. I shouted: "Don't touch her, you promised to be gentle with her." He just took her by the collar and left, turning back and saying, "I have to train her."

Packing for America

Obviously we did not have too much time to prepare, but had to arrange for an inspector to come to the house to seal the large crate that someone had made for us to pack our belongings for transport to the United States. We had to pack in front of the inspector. Every time we wanted to pack some crystal or porcelain, he objected to it, saying we could only pack our clothes, linen and household objects, but nothing valuable. We could not persuade him to be a little more lenient. He also told us, off the record, the reason for his diligence. Some or most of the people that had left Czechoslovakia before us, had managed to either pay off the inspectors or keep them occupied enough so they could slip all kinds of valuable objects into the crate. The problem arose when they wrote back to their relatives and friends and bragged about how easy it was to outsmart the inspectors. They took a lot of diamonds, paintings and other items without too much trouble. At that time letters from abroad were very often censored. Naturally the authorities became angry when they read these letters, and became very strict with the next group of immigrants, which was us.

My brother Leonard had pre-paid for the whole trip. This included the hotel room in Prague, the train from Prague to the docks in Poland, and the boat (barge) ride across the Baltic Sea to Scandinavia. The train ride to Goeteborg, Sweden, and the ship to New York.

December 28th arrived, and we had to leave. Most of the merchants from the village came to say goodbye, and the neighbors kept telling us how happy they were for us; they would give anything to be in our shoes. I believed them. We left with tears in our eyes. It made me think of the many homes I had had to leave in this short time. This was different; we were making a change for the better.

We boarded the bus to go to the train station in Libouchec for the last time. We arrived in Prague in the late afternoon on December 28th. We registered at the consulate, and they gave us vouchers and transportation to our hotel room. Javor and I were told to be ready in the morning, and we would be picked up in front of the hotel. While waiting in Prague, we bought a few pieces of beautiful crystal and a good set of dishes to take with us. We wanted to spend our Czech money.

We slept restlessly that night, hoping to get out of Prague as soon as possible. I do not even remember if we ate anything in the morning. When our transportation arrived, we were told to take our suitcases with us. The driver would not tell us anything else. When we arrived at the Immigration Building, I was worried. Some old memories came to mind, as if I had been there before.

We had to drag the suitcases and the baby into the building. The immigration officer told us to wait our turn for inspection. We had a long wait. Lunch time came and we still had not been called in. Now at twelve the office closed for lunch, and we had to wait until two in the afternoon. We ate lunch also, and finally our time came. We passed inspection and were taken back to the hotel, which was close by.

Many relatives and friends came to say goodbye, including Uncle Andor from Luchenec and a friend from Uzhorod. All of us went to the train station, and to our surprise, there was another inspection. To our big shock, the inspector would not let us take the bag with the crystal and dishes. He also demanded that I leave my wedding ring. I got very upset and told him that I was allowed to leave with my wedding ring. He then let me keep my ring. We gave away all these items to the relatives and friends who were still there.

We were in Prague only for a few days, but it seemed like a month. We still did not have our passports. I thought that since we had passed inspection, we would be ready to leave, but each time something illegal was found in anybody's suitcase, they ordered a new inspection for all of us. This did not make much sense to me, but the officers were very careful.

I do not remember how many days we spent like this, until one day we were given our passports, the visa and whatever else we needed. I was very relieved, when they told us we could leave. Until then I was not sure that they would ever let us go.

We were taken to the train station. While we were waiting for the train, suitcases were checked and rechecked. I remember, one lady had lined her suitcase with American gold coins and covered it with another lining material. Somehow they found out what she did and detained her. She called out to me: "If you should see my children in New York, they are tall and red-headed. Please tell them that I tried to make them rich and it backfired." I didn't see her children because by then I had my own problems.

I told Javor that I needed to talk to him. We set down in a coffee shop and after we had ordered something, I said to Javor, "Now that we are allowed to leave, I have to tell you that things will have to change. Until now I was by myself, and you were surrounded by your family. When we get to America, the situation will be reversed. I will be the one with a family and you will be by yourself. I had experienced that awful feeling, and I would like to save you from it. I would like you to join us and help create a togetherness. He agreed with me and thanked me.

We said our last goodbyes while still on Czech soil and boarded the Polish train for our next destination. The train was filthy, uncomfortable; the smoke was heavy from the chain smoking drunk or semi drunk men that traveled from work. The worst part was that we did not know how long this situation would last.

I remember arriving somewhere on a dock where we were put on a ship with one big room, where everyone sat on the floor and most of us got sick. I cannot think of the name of that ship. Someone brought the baby some milk and a bouillon for Javor and me. It made us feel a little better. Shortly, we arrived at a place whose name I do not recall. We were put on a nice, clean train. It even had water to wash our hands, and cloth towels. We were astonished at the difference between the two train rides.

When we got off the train and looked around the station, the first thing we noticed was a stand where oranges were being sold. We ran to it, afraid that they would be sold out before we got there. Luckily they accepted our Czech money, because that was all we had. We ate the oranges with great pleasure, and saved some for later. Little Jirka ate them for the first time in his young life and enjoyed them a lot.

Goteborg-Sweden

A man approached us and said: "Welcome to Goteborg, Sweden." We were informed that he was our guide while staying in the city. He was the travel agency representative in Goteborg. He had a funny name, Gunnar, which in Hungarian meant "gander." He took us to a restaurant, clean as a whistle. On every table stood a large pitcher of milk, and glasses.

As we sat down, we were encouraged by the waitress to drink milk, while she tried to explain the menu in Swedish. We did not understand a word. Somehow, the table was filled in no time with all kinds of good, healthy food, like cheeses, vegetable and fruit, all this in the midst of winter! At the table, a young girl sat next to me, and we started to talk. Her name was Marianna. She came from Prague also, but I did not remember having seen her before. She seemed to speak several languages, which came in handy on the trip. She was fluent in English also. Now we had a translator. Afterwards, Gunnar showed us where to change our currencies for Swedish money. When that had been taken care of, he took us to a hotel, where we would stay for five days or until our ship the "S.S. GRIPSHOLM" would be ready for us to board.

The "Hotel" was a building on a hill on the outskirts of town where young traveling students stayed, nothing fancy but clean and spacious. Each room had two beds and a closet; we had to ask for another bed for little Jirka. The bathroom for the whole floor was down the hall. This time, the people waiting for the ship to the U.S. were the only occupants, so it was not too bad. It was a luxury. We did not have to go to an outhouse. We opened the closet to put our coats in, and there were a whole bunch of clothes that had been left there. Javor made me call the woman who had brought us to the room, and tell her. She spoke German and so did I. She told us to just leave the clothes there, but if we needed some, we could help ourselves. We did not need anything.

As soon as we were settled, little Jirka wanted to go outside, so we went to look around. We found out that a shuttle would take us to town at no charge. Promptly we asked about the schedule and took advantage of the free transportation. Goteborg was a large city. We did not know where to go, so we stopped at the same restaurant where we had eaten earlier. The proprietor came over and started to talk to us in German. He 1informed us about the city and told us where we could go to see some interesting sights. We left that for the next day, since it was getting late.

The next morning we got up early and ate breakfast in the restaurant. There on the table at which we were seated we saw a wrist watch. We brought it to the waitress's attention, and she told us that someone had left it there and would probably return to claim it; we should just ignore it. When we had finished our food, we went to look around, visiting some places of interest.

We passed stores where merchandise had been delivered during the night and had been left in front of the door. We could not believe that no one stole any of it. In Czechoslovakia, all of it would have disappeared almost as soon as it was left there. Amazing! We asked some people about it, and were told that in Sweden no one steals. Actually no one ever did, until the refugees came. Once in a while, they tried to take things. The courts sentenced those people to spend time in an insane asylum, claiming that they had to be insane to steal in Sweden, where they could get everything they needed.

In a few days we were notified of our next move. We boarded the ship the next day. There was a big send-off, a band was playing and lots of people came to see the S.S. Gripsholm leave.

The SS Gripsholm

The Trip to Our New Home

We were luckier than most of our fellow passengers, because, when I had been pregnant and so sick, I had written to Leonard that maybe I might not be able to travel on the ship. He promptly changed our tickets for second class accommodations. At the time it did not mean much to me, but when we went to see the other people and saw them all the way in the bottom of the ship, where all the machinery was buzzing and giving out a horrible smell, I realized what a gift my brother had given us. Our cabin was not luxurious, it had bunk beds, and the bathroom was in the hall, but it was paradise in comparison. At first Jirka and I were assigned to bunk with another lady, Marianna. Emil, as he was now called by his registered name, (to me he remained Javor for the rest of his life.) was given a single cabin, where he was to stay by himself. We did not like that arrangement very much, and complained about it. It did not help. We were told that males and females had to be separated. It was Marianna's idea to get Emil to move in with us, and she would take the cabin for herself. This was a much better arrangement for both of us.

We got settled. There were two triple bunk beds, Jirka was sleeping on the middle bed and we both slept on the top layer of each bunk bed. We were not bothered by anyone after that. I did not know what to do next. Marianna asked me to go with her to the beauty shop, and I went and also had my hair done. I did not know what for. Later, when we went to eat dinner in the beautiful large dining room, I was glad about my new hair-do; I felt very good. Little Jirka enjoyed everything and everybody. He was a little over two years old and he was so friendly that the rest of the passengers were crazy about him.

I looked around wild-eyed. Everything was so beautiful and grand I had never seen anything like that; I did not even know how to take it all in. The rest of the passengers were dressed very stylishly, I was wearing a good outfit and was hoping that it was passable. Before we started out on our trip, I had tried to find some catalogs from America to see the current styles, but I was not successful. I was informed by some people, that the dresses were much longer that year than the previous year. I found a tailor who made me a beautiful navy blue coat that reached my ankles. Two or three long dresses were also custom-made; they were very pretty. Most of the passengers wore long dresses for dinner, so my outfit blended in beautifully. I felt so insecure among all those strangers. They spoke so many different foreign languages. If I had not been able to speak some German, I would have felt lost. At least I could order or rather ask the waiter to suggest something for us to order, and we ate well. After dinner we listened to the music for a little while and then we went back to our cabin. It was past Jirka's bed-time. I heard Marianna come in early in the morning. The next day she told me what a great time she had had and how much fun one could have on the ship. She asked me to come with her the next night. I was 24 years old at the time and I would have liked to go and have some fun also, but I had to face facts. I was a wife and mother and not free like Marianna.

We were exhausted, so we slept well that night. In the morning we went to eat breakfast and we noticed people eating something I had never seen before. It was a grapefruit and I wanted to taste it, so I ordered it, and it was very sour. Marianna told me to put some sugar on it, and now it was delicious. Javor asked for a schnapps. The steward gave him a funny look, but brought him the schnapps (Liquor). He probably thought that he was an alcoholic, drinking so early in the morning. Javor said that his father and grandfather had had schnapps every morning, and they were not alcoholics. Lots of men had a drink in the morning, if they were able to afford it. It was not unusual.

The rest of the day we spent looking around on the ship. What we saw was amazing. It was like a small town. It had everything, only in small scale. Jirka kept us busy; he was a very inquisitive and curious child. When the time came for us to eat dinner, I wore my second new outfit. I felt well dressed.

Dinner, like all the meals they had served so far, was delicious and different. At the time I had no idea that the next dinner would be served without us. The following morning I could not finish breakfast. I felt sick and had to leave in the middle of it.

I went back to the cabin and was violently sick, and when Javor came in and saw me using the bag, he got sick also. This went on for the whole trip. The steward was very sympathetic and kept bringing us food that, according to him, was good for us, but our stomachs did not agree with him. We tipped him generously, because we had no idea of the value of Swedish money. He took real good care of us; he kept telling us how important it was to eat, to keep up our strength, and encouraged us to leave the cabin to get a breath of fresh air. That night there was a big storm. The waves came up so high that they covered the windows. It lasted a couple of days and caused a big delay in our arrival at our destination. After the storm subsided the steward convinced me to go out on the deck and take a few deep breaths. When I came out, the waves were still high and wild, the water was so dark that I had to run to the railing and was sick all over again. After that, I went inside and stayed there until we arrived in New York.

All this time Jirka was fine, but bored. He managed to figure out that, if he said that he had to go to the bathroom, I had to take him out. He made it happen more and more often, and it was very hard for me to take him each time, but I did it. Once he ran away from me, and I had a hard time catching up with him.

Because of the storm the trip lasted much longer than anticipated. I felt weaker each day. I could not keep anything down. One day Jirka slipped out of the cabin without our noticing it. When I discovered him missing, I panicked. Somehow I got dressed and went looking for him, but I could not see him. I saw an officer approaching. I stopped him and asked in German if he had seen a small, blond baby. He told me: "Don't worry. The baby is sitting on the band leader's lap." And he took me there. Jirka was very comfortably playing with the band instruments and constantly talking to the conductor in Czech. He kept all the musicians entertained, even though none of them understood a word he was saying. He was such a friendly and lovable child. I thanked all the men for being so good to him and took him back to the cabin.

Finally in America

The day of arrival had come, and about four in the morning the commotion started. Marianna knocked on our door and asked us to come out to see the Statue of Liberty. We were in New York. This was an experience to be remembered for the rest of my life. When I went out and saw Lady of Liberty for the first time, I felt free as a bird. I was crying and laughing at the same time. I felt sad that my family could not be there with me.

It was about mid-morning on February 16, 1949, when we had to get our suitcases and stand in line for departure. I was told later that we had landed at Ellis Island. It was a slow-motion operation, and standing in line brought back lots of bitter memories from the past, but gradually we reached the officer. He asked for our passports and affidavits, looked at them, but did not return them to us as he had to the people before us. He pulled Emil out of the line. We kept walking together until the officer told me to wait outside, and he took Emil into a building. I did not know what to make of this and was frightened. From where I was standing I could see lots of people waiting behind a fence. I wondered if my uncle Adolf was one of them. This delay really ruined my pleasure at entering the land I hoped to make my home for a long time. At that point I was very uncertain of our future.

I do not know how many hours had gone by, but Jirka was getting hungry and tired, so I decided to knock on the door through which Emil had disappeared and walked in. I demanded to know why they were holding him there. I spoke in German, and they understood. It was explained to me that the medical records were showing that Emil had an enlarged heart, and they had to check it out. Just then Emil came to the door and said in Czech, "No matter what happens, you and Jirka stay in America, even if they send me back."

I started to cry and I guess the officers felt sorry for me, because one of them ran to get the person who had the final say. He came out, gave us back our papers and told us to go. We quickly claimed all our suitcases.

I had a photo of my uncle, and as we were walking toward the exit I was scanning the people that were still standing there, waiting for their loved ones. There were not too many left. I heard someone calling, "Lilly, Lilly," I turned toward the sound, and there was my uncle. We ran toward each other and the hugs and kisses were sweet and brought a great deal of relief.

Part IV: The Verification
By Dennis L. Judd

Life in America

In 1949, Lili (Lillian), Javor (Emil) and Jirka (Irving) settled in Los Angeles, California near where her brother and sister, Leonard and Herczi were living. It was a very hard yet special life as they struggled to find and make a new home, learn the English language, and find work to support the family. Javor's brothers and sisters also came to Los Angeles with their families. Many other Holocaust survivors from the Ungvar area also settled in Los Angeles where they kept up their close friendships.

Emil found work at Canter's Deli and later Langer's Deli. After years of hard work and saving whatever they could, they were able to buy their home in 1953. Their second son Dennis (Denny) was born 1955. In 1957, Emil and Lili bought their first restaurant (Judd's Fat Boy) in the San Fernando Valley.

There were many happy occasions including celebrations of holidays and birthdays, weddings, children being born and Bar Mitzvahs. Irving had his Bar Mitzvah in 1960 and all of the "Ungvaries" (friends and family who had emigrated from Ungvar after the war) came. Dennis had his Bar Mitzvah in 1968.

Life was hard, but good, as the families grew and became established in the community. Then a terrible tragedy happened when Irving lost his life in a car accident at the age of 21, while a student at UC Davis. Life was never the same after the loss of Irving.

Throughout their lives in America, both Emil and Lili continued to suffer from terrible nightmares from their experiences in the concentration camps. In 1986, after a terrible nightmare, Lili came to the realization that it was time for her to start writing her book. Over the next 15 years Lili wrote her memoirs. As she wrote them, her nightmares stopped.

In 1996 Emil and Lili moved to Santa Rosa, California to be closer to their new grandchild Sarah. They became very active in the local synagogues. In 1997, at the age of 81, Emil passed away from pancreatic cancer. He had suffered a lot during the last few years of his life.

Lili missed Emil a lot. Over the next few years, Lili then started giving talks about her life experiences and the Holocaust to schools, churches, synagogues, and service clubs. Her talks gave a personal firsthand experience of living in Eastern Europe as the German Nazis took over. Specifically, about what hatred, anger and prejudice can do to people.

She also had a vision of having her Bat Mitzvah. This was an impossibility for her as a young girl back in Europe. With the encouragement of Rabbi Schlesinger, she began studying her Havtorah (prayers). At the age of 80 she was Bat Mitzvaed at Beth Ami Synagogue in Santa Rosa. It was a very special event that made the front page of the Santa Rosa Press Democrat. Lili is still active in her synagogue, and enjoys spending time with Dennis and Anna, her son and daughter-in-law, and especially her two grandchildren, Sarah and Daniel.

She continues to give talks and has received hundreds of letters from teachers and students who are deeply touched by her message to let go of their anger, become tolerant, and make a positive difference in their lives, and the lives of others.

Irv and Denny 1957

Family portrait of the Judd Family in the mid 1960's.

The Judd Family in 1968 at Denny's Bar Mitzvah.

This was one of the last photos of Irv before he died in the auto accident.

Emil at Judd's Restaurant in the 1970's.

Lillian, Emil and Dennis at Emil's 70th Birthday Party in 1985.

Emil and Lillian on a cruise after retirement in the late 1980's.

Dennis, Anna, Sarah, Daniel and Lillian.

The Photographs from Auschwitz

Helping Mom edit her autobiography has been a special, yet difficult and long process. Her story and writing style are very complementary as she personally walks us through some of the most horrific times in human history. However, growing up as a second generation of the Holocaust, I felt the need to conduct further research in an effort to document what she experienced firsthand. I know that Mom's story will help educate people in society who are ignorant about what happened in the Holocaust. I also know that even with this documentation, it will not stop the hateful anti-semitic individuals who deny that the Holocaust ever happened.

During the writing period, in 1996, I drove to visit Mom and Dad at their home in Oakmont. Mom had just received a brochure from the United States Holocaust Memorial Museum and showed me the picture of "Hungarian Jews arriving at Auschwitz." Mom said that she and her mother and sisters were in the photo. I looked and said "Sure Mom". Then she showed me a photo of her family that was taken and sent to relatives in America just before World War II and I could definitely see the same faces.

What a coincidence that out of the millions of Jews who were murdered, among the only surviving photos of Jews being processed at Auschwitz, taken by a Nazi photographer, would have included a picture of her and her family just after my grandfather was murdered. I knew then that Mom's story had to be published to document what happened and to be used as an educational tool to stop anger and intolerance which could lead to future genocides.

The photograph is part of the "Auschwitz Album" of photographs documenting the arrival, selection and processing of one or more transports of Jews from Subcarpathian Rus (Carpatho-Ukraine). The album was found after the liberation by Lili Jacob (later Zelmanovic, now Meier), herself an Auschwitz survivor who appears in one of the photographs.

Many of the Jews in the photographs came from the trains that were transporting Jews from the ghetto at the brick factory in Ungvar (Ushorod). The Nazis rounded up Jews from the "Sub Carpathian Rus" area and forced them into the ghetto where Mom and her family were also imprisoned.

The following photographs are just a few that I chose to include to visually document the evil selection process that occurred when the long trains full of innocent Jewish families arrived at Auschwitz-Birkenau. They provide photographic documentation of the Nazi German processing of Jews including Mom's family. I have included my own comments with the original captioning. We would like to thank the United States Holocaust Memorial Museum for providing these photographs and giving us permission to publish them in our book.

(USHMM, photo #77220)

"SS guards walk along the ramp at Auschwitz-Birkenau."
Was it one of these guards who viciously murdered my grandfather?

(USHMM, photo # 77321)

"A transport of Jews from Subcarpathian-Rus is taken off the trains and assembled on the ramp at Auschwitz-Birkenau." After four days in the sealed train cars, the innocent and unsuspecting Jewish families are ordered to exit the train cars. This is when Grandfather Elemer was murdered in front of Lili.

(USHMM, photo #77229)

The view from on top of the train car as the "transport of Jews are taken off the trains"

(USHMM, photo # 77225)

"Jews from Subcarpathian-Rus unknowingly await selection on the ramp."

(USHMM, photo # 77218)

Jewish brothers from Subcarpathian Rus await selection on the ramp at Auschwitz-Birkenau. Not just a mass of faceless people in the photographs, but two scared unsuspecting little boys.

147

Renee   Hajnal   Iren   Herczi   Lili

(USHMM, photo # 77295)

"Jewish women and children from Subcarpathian-Rus await selection on the ramp at Auschwitz-Birkenau." This is the photo of Mom (Lili), Grandma Hajnal, Aunt Herczi, Aunt Renee, and Aunt Irene. It is the last picture of my Grandmother and my two aunts alive. What kind of men, people and culture could so easily select these young innocent girls and all of the others to be separated from members of their families, stripped naked, shaved, and then forced into the showers – Gas Chambers, where they died gasping for air. After which their lifeless bodies were then thrown into the German engineered crematorium and burned to ashes to be disposed of as waste?

(USHMM, photo # 77319)

"Jews from Subcarpathian-Rus await selection on the ramp at Auchwitz-Buirkenau." The men on the right have been separated from the women and children on the left. They stand in rows of five waiting for the unknown.

(USHMM, photo #77233)

"Jews from Subcarpathian-Rus undergo a selection on the ramp at Auschwitz-Birkenau."
WHO SHALL LIVE AND WHO SHALL DIE? The SS are separating the children along
with their mothers, and the older women to one side (their right), and the women who do
not have children and appear strong enough to make good slave laborers who go to their
left. They did not separate the mothers from their children because it would cause too
much commotion and because grieving mothers separated from their children would not be
good slave laborers.

150

(USHMM, photo # 77298)

"Jewish women and children who have been selected for death, walk in line towards the gas chambers." The long line, unknowingly walking to their deaths. The SS Officers standing in front of the truck do not pay any attention to the walking dead. The young SS guard standing with his rifle at the bottom of the photograph surely knows what is going on.

(USHMM, photo #77309)

"Jewish women and children from the Subcarpathian-Rus who have been selected for death at Auschwitz-Birkenau, walk towards the gas chambers." Innocent mothers and their children walking unsuspectingly, each one an individual, each one murdered.

(USHMM, photo # 77313)

"Jewish women and children from Subcarpathian-Rus who have been selected for death at Auschwitz-Birkenau, unknowingly wait to be taken to the gas chambers."

(USHMM, photo # 77314)

"Jews from Subcarpathian-Rus who have been selected for death at Auschwitz-Birkenau, wait in a clearing near a grove of trees before being led to the gas chambers." Look at the faces of the little kids.

(USHMM, photo# 77353)

"**Jewish women and children from Subcarpathian-Rus who have been selected for death at Auschwitz-Birkenau, wait to be taken to the gas chambers. Each child and mother; no more birthdays, no more laughter, no more singing songs, no more learning, no possibility to make this world a better place, no more life because they were Jews.**

(USHMM, photo # 77378)

   "Jewish women from Subcarpathian-Rus who have been selected for forced labor at Auschwitz-Birkenau stand at a role call in front of the kitchen." The Nazi German industry now had free labor to make their products. How many of these companies, and their owners, and their families who survived World War II benefited financially from the forced labor? How many of them supported and encouraged the Holocaust for their own personal financial gain? How are their descendants coping with what was done?

(USHMM, photo # 77370)

"Jewish women from Subcarpathian-Rus who have been selected for forced labor at Auschwitz-Birkenau, march towards their barracks after disinfection and head shaving" Lyda Hausler Lebowitz a friend of Lili's from Ungvar stands in line in the second row next to the lady with darker hair. Lyda survived, and is giving talks to classes in Las Vegas, Nevada. She was inducted into the "Hall of Fame" by the Clark County School District

157

(USHMM, photo # 77381)

"Prisoners in the Aufrasmungskommando (order commandos) sort through a mound of personal belongings confiscated from the arriving transport of Jews from Subcarpathian-Rus." The Nazi Germans utilized the Holocaust to steal businesses, homes, furniture, clothing, money, jewels, art... everything owned by Jews, including their hair, dentures, teeth fillings, and eye glasses.

(USHMM, photo # 77384)

"Prisoners in the Aufrasmungskommando (order commandos) sort through a mound of personal belongings confiscated from the arriving transport of Jews from Subcarpathian-Rus."

Nazi German Prisoner #A-10946

Further research with the help of Jude Richter of the Holocaust Survivors and Victims' Resource Center, United States Holocaust Memorial Museum found the Nazi German documentation of prisoner A-10946 (Lili Klein).

German Concentration Camp Documents

Dear Mr. Judd,

Thank you for your request for information on your mother, Lili Judkowitz, from the International Tracing Service (ITS) collection held by the United States Holocaust Memorial Museum.

My search of the ITS records and other resources yielded the following results. Where relevant, I have included an archival cover page and the first page of the list as well as the page on which your mother is named.

According to the documents, prisoner number A-10946 (Lili Klein) was in Auschwitz from June 1944 through December 12, 1944 (529264_1, 529298_1, 529340_1, 529380_1, 529425_1, 529482_1, and 529530_1). She was in Bergen-Belsen (Lili KLEIN Bergen Belsen.doc). From there she was sent to Flossenbürg's subcamp Graslitz, where she arrived on February 1, 1945. Her Flossenbürg prisoner number was 61449 (10796551_1; 10797538_1, 10797539_1, and 10797562_1; 11071363_1, 11071364_1, and 11071364_2). She is listed as person number 120, Lilli Kleinova, on a list of persons who returned to Uzhorod after the war (78810594_1 and 78810596_1). The Regional Restitution Office in Trier sent an inquiry about her to ITS.

If you have questions regarding German terminology on the documents, please visit http://itsrequest.ushmm.org/its/Glossary.pdf for a basic glossary of those terms.

We have completed our research on this case. I am compiling the documents I have found about your father (case 13307) and will send those to you in the next few days.

Sincerely,

Jude C.Richter

Holocaust Survivors and Victims Resource Center

United States Holocaust Memorial Museum

100 Raoul Wallenberg Place, S.W.

Washington,D.C.20024

www.ushmm.org/resourcecenter

Auschwitz Log; June1944;

Lili Judd, AuschwitzPrisoner#A-10946. Arrived June 7th 1944

Monthly Logs of Auschwitz

Arrived June 7th, 1944 – Left December 12th, 1944

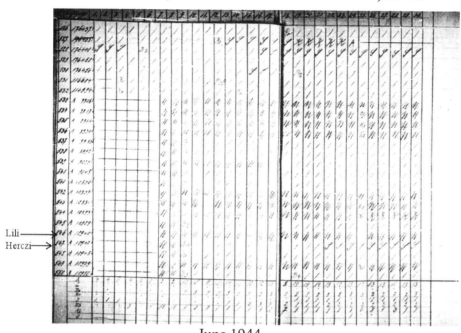

June 1944

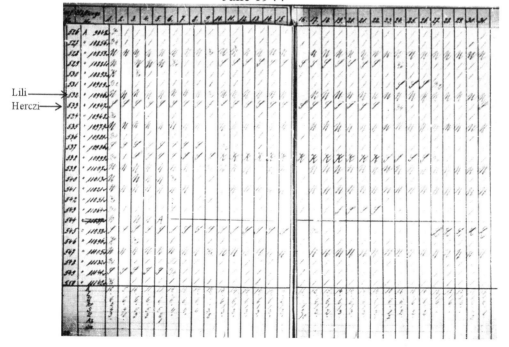

July 1944

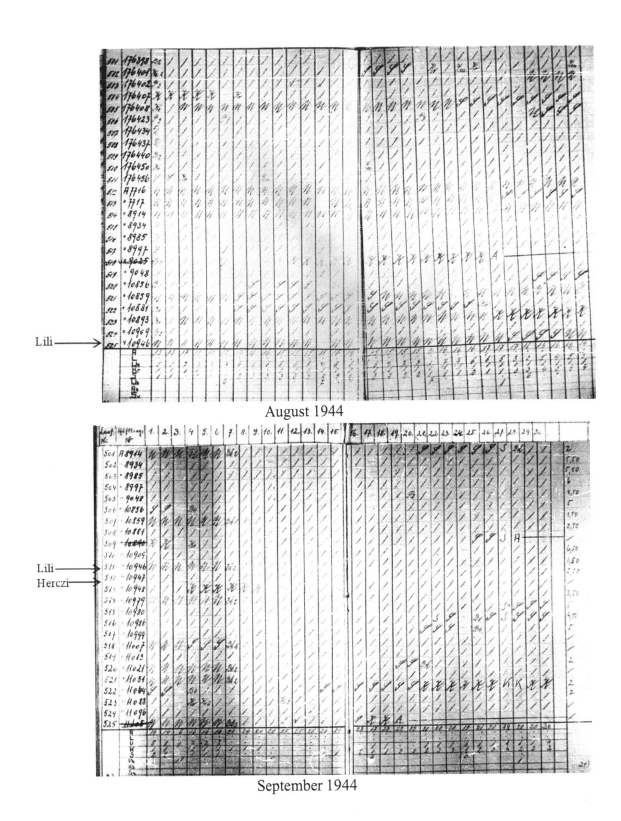

August 1944

September 1944

From Nightmare To Freedom

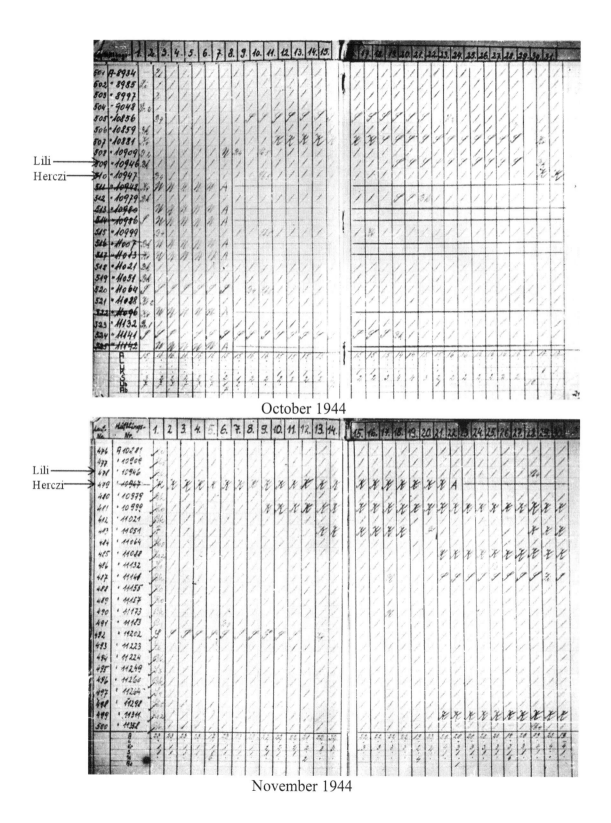

Lili ——

Herczi ——

October 1944

Lili ——

Herczi ——

November 1944

163

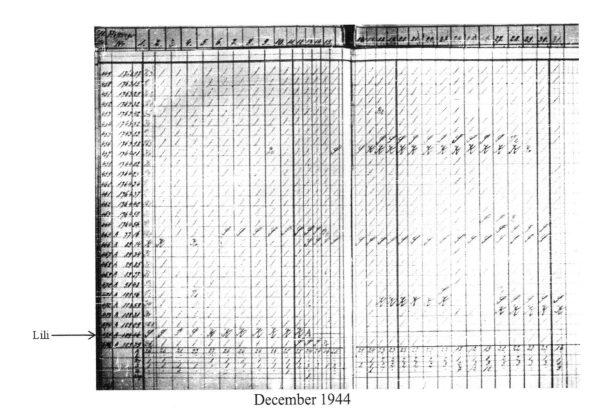

December 1944

Bergen-Belsen Concentration Camp Record

67.441	J. Ung.	Katz	Dora	16. 12. 22.	Bergen-Belsen 4.445.	28.3.45	Graslitz
2	-"-	Katz	Elisabeth	3. 3. 23.	-"-	1.4.45	Rochlitz - Mech
3	-"-	Katz	Hermin	6. 8. 24.	-"-	1.4.45	Rochlitz - Mech
4	-"-	Katz	Rozsi	24. 5. 23.	-"-	28.3.45	Graslitz
5	-"-	Katz	Sari	25. 7. 27.	-"-	1.4.45	Rochlitz - Mech
6	-"-	Katz	Szeren	8. 12. 27.	-"-	28.3.45	Graslitz
7	-"-	Katz	Szeren	26. 10. 20.	-"-	1.4.45	Rochlitz - Mech
8	-"-	Klein	Eta	28. 5. 24.	-"-	28.3.45	Graslitz
9	-"-	Klein	Lili	29. 10. 23.	-"-	1.4.45	Rochlitz - Mech
67.450	-"-	Klein	Eva	5. 3. 27.	-"-	28.3.45	Graslitz
1	-"-	Klein	Hedvig	12. 12. 22.	-"-	1.4.45	Rochlitz - Mech
2	-"-	Klein	Hermin	15. 11. 25.	-"-	28.3.45	Graslitz
3	-"-	Klein	Hermina	16. 3. 26.	-"-	1.4.45	Rochlitz - Mech
4	-"-	Klein	Johanna	1. 8. 09.	-"-	28.3.45	Graslitz
5	-"-	Klein	Maria	29. 10. 20.	-"-	28.3.45	Graslitz
6	-"-	Kleinberger	Etel	26. 2. 25.	-"-	1.4.45	Rochlitz - Mech
7	-"-	Kleinberger	Hanna	15. 9. 23.	-"-	28.3.45	Graslitz
8	-"-	Kleinmann	Erzsi	1. 5. 27.	-"-	28.3.45	Rochlitz - Mech.
9	-"-	Kohn	Ilona	17. 3. 17.	-"-	28.3.45	Rochlitz - Mech. Graslitz
67.460	-"-	Kohn	Janka	13. 9. 14.	-"-	28.3.45	Rochlitz - Mech. Graslitz
1	-"-	Korn	Sari	14. 12. 19.	-"-	28.3.45	Rochlitz - Mech
2	-"-	Kornhauzer	Rozsi	5. 5. 24.	-"-	28.3.45	Rochlitz - Mech
3	-"-	Kovacs	Valeria	17. 3. 17.	-"-	28.3.45	Rochlitz - Mech
4	J. Pol.	Kleimnitz	Paula	16. 2. 23.	-"-	28.3.45	Rochlitz - Mech
5	J. Ung.	Krausz	Erzsebeth	28. 6. 19.	-"-	28.3.45	Rochlitz - Mech
6	-"-	Landov	Berta	26. 12. 19.	-"-	28.3.45	Rochlitz - Mech
7	-"-	Langamer	Estera	19. 3. 14.	-"-	28.3.45	Rochlitz - Mech
8	-"-	Lazarovits	Gizi	10. 6. 27.	-"-	28.3.45	Rochlitz - Mech
9	-"-	Lazarovits	Kato	25. 9. 16.	-"-	28.3.45	Rochlitz - Mech
67.470	-"-	Lazarovits	Roza	26. 12. 22.	-"-	28.3.45	Graslitz

165

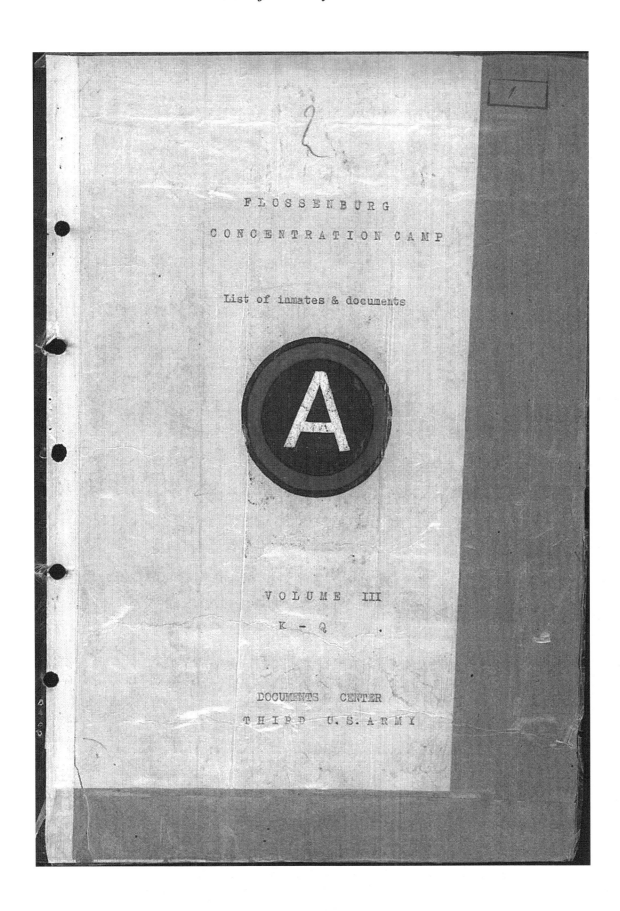

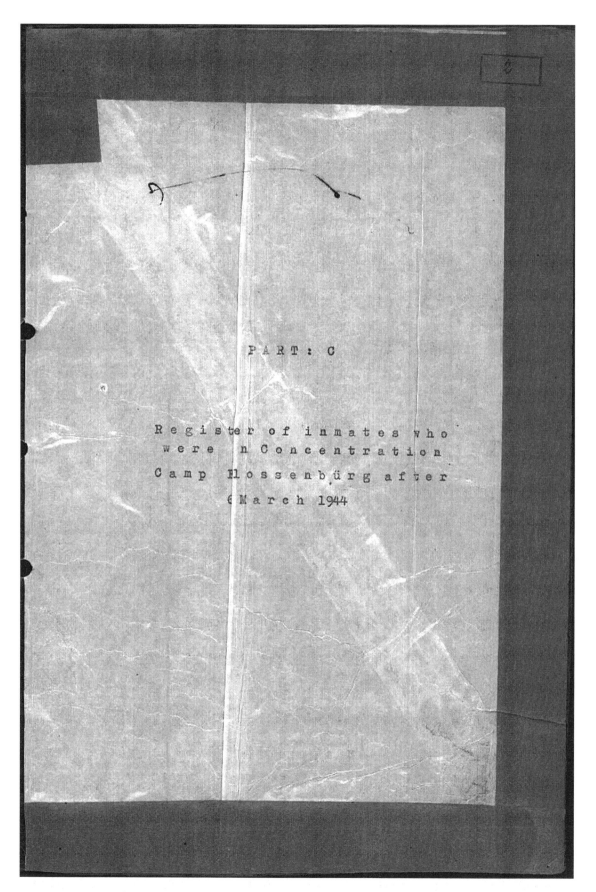

PART: C

Register of inmates who
were in Concentration
Camp Flossenbürg after
6 March 1944

Flossenbürg's Subcamp Graslitz

- 499 -

Klee,	Rachel ✓	63041	HJ	5. 3.09	28. 2.45	
Klein,	Lajos	33166	UJ	17.11.20	9.11.44	
Klein,	Lajos	82301	UJ	24.11.24	25. 2.45	
Klein,	Laszlo	33734	UJ	20. 7.98	9.11.44	26.11.44 Bu
Klein,	Laszlo	40730	UJ	24. 2.14	25.12.44	
Klein,	Laszlo	33167	UJ	27. 9.20	9.11.44	26.11.44 Bu
Klein,	Laszlo,	34376	UJ	3. 6.20	9.11.44	
Klein,	Laszlo	33733	UJ	15. 2.21	9.11.44	26.11.44 Bu
Klein,	Laszlo	40729	UJ	28. 3.21	25.12.45	
Klein,	Laszlo	81407	UJ	7. 9.22	25. 2.45	22. 3.45 Na
Klein,	Laszlo	48446	UJ	14. 7.26	13. 2.45	
Klein,	Lazar	34381	UJ	25.12.16	9.11.44	16. 3.45 T
Klein,	Lazar	81408	UJ	25. 3.26	25. 2.45	10. 3.45 Bu
Klein,	Leib	15216	PJ	2. 5.12	4. 8.44	13.10.44 Da
Klein,	Leisor	83898	UJ	1. 2.26	3. 3.45	
Klein,	Lenke	53067	UJ	26.10.25	8. 9.44	
Klein,	Lidia	64453	UJ	18.12.19	8. 3.45	
Klein,	Lila	62001	UJ	24. 2.05	15. 1.45	
Klein,	Lili	54912	UJ	20. 3.15	10.10.44	
Klein,	Lili	54900	UJ	28.10.22	10.10.44	
Klein,	Lili	61449	UJ	29.10.23	1. 2.45	
Klein,	Lilli	61997	UJ	2. 2.24	15. 1.45	
Klein,	Lipol	34395	UJ	13. 3.00	9.11.44	
Klein,	Lipot	33735	UJ	13. 5.07	9.11.44	
Klein,	Lipot	33168	UJ	14. 9.07	9.11.44	26.11.44 Bu
Klein,	Lizzi	63763	UJ	12.11.20	5. 3.45	
Klein,	Ludwig	33736	UJ	15. 8.07	9.11.44	28.11.44 T
Klein,	Ludwig	16409	D	10. 1.15	27. 5.44	
Klein,	Ludwig	16415	D	23.10.23	27. 5.44	
Klein,	Magda	64454	UJ	24. 5.14	8. 3.45	
Klein,	Magda	63414	UJ	1. 6.22	26. 2.45	
Klein,	Magda	56023	UJ	3.12.18	18.10.44	
Klein,	Magda	63055	UJ	9. 8.24	8. 3.45	
Klein,	Magda	56018	UJ	29. 9.24	18.10.44	
Klein,	Magda	58885	UJ	28. 4.26	22.11.44	
Klein,	Magda	54897	UJ	25. 5.26	10.10.44	
Klein,	Magda	63298	UJ	26. 9.26	28. 2.45	
Klein,	Malvin	54907	UJ	16. 5.12	10.10.44	
Klein,	Melvin	54910	UJ	28.10.26	10.10.44	
Klein,	Mania	53331	UJ	15. 9.24	8. 9.44	
Klein,	Mano	81409	UJ	10. 4.00	25. 2.45	10. 3.45 Bu
Klein,	Margit	63415	UJ	10. 9.10	26. 2.45	
Klein,	Margit	54137	UJ	11. 9.16	12.10.44	
Klein,	Margit	56030	UJ	18.10.16	18.10.44	
Klein,	Margit	56007	UJ	4.12.27	18.10.44	
Klein,	Maria	54906	UJ	29. 5.17	10.10.44	
Klein,	Maria	62604	UJ	28.10.18	15. 1.45	
Klein,	Maria	61455	UJ	29.10.20	1. 2.45	
Klein,	Maria	53235	UJ	1. 8.23	8. 9.44	
Klein,	Maria	50065	DZi	20. 9.24	1. 9.44	
Klein,	Merianne	62470	DA	16. 8.22	19. 1.45	3. 3.45 F
Klein,	Marie	50064	DZi	9. 3.25	1. 9.44	
Klein,	Margarette	50991	DA	13. 4.20	1. 9.44	
Klein,	Markus	47510	UJ	10.10.97	6. 2.45	
Klein,	Martin	89691	SJ	30. 7.16	31. 3.45	
Klein,	Marton	33738	UJ	4. 6.20	9.11.44	4.12.44 Mi
Klein,	Merzell	34402	UJ	21. 1.06	9.11.44	4.12.44 Mi
Klein,	Matthias	47511	UJ	10. 5.06	6. 2.45	
Klein,	Matyas	48873	UJ	2. 1.11	13. 2.45	3. 3.45 T
Klein,	Mayer	81410	UJ	20. 8.27	25. 2.45	10. 3.45 Bu

Flossenbürg Documentation

KL. FLOSSENBÜRG T/D Nr. | 8 | 3 | 6 | 3 | 6 |

KLEIN,   Lili
NAME   Vorname

29.10.1923   61449
Geb.-Datum   Geb.-Ort   Häftl.-Nr.

Häftl. Pers. Bogen . . . ☐		☐	Dokumente:
Häftl. Pers. Karte . . . . ☐		☐	
Effektenkarte . . . . . . ☑		☐	Inf. Karten:
Transportkarte . . . . . ☐		☐	
Häftlingskarte . . . . . ☐		☐	Bemerkungen:
Postkontr.-Karte . . . . ☐			
Krankenblätter . . . . . ☐			
Todesmeldung . . . . . ☐			
Leichenschauschein . . ☐			
Sterbeurkunde . . . . . ☐			
Korrespondenz . . . . ☐			

Umschlag-Nr.:
004887

Vor- und Zuname: K l e i n Lili   Ung. Jüdin   Haft-Nr. 61449

Beruf: _____ geboren am: 29.1o.23   in: _____

Anschrifts-Ort: _____

Eingel. am: 1.2.45 / Uhr von K.L.B.Belsen Entl. am: / Uhr nach _____

Bei Einlieferung abgegeben: Koffer   Aktentasche   Paket

Paar Schuhe, halb	Schlüpfer, Makko	Mantel: Tuch	Paar Handschuhe: Stoff	Effektensack
Paar Schuhe, hohe	Leibchen	„ Leder	Handtasche	Invalidenkarte Nr.
Paar Schuhe, Haus	Korsett	„ Pelz	Geldbörse	Invalidenquittung
Paar Schuhe, Überzieh	Strumpfhaltergürtel	Jacke: Tuch	Spiegel	Arbeitsbuch
Paar Strümpfe, Wolle	Unterrock	„ Leder	Messer	Photos
Paar Strümpfe, Seide	Bluse	„ Pelz	Kamm	Schreibpapier
Paar Söckchen	Kleid, Rock	„ gestrickt	Ring	
Hemd	Schürze: Kittel	Hut	Uhr m. Kette	
Hemdhose	Schürze: Träger	Mütze	Uhr m. Armband	
Büstenhalter	Taschentuch	Schal	Halskette	
Schlüpfer, Seide	Pullover	Paar Handschuhe:Wolle	Armband	
Schlüpfer, Wolle	Trainingsanzug	Paar „ Leder	Koffer	

Bemerkungen:

Abgabe bestätigt: Effektenverwalter:

J U D K O V I C Lillian   836 366
oder JUDD geb. KLEIN
Elmemer & Hanna geb.Friedmann   jüd.

29.10.23   Uzhorod   USA
Ende 3.44   Besohr. i. Uzhorod CSR,
    5.44   i. Auschwitz verhaft., Gh.,
            KZ Auschwitz, H.Nr.A-10946, C Lager,
  1.1.45   - Bergen-Belsen,
    5.45   befr., war i. Hospital Bergen-Belsen,

  3.2.49   v. Goeteborg/Schweden m.SS Stockholm
            n. d. USA ausgew.

BA.f.Wg.Trier   JF.

Podkarpatske Rusi

```
- 1 -                    Majetek American Joint Distribution Committee
                                        v Praze.
Osoby, žijící na               Zapůjčeno k účelům informačním a statistickým.
Podkarpatské Rusi
       Užhorod.
                                   odd. pro stát. příslušníky
         1771
                                        Dr. Marek Gordon
```

Ptot.č.	Jméno	Jm.matky	dat.nar.	Jm.lágru	bydliště	č.
1.	Jakubovics Ignátě	Weiss Cilli	1913	Buchenwald	Užhorod	77843
2.	Grünfeld Ignátz	Markovič Berta	1909	Günskirchen	"	
3.	Weiss Benjamin	Grünberger Ilona	1927	Allach	"	88594
4.	Mermelstein Samuel	Schwartz Helena	1925	Buchenwald	"	119210
5.	Kirschenbaum Abr.	Weingarten Berta	1916	Theresienstadt	"	7261
6.	Neubauer Herman	Weiss Fani	1930	Bronthal	"	25824
7.	Neubauer Fani	Hartberg Etel	1900	Bronthal	"	25825
8.	Mendlovič Wolf	Hönig Serena	1902	Neuburg Belind	"	12820
9.	Klein Arminova	Rosenspitz Terés	1886	Walpstadt	"	11807
10.	Markovics Aranka	Diamanstein Amali	1919	Grunthall	"	35740
11.	Weiss Margita	Weiss Fani	1916	Wurzen	A	45477
12.	Kaufmann Gizella	Grünberger Éva	1928	Brunnthal	"	35758
13.	Dreisen Éva	Welisch Etelka	1924	Auschwitz	ga	11184
14.	Grünfeld Hugo	Feuerstein Pepi	1923	Murfold	"	
15.	Weinberger Desider	Izakovič Léni	1910	Dachau	"	4114?
16.	" Alexander	Grünwald Mária	1926	Auschwitz	A	11762
17.	Moskovics Heinrich	Merkovics Gizi	1893	Flossenburg	"	
18.	Moskovics Jan	Junger Berta	1928	"	"	35502
19.	Malbaum Jakubova	Grünbaum Laura	1896	Neumark	"	61336
20.	Malbaum Marta	Lang Ella	1921	Neumark	"	61335
21.	Schwartz Rozalia	Braun Fani	1907	Bochlurin	"	11943
22.	Mermelstein Hugo	Schönberger Rosa	1919	Mittenwald	"	150152
23.	Kormann Ludvíková	Schindler Pepi	1909	Freudenthal	A	25762
24.	Bernát Serena	Katz Ida	1901	Weiwasser	A	10700
25.	Paktorovič Magd	Katz Dorotya	1924	"	A	11013
26.	" Rozália	Keller Ida	1927	Grunthal.	"	25832
27.	" Vojtěchova	Steinberg Adéla	1907	" "	"	25835
28.	" Edith	Keller Ida	1926	" "	"	25831
29.	Ecker Tomáš	Paktorovics Berta	1930	Budapest		
30.	Mittelmann Jolán	Roth Ida	1929	Prast	Dovh.Pole	3045
31.	Jakubovics Lipot	Friedmann Mária	1925	Schönwerk	Užhorod	38414
32.	Mermeletein Bernáth	Ausländer Vilma	1927	Javišovic	a	7408
33.	Rothmann Mozes	Kleinberger Fani	1929	Dachau	"	112345
34.	Rubin Ibolya	Gross Jolán	1930	Allach	"	20770
35.	Klein Vasil	Juskovics Bella	1925	Brno	"	38491
36.	Klein Desider	Srulovics Mária	1901	" "	"	39467
37.	Goldberger Vojtěch	Biedermann Hermi	1928	Neuburg	ga	7180
38.	Marglerski Michael	Marglerski Paulina				
			1908	Pisn n/Vltava	"	
39.	Silinec Štefán	Grasz Iréna	1911	Steier	"	8306
40.	Lieber Samuel	Grünfeld Gizella	1892	Manovic	A	5967
41.	Kreuzler Margetta	Weiss Roza	1917	Užhorod	Vel.Lipa	11923
42.	Rosenberg Bernát	Frič Hani	1907	Graz "	Užhorod	
43.	Reimann Judit	Leichtmann Szeréna				
			1925	Bonzer	"	11932
44.	Gelo Karolina	Lefkovics Laura	1919	Praust	"	38470
45.	Kaufmann Serena	Grünberger Éva	1926	Brunthal	"	25730
46.	Markovics Olena	Ausländer Reige	1920	Warschewa	"	61342
47.	Markovics Herman	Merovics Lilli	1912	Auschwitz	Koritnya n B	7556
48.	Perlmann Josef	Friedmann Záli	1914	Dorngott	"	44565
49.	Misikovics Judit	Misdorfer Gizella	1920	Teresiens.	Užhorod	54711
50.	Speiserova Helena	Misonberger Roza	1920	Reichenbad	"	ga 12252
51.	Tendler Jolán	Roth Éva	1920	Mittan	"	83600
52.	Moškovič Herman	Braun Serena	1922	Ilz	"	
```
Searched - 9 JAN 1946   87
```

171

- 5 -

```
114.  Goldberger Maria     Weiss Zseni      1925   Užhorod   Freudenthal    A 25712
115.  Liebermann Magda     Kleinová Serena  1922     "       Sinov            54871
116.  Weissová Matilda     Kessler Regina   1924     "       Reichenbach.ga  12311
117.  Weissová Helena      Kessler Regina   1922     "       Reichenbach ga   1 310
118.  Goldberger Cecil     Weiss Zseni      1926     "       Freudenthal     25215
119.  Moškovič Klara       Junger Berta     1926     "       Pučing          37855
120.  Kleinová Lilli       Friedmann Hajnal 1923     "       Kolnava         10948
121.  Berger Peterova      Weiss Roza       1915     "       Žitava          83998
122.  Mermelstein Laura    Ausländer Vilma  1925     "       Freudenthal   A 25823
123.  Weissová Regina      Weiss Dora       1926     "       Paršnic         52709
124.  Laxová Margita       Ickovič Fani     1920     "       Newmark         28992
125.  Klein Henriková      Weiss Regina     1908     "       Krone           68148
126.  Roth Klara           Rosenfeld Margo  1915     "       Cino            55034
127.  Pollák Elisabeth     Weinberger Eta   1913     "       Praust Hochstadt 7795
128.  Liebermann Klara     Kleinova Serena  1926     "       Sinov           54872
129.  Neumann Brigita      Schwartz Mali    1898     "       Neudorf         38045
130.  Braun Lilli          Klein Hanči      1924     "       Kromberg     A  18475
131.  Tischler Alfred      Augner Maria     1928     "       Wüstegiersdorf  30685
132.  Szuk Ernest          Schäffer Pavlina 1912     "       Günskirchen
133.  Bergida Ignatz       Bergida Fani     1899     "       Ebensee         70450
134.  Ackermann Sara       Bergida Ilona    1923     "       Barth           91506
135.  Ackermann Magda      Bergida Ilona    1919     "                       81510
136.  Samlovič Sara        Neumann Cila     1919     "       Vurzen          15407
137.  Fried Vilhelm        Berkovič Fani    1907     "       Sachsendorf   a  12
138.  Klein Lilli          Kessler Linka    1924     "       Libau         za 9958
139.  Ausländer Eliašova   Friedmann Esti   1909     "       Görlitz         54761
140.  Herskovič Martin     Weiss Cimella    1924     "       Buchenwald    A  9088
141.  Tuchmanová Cecilia   Grünberger Malvin
                                            1919     "       Zittau          83904
142.  Grünberger Regina    Mann Ester       1913     "       Kraso           67922
143.  Rosenfeld Alice      Rosenfeld Magi   1917     "       Cino            55033
144.  Ehrlich Helena       Weineberger Ete  1907     "       Praust Hochst.  37794
145.  Deutsch Ernest       Duber Helena     1920     "       Kempten        158560
146.  Orovan Irena         Engländer Jolana 1921     "       Frauberg        13549
147.  Ackermann Aron       Ackermann Betti  1909     "       Terezín         95060
148.  Glanz Frida          Schönberger Boris
                                            1921     "       Grossenan       56007

149.  Frojmovič Ferdinandová Mermelstein
                           Rosa             1902     "       Paršnic         54766
150.  Frojmovič Lenke      Gross Hajnal     1925     "       Paršnic         54769

151.  Moškovič Regina      Rosenfeld Roza   1924     "       Paršnic         52601
152.  Schwartz Rezsi       Lefkovič Sali    1918     Szurti  Zittau         84083
153.  Dr Sándor Jozef      Selesinger Ana   1894     Užhorod Dachau         78012
154.  Srulovičová Irena    Grünfeld Mária   1922     "       Žitava          91.290
155.  Ausländer Rozalia    Fuchs Dora       1920     Leginec Chrastava      48.905
156.  Bergida Jakubova     Moškovics Sali   1903     Dubrinič Zittau        83919
157.  Schwartz Béla        Klein Roza       1909     Užhorod Berndorf
158.  Adlerová Maria       Guttmann Zseni   1904     "       Berlinska      70463
159.  Deutsch Zoltán       Kohn Lina        1897     "       Ebensee        89920
160.  Weller Ignátz        Winkler Zseni    1897     "       Buchenwald   A 13767
161.  Kronner Ber
                           Kronner Esti     1908     Vel.Berez Plzeň       101361
162.  Niemann Lilli        Keszler Zseni    1922     Užhorod Leipzig      gal8588
163.  Srulovičová Rezsi    Grünfeld Maria   1924     "       Žitava         83991
164.  Bergidova Cecilie    Srulovič Zeni    1907     "       "              83988
165.  Ickovics Hanna       Lebovičová Serena 1920    Zaričova Charchiv   A 11989
166.  Schneider Herman     Keszler Pepi     1907     Užhorod Harka
167.  Jakubovič Klara      Weiss Serena     1929     "       Freudenthal  A 25781

168.  Deutsch Jakub        Schwimmerova Lina 1915    "       Terezín
169.  Mermelstein Aranka   Schwartz Hermin  1929     "       Gerlic         54780
170.  Glüc Fani            Kaufmann Hermina 1917     "       Harpstadt      66565
171.  Grünwald Tibor       Adler Paula      1918     "       Vena

                                                              Dr. Marek Gordon
```

Searched – 9 JAN 1946

89.

Visions from the Second Generation

As Lili Klein Judd's surviving son; I am one of the "Second Generation" of survivors of the Holocaust. The atrocities of the Nazi German "Final Solution" to destroy all Jews didn't just impact those who were in the Holocaust; it doesn't just end when their lives do. The reality of the horror and atrocities that my parents went through continues on through me and through my children. As I encounter more survivors of the Holocaust and other genocides, it is clear that the impact is on all of us.

I was born and raised in the San Fernando Valley of Los Angeles California. I grew up in the baby boomer generation in what seemed to me to be a typical American family. We went to public schools, we watched the Saturday matinee movies at the local movie theatre. We played miniature golf, went bowling, played in Little League baseball. We loved going to Santa Monica Beach in the summer. Our friends included the whole gamut of society of different religions, ethnicities, and countries of origin. Yet, we carried an extra layer of reality that most of our friends did not have.

I, (and all the second generation descendents of Holocaust survivors), grew up without grandparents or any elders in my family. My family of aunts and uncles, and other friends from Ungvar were all the same age. There was no one over the age of my parents. There was also a gap of life between the age of the new-born children and their parents. There was a minimum of a 15 year gap between the eldest child survivor and the youngest survivor.

We were routinely woken up in the middle of the night by the screams of my father as he was having another terrible nightmare reliving his experiences at Auschwitz or Buchenwald. There was always the sadness of those missing from our dinner table: my cousins who were murdered when they were little kids; their parents - my aunts and uncles; and my grandparents from both sides of the family.

I remember being told the stories of the old days before the war. It was usually after the Passover Seder, when the extended family of survivors would be together. They would talk about when life was so good and so hard in Europe. How fun it was to pick and eat the pears from great grandpa's tree; doing the family chores including working in the vegetable garden; playing games and going to school (each year as the stories were told, the snow got a foot deeper, and the walk to school got even longer). I especially enjoyed hearing the stories of the mischief my father would get into as he grew up.

There were parts of the old country that our parents missed, but the reality was that they were glad to be here in America. They were proud to be Americans. While it was a hard place for them to start over, it was a land of opportunity and freedom. It was a country with religious freedom, educational and work opportunities, and many nice and caring people.

That extra layer of reality as the son of a survivor of the Holocaust that I carried in my childhood continues to impact me even today. I am very aware of the need to make this world a better place for everyone. I am aware of the ignorance and thoughtlessness of many individuals towards other people. Many times it is covered up or justified by their misperceptions of acceptable business practices, religious views, and/or their racial and ethnic stereotypes.

Or perhaps it is from an even deeper place inside of us, a trait that can begin to surface in us when we are little children. A form of intolerance that spilled out when we teased that one kid who walked funny, or the one who was homely or uncoordinated. Perhaps it is that human trait, that can continue to expand from that one funny or weird kid to that small group of people who look or act differently; and ultimately to that "other" different race or religion.

Sadly, all too often throughout history, and even today, this trait of negatively "othering" is utilized as a rallying point for many of our world leaders. They focus on finding and blaming a "scapegoat" as a method of uniting masses of people to support them as leaders. A problem in our economy? Blame the (fill in the blank). Hard to find a job? Blame those _____. Couldn't get into the school you wanted to? Blame the _____.

Which group's name have you heard used to fill in these blanks? Jew, Catholic, Protestant, Moslem, Sunni, Shiite, Gypsy, Kurd, African American, Latino, Asian, Gringo, Hutu, Tutsi, poor people, rich people. It's the minority group that visibly looks or acts different then the norm, or comes from a different part of the world. They are easy to be picked out, when there are not so many of them in our midst.

Hitler did it with the Jews. They were his scapegoat to power. Hitler knew that the world would not care about the Jews being slaughtered. He knew the world had not cared about the million or more, Armenians who were slaughtered by the Turks just thirty years before the Holocaust. Even today, the Turkish government refuses to acknowledge their role in the Armenian Genocide.

The Nazi regime which spread its hatred and destruction throughout much of the world was only able to succeed to its level because so many individuals acquiesced to it. It was alright for Germany to occupy the peaceful democratic country of Czechoslovakia, to split up Poland with Russia, to make scapegoats of Jews, Gypsies, homosexuals and the disabled, taking their belongings and their lives.

When so many individuals conformed to the hatred and anger-stirring preachings of their governments, they gave up their individual sense of fairness and justice. That is what allowed and supported the rise of the Nazi power throughout Europe. All of those people who did so share the responsibility for the atrocities that occurred. It is not just those who commit the atrocities that are responsible, but also those who show their indifference by allowing it to happen.

Thankfully, humans also have the ability, as individuals to think and act in a manner that is based on tolerance, caring, respect and love. We must always realize that we, as individuals, must take responsibility for our actions and inactions. Remember, there also were those few, (called the "Righteous Gentiles" by the Jews) who risked and often lost their lives when they choose not to cooperate with the Nazi atrocities toward the Jews. Among others, many of who are honored at the Yad Vashem Holocaust Memorial Museum in Jerusalem, there were individuals like Raoul Wallenburg, the Swedish diplomat who risked his life to save more than 30,000 Jews of Hungary.

But, there was another level of individual caring that must also be remembered. Perhaps it was not as strong as the Righteous Gentiles, but it made a great difference to many. It was the times when those with power inside the "system" individually chose to do the right thing. In my mother's experience, as described in her story, it happened several times.

These are the times that an individual chose to make a difference. One example was when the Nazi SS soldier at Auschwitz caught my mother and her sister washing themselves at night outside of their barrack. He could have "justifiably" killed them on the spot, like so many other SS soldiers would have done, but he was able, as an individual, to be kind, and let them live. The thought of an SS soldier being kind is almost incomprehensible; it was an SS soldier that brutally murdered my grandfather in front of my mother as he got off the train at Auschwitz. Yet, the one SS soldier who let my mother and aunt live, when they were washing, took a greater risk than the one who murdered my grandfather. The SS institution supported actions of murder and did not support actions of kindness. Who was braver, and who was the more righteous?

More education, tolerance, and kindness is what we need in this world to survive. Education alone, without tolerance and kindness, is not enough. The Germans were one of the most highly educated people in the world in the 1930's, yet, it was their highly educated doctors and medical personnel who conducted the brutal experiments on innocent prisoners in the concentration camps. It was their engineers and scientists who designed the efficient mass murder xylon gas facilities and crematoriums. Education without conscience can be extremely dangerous.

The German society was able to accept and support the teaching and preachings of their Nazi government because they had been educated to believe that they were the special Aryan Society, and that Jews were the inferior race.

(USHMM, photo # 77356)

Yes, the million families which included the women and children in the above photograph from the Auschwitz Album, were seen as sub-human and "justifiably exterminated" in accordance with Hitler's Nazi Aryan psyche that the German society and their allies readily accepted.

This psyche of creating a sub-human label or category for the specific group/race/religion of people allowed the people in German society to live their lives in comfort and total disregard for the genocide that their society was perpetrating.

176

(USHMM, photo # 91530)

Aerial photo of Auschwitz-Birkenau. See the proximity of the SS Headquarters and Barracks to the extermination camp (upper right).

The above aerial photograph of Auschwitz shows how close the SS Soldiers and Officers lived to the human slaughter house and slave camp at Auschwitz. Yet the following photographs that were discovered in the "Hoecker Album" show how these special privileged German SS were able to drink, sing songs, laugh, and socialize "on the other side of the wall." The photographs in this album were taken between June 1944 and January 1945 at Auschwitz during its most lethal period, coinciding with the murder of 400,000 Hungarian Jews, including the majority of our family.

(USHMM, photo # 42784)

Nazi German SS officers/guards socializing and singing songs while one plays the accordion.

(USHMM, photo # 42792)

Auschwitz Commandant Hoecker, relaxes with the SS women. "On the terrace of the Lodge"

(USHMM, photo # 42792)

Nazi German SS Officers including Commandant Karl Hoecker enjoying themselves with their German "Blueberry Girls" at Auschwitz during the same period that they are systematically murdering tens of thousands of Jewish men, women, and children daily at Auschwitz.

(USHMM, photo # 42798)

"Julfeier 1944." Commandant of Auschwitz, Karl Hoecker lights candles on the Christmas Tree at Auschwitz in 1944.

How is it possible that the minds and souls of individuals such as Commandant Hoecker and so many millions of German soldiers and civilians could celebrate Christmas, the birth of Jesus Christ, while at the same time feel totally morally right, or at least indifferent, while they are murdering innocent families by the millions? The "other side of the wall" does not just include the SS barracks at Auschwitz, it includes the neighboring towns and cities; it includes the entire country of Germany; it includes the world that turned a blind eye to the genocide that was occurring to the Jews in Europe.

The questions that must be answered and understood are:

How was an educated, caring society of people, able to be transformed into a society that accepted the concept of dehumanizing a specific group of people with whom they had been peacefully interacting with for generations?

How were the Germans able to dehumanize the Jews to the point of accepting that it was totally justifiable to conduct a mass genocide of these people?

Perhaps it was a sense of economic and physical vulnerability in Germany that enabled Hitler and the Nazis to invoke anger, hate and intolerance within the German society as the Nazis rose to power. Germany had lost World War I twenty years earlier, and was undergoing extreme inflation. The vulnerability that existed in the German society was manifested by blaming all of the Jews (as the scapegoat) for the population's problems. We must understand that these circumstances of vulnerability can also happen to us.

Sadly, it did happen to some Jews in the Nazi system. The Nazis designed their operating system to take advantage of the vulnerability of prisoners at Auschwitz and other concentration camps. For some who were offered the chance to not be taken to the gas chambers, and to be fed more rations, they became the *blockalteste* and kapos. While some of them were decent and caring for the prisoners within their control, many became as ruthless as the Nazis. As in my mother's autobiography, it was a Jewish *kapo* that so brutally beat her on her head when she saw Mom and the others trying to observe the sacred holy day of Yom Kippur.

Yet again, as stated in her story, it was some kind hearted Jewish women, working at the kitchen who risked their lives by secretly giving Mother some extra food to take back to her sister Herczi when they were starving. There are so many examples of the individual making the difference. Be it through caring and kind actions or through ruthlessly brutal actions.

Never Again! That is the mantra of the surviving Jews, which I grew up with. Never again will there be a Jewish Holocaust. That is why Israel, the Jewish homeland since before the founding of Christianity and Islam, is so important for the Jews. During the Nazi Holocaust, the majority of the world refused to help or allow Jews to escape. There was no recognized country of Israel at that time. Now, Israel is available for Jews from throughout the world to escape to and live in dignity and freedom.

Since Israel was established it has been the country for Jews to return to and prosper. Yes, it was the one country that completely opened its doors to the Jews who lived for centuries throughout the Middle East when they were forced to leave Iraq, Lebanon, Egypt, Yemen, Morocco, Syria; the list goes on and includes virtually every Arabic country. More recently it has included the Black Jews who had lived in Ethiopia for centuries, and the Jews from the former Soviet Union.

As the years have flown by, I realize that the statement "Never Again!" regarding the Jewish Holocaust, must be expanded to include everyone in this world. It must be "NEVER AGAIN TO ANY GENOCIDE!"

Since the Holocaust, there have been too many genocides. Again, in each of these genocide examples, would-be leaders, for their personal gain, used lies and deceit to manipulate the masses into justified hatred for the scapegoat. As it happened with the German people toward the Jews in World War II, genocide is now occurring in Darfur and the Congo; and has since happened in Rwanda, Cambodia, and Serbia.

We must also never forget the genocides of the Armenians and indigenous peoples all over the world, to name some that occurred before the Holocaust. Since the Holocaust, too many people are not even educated about genocide and the Holocaust. Since the Holocaust, too many, usually for political reasons, falsely deny it even happened. Understand, that the rulers and would be rulers of these genocidal societies have used deceit, lies, greed, and a lust for more power, coupled with a vulnerable ignorant and economically challenged population to achieve these genocides.

This aspect of hatred, anger, and intolerance has to be exposed to the general population so that this evil power is taken away from deceitful leaders and would-be leaders. So that individuals within each population are educated and empowered to think and act in a tolerant manner without anger and hatred affecting their judgment.

For the victims of genocide, and their families; healing, and day to day survival in life requires its own important process. The survivors of the Holocaust had to learn to disengage themselves from the unthinkable and unimaginable horror, terror, and pain and suffering that they were put through. They had to learn to live in society again with other peoples. They had to learn to forgive, at least to an acceptable level for each of them. My mother was able to heal and forgive through the process of writing her story.

When I hear my mother tell her story to children and adults, I feel the silence and intensity of the audience as they listen. I feel and see the opening of their hearts as they ask questions and come to give my mother a hug, or have a picture taken with her. Those she touches include the professionals and business people in service clubs, the troubled youth at juvenal hall, the students (Anglo, Hispanic, Black, Native American, Asian) in public schools and University of California campuses. Male or female, young or old, highly educated or working class; they all are touched by my mother's story. (See some letters from students and teachers in Appendix A.)

As a result of helping my mother prepare her book, I too am learning about the necessity of letting go of my anger and intolerance. I am realizing that it is best for my healing if I forgive the second generation of Germans and their allies who's previous generation murdered so many of my family, and stole so much from my culture. Holding on to the anger and hatred toward all German descendants for what happened during the Holocaust must be released.

I must also respect the German people of today, who not only have acknowledged the terrible genocide that their parents' generation participated in, but are on the forefront of educating and standing up against other genocides. I must forgive them because this generation of Germans are not responsible for what their previous generation, who were misled by the deceit, lies, greed, and lust of power of the Nazi leaders, did. However, my forgiveness can only represent my own personal experience as a second generation of the Jewish victims of the Holocaust to the second generation of the Germans who carried out the Holocaust. It is not forgiveness to those individuals who participated in the Holocaust. It is not meant to be, and in fact can never be forgiveness from all of the other individuals who were, and still are impacted by the German Holocaust or the millions who were murdered by them. Only they can forgive the Germans for the suffering and losses they themselves incurred during the Holocaust.

We are happy and proud to finally be able to have mother's story published and available, so that many more can be touched, and so that many more people can become aware of the need in this world for them to let go of their anger, prejudice, and hatred so that they can take a stand to make this world a better place for everyone to live in, so no more genocides would ever happen again.

It is our intention that this book does not just tell my mother's story, but also delivers her message that "we must get rid of our anger and hatred and learn to forgive." For me, if you are moved by this book to examine your own thoughts of life and to act accordingly, then I will feel that all of the suffering and loss of my family will not have been in vain.

Part V: Discussion Items

Using this book as a teaching tool

April is a month when many Holocaust commemoration events are held. However, it is important to remember the Holocaust all year round, and not only the Holocaust, which happened during World War II, but all the recent ones as well, for example the terrible Holocaust in Darfur, that is going on while we are writing these words.

It is easy for present day students in America to forget the Holocaust because it happened long time ago and far away from us, and yet it is critically important for everybody's well-being, here and now, to remember this incredible event. We must remember because if we forget it can happen again, and millions of Jews, or Mexicans, or Arabs, or simply redhead or brown-eyed people, or whatever other minority may be, can be singled out and killed while others watch in silent cooperation.

There is a short poem, attributed to Martin Niemolle (1892-1984), a priest in Germany who in 1937 was arrested and eventually confined in the Sachsenhausen and Dachau concentration camps. (http://en.wikipedia.org/wiki/First_they-came) which sums it all up and really gets to the point:

"First they came for the communists,
And I didn't speak out because I wasn't a communist.

Then they came for the trade unionists,
And I didn't speak out because I wasn't a trade unionist.

Then they came for the Jews,
And I didn't speak out because I wasn't a Jew.

Then they came for me,
And there was no one left to speak out for me".

We are very fortunate to still have amongst us a few very brave Holocaust survivors, who personally went through unimaginable horrors of the World War II, and who are here still going strong and speaking out for all those who perished during the Holocaust who obviously are not able to advocate for themselves.

Lillian Judd, the author of this book, is one of the people who are still here to tell their story. Lillian is the most amazing person you would ever meet in your life. She is a true survivor, in every possible meaning of this word. Every year, for the last 15 plus years, Lillian has given presentations of her Holocaust experiences in many local high schools, colleges, churches, synagogues, rotary clubs, and juvenile halls.

"I feel motivated to tell my story" - says Lillian Judd, "especially to the kids, so that they would know, without any doubt, that the Holocaust did really happen and it can happen again if we will not defend any minorities, which are being singled out and prosecuted unjustly. I always finish my presentation by inviting the kids to look inside themselves and check if they harbor any anger towards anyone. And if they do, I ask them to let it go. Control your anger or your anger will control you."

Most people, young and old, are profoundly touched by Lillian's story and her calm, simple, down-to-earth way of telling it. We have several huge boxes of letters Lillian received from students thanking her for coming to their class and personally sharing with them her incredible life journey. Here are just a couple of excerpts from students' letters, which Lillian received after her recent speech at the Santa Rosa High School:

"When you told us about your experience and your story, I had tears falling from my eyes, because I felt your pain. I am currently using your advice as a part of my daily life."

"I can never imagine what you went through. It is through people like you that experiences live on and people learn from mistakes."

"It was a great story and it touched everyone's heart. I hope you will come back soon."

"It is liberating to meet someone, who despite experiencing the extremes of hatred can maintain a positive outlook and condemn anger."

"Thank you for being loving and for not giving up your will to live."

"You have given me a lot to think about."

"Thank you for changing my life!"

Last fall Sonoma County resident, Professor Laurie Lippin, who is teaching classes at UC Davis, invited Lillian Judd to be her guest speaker, and all the students were very impressed with Lillian's story. Here is an abstract from one of the student's letters:

184

"Ms. Judd, I want to say thank you from the bottom of my heart. By speaking to my class you gave me a glimpse into a situation I was always aware of and never realized the extent of its horror. I have no idea how you had the will to survive. You are a strong women, I would be blessed to be able to possess half the strength you do. You are an inspiration. Because of you, I am walking away with the knowledge of survival, strength, forgiveness and love. I will forever be grateful to you. Thank you, Sara D.H."

Some students write poems about Lillian, most of them share her story with their parents and friends. Getting to know Lillian is a precious gift. Rarely do we get to meet living history face to face. As a result of listening to Lillian's story and traveling with her through the war-torn Europe, from one concentration camp to another, we are profoundly transformed. The story of the Holocaust becomes very real and close to the heart. We come out more resolved to do everything in our power to cherish every day and to stop anyone from trying to hurt other people because of their religion, culture, or beliefs.

At the present time, Lillian Judd continues to be a voice for tolerance and peace in our Northern California community, and she is constantly asked to be a guest speaker at various schools and colleges. However, she can't come in person to all the classrooms, so her book can speak for her. We invite all the teachers to use this valuable book as a teaching tool, to empower their students to never again let another genocide occur.

"God gave me life and I try to make the best of it." – says Lillian Judd, "I survived, so I can tell the young people to work off their anger, hate, and prejudice, to live in peace with each other, and to prevent another Holocaust from happening in their lifetime."

We must continue to spread this message even after the last Holocaust survivor is no longer alive. Please use this book as a springboard for heart-to-heart discussions with your students. It gives you rich material for going deep into the meaning of life and death, fairness and dignity, freedom and human rights. These discussions can bring profound long-lasting results in the lives of your students and your own life. Please feel free to contact us if you need any support in doing this important work. We would be also truly grateful for your feedback and sharing any essays, poems, or class projects which resulted from the discussions of Lillian's book.

By bring these discussions in your classroom you as a teacher will be *personally* participating in making this world a safer place. Your students will be touched in more ways than you can imagine, and will remember your discussions for years to come. Thank you for opening your hearts to this important work!

Discussion Items

I. This section is meant to be used by readers and teachers to stimulate thinking and feeling (empathy) of what it would be like if they were going through the Holocaust.

How would you feel and what would or could you do under these circumstances?

Having your right to earn a living taken away by the new government.

Having the right to worship and pray to G-d taken away.

Having the right to attend school for education taken away.

Having the right to attend community functions taken away.

Having the right to travel taken away.

Having the right to listen to a radio and read the news taken away.

Having the right to communicate by mail, censored and taken away (no phones, radios or computers).

Having all of the working age men taken away and put in forced labor camps by their new government.

Having your belongings and homes taken from you by the new government and your neighbors.

As a selected community (being a Jew), having to endure indiscriminant (at any time for no reason) arrests, imprisonment, torture, and murder.

The sense of complete uncertainty and control when your whole family must leave everything they have ever known and owned as they are forced into ghetto prisons without sufficient food, shelter, or clothing for no reason and with no knowledge or communication as to why, for how long, and what was next.

Being forced into crammed cattle trains with no food, water, toilet facilities, no place to even sit, while you and your family are taken away with no knowledge of where you are going, when you would get there, and what was in store for you.

After arriving at your destination, being greeted by machine gun pointing German SS soldiers yelling and screaming orders and their barking, growling, snarling German Shepherd dogs.

Having your families torn apart and separated, first the men from the women and children, then again those, as decided by the German officers (Dr. Mengele), who were fit for slave labor, from the elder, the children and their mothers, who were marched into the gas chambers.

Where do you think you would have ended up at this point?

Having what belongings you have left in your possession taken away.

Having the clothing you were wearing ripped off of you and taken away so you are left standing naked.

Having your hair shaved off of you.

Being forced to stand naked in the freezing cold rain in lines for hours at a time.

Being tattooed with a number (even your name is taken from you).

Being starved.

Being forcibly worked.

Being beaten.

Selections; the fear and terror of what is next.

Imagine yourself, today going through the following aspects of that genocide; having so many of your neighbors and friends turn on you with hatred and greed because it was promoted as the "proper thing to do" by the new government, and minimized by the majority of religious institutions.

II.   Intolerance and scapegoating

Intolerance and scapegoating occurs in many societies. Now imagine that you and your family live in a country where a different minority of your community is being affected by these conditions.

Can you think of any minorities in your country that are being discriminated against?

List them.

Why and how are they being discriminated against?

What could and what would you do as an individual to change this situation ?

III.   Daily Life Experiences

Can you take the concept of the above; and compare it to some of your   daily   life experiences growing up such as:

Bullying.

Teasing.

How did you feel when you bullied or teased someone?

How did you feel when you were bullied or teased?

How do you think the other person felt?

Why does bullying and teasing occur?

Can it lead to bigger problems?

IV.   Our perception of what is the norm.

Each of us individually, or as a part of our family unit, often experience something that is different from our perception of the norm. It could be issues related to relationships, health, school, employment, and/or finances just to name a few. Sadly, sometimes these can lead up to substance abuse, or feelings of anger, hatred, and intolerance that can spill out onto those we love and are close with.

What is your perception of what a normal life is like?

Of what a normal family is like?

Of what a normal school is like?

What in your life is different from the norm?

How does it make you feel?

How do you act or react when you think about it?

Do you get angry?

Do you accept what it is, or do you want to try to make a change for the better? Sometimes under certain conditions, one of these choices may be better than the other.

Do you think most other people are "normal", or do you think they have issues and problems also?

V.   Dehumanizing others.

Have you ever been labeled by others? Nerd, jock, gang bangers, geek, retard.

Have you ever been labeled by your own race, religion, gender, or national identity?

Isn't it kind of easy to do that when you think or talk about others? To lump them into a group that focuses on the negative versus the positive? A group that takes away their individuality?

VI.   Individual Empowerment.

Do you realize the good power you have as an individual?

The power to listen.

The power to be nice.

The power to love.

The power to care.

The power to help.

The power to make a difference in someone else's life.

The power to heal.

The power to forgive.

VII.   Becoming Aware.

Do you read and understand the news and issues of today?

Do you routinely accept what you read as the actual truth?

Do you know how to evaluate the media sources and to use your judgment to understand what their biases are?

Do you know what genocides are going on today?

Do you know which communities are suffering at the hands of other communities?

Do you know of people who are suffering at the hands of other people?

VIII.   Making the Positive Difference

How do you start to make the positive difference in your own community, and in the world?

First let go of your own hatred, anger and intolerance. Talk it out with someone, friends, parents, teachers, religious leaders or even the police. Or write about it. Putting your feelings down on paper is a good step toward healing.

IX.   Begin to forgive.

Realize that most people have needs and desires similar to yours. Food, water, shelter, freedom, security, comfort, love, and friendship.

We are all God's children and we should love each other.

Stand up to injustice when you see it. If we see a person in the minority being abused by others we should help by calling the police or getting others to help. Depending on the circumstance, bringing it to other people's attention often works better and is less dangerous than going to help by yourself.

Have you ever participated in a service organization that helps the community such as Rotary, Kiwanis, or Boy/Girl Scouts ?

What difference can you make as an individual?

X.   Reference Web Sites

The following websites and groups are good references for gaining further knowledge about the Holocaust and other genocides:

All students and teachers should be led to:

The United States Holocaust Memorial Museum site:

http://www.ushmm.org

On Genocides in general:

http://www.historyplace.com/worldhistory/genocide/index.html

On the Cambodian Genocide:

http://www.khmerlegacies.org/

On Darfur:

http://www.savedarfur.org/

Letters from Students and Teachers

May, 2010

Dear Lillian,

I'm writing you in light of a new awaking I've recently experienced. My transformation is difficult to explain but I hope you understand my ramblings. When Dr. Lippin told the class we were going to have a guest speaker, I didn't jump for joy nor was I enthusiastic about listening to some old White lady talk for three hours. However, it only took a few moments from the time you began speaking until I found myself still with anger, hurt, and uncertainty. How dare you speak of my pain? Who let you inside me? You can't be my sistah can you? As you spoke of how your father's blood soiled the ground beneath him, I thought about how my daddy's blood made puddles too, beaten by White men dressed in blue. I convince myself once more you can't be my sistah our hair, our skin, and clothing so different. But here you go again telling your story for which I can relate to, STOP! Please stop, I don't want to feel your pain you are my oppressor and I your slave. Aren't I? I'm overwhelmed at this point I cannot tame the churning inside that makes me hurt for you. I want to harm those who have harmed you; see you are me and I am you. Oh dear sistah you have released me, from what I am still not sure...............

Eboni Cooper

Dear Ms. Lillian,

Hello, my name is Astrid Berrios and I was privileged to listen to your life story in my Ethnicity and American Communities class at UC Davis. I wanted to thank you for sharing your story not only to our class but, for continuously reliving the heartache.

Your message of peace and acceptance was one that I needed to hear. I believe in fate and I truly believe I needed to hear your message that day. I am currently facing difficulties that have led me to depression which in turn has led me to internalized anger. Your message of love and inner peace has struck me and is helping me cope with my resentments and move forward.

I admire you for sharing your story and reliving the traumatic moments, I can only imagine how much strength and courage you have. I also wanted to thank you for educating people on the message of peace amongst communities different than our own. Still even in modern times there is encouragement of segregation and marginalization. I am devoted to helping do away with such things from our society. I want to be a part of the change I would like to see in the world and I believe it starts with individuals like you who spread that message.

I cannot express to you how much your story has affected me and given me courage to push through my personal hardships. I was given love, peace, and encouragement during your visit. My heart was touched to see how much resilience and courage you had at such a young age in such tragic times. This gives me hope to overcome my own hardships and find my way towards a more positive outlook. I am eternally grateful.

With love and respect,

Astrid Berrios

I want to thank you, Mrs. Judd, for coming to our CRD class a few weeks ago and talking to us about your experience with the Holocaust. I deeply respect all that you have shared and hold it in high regard. I believe you are a hero for surviving the terrible ordeals you faced and you are a truly courageous person for being able to talk to us openly about your experience, your feelings, your memories, and your personal life story.

I was deeply moved when you talked about the loss of your mother and sister, and also the brutal beating of your father. To imagine that happening to my family or somebody I loved would be unimaginably gut-wrenching. I can't completely swallow the fact that you even witnessed those things, much less dealt with them with patience and anger and hurt. I don't know what I would have done in your position but I am proud that you survived and were able to escape your prison. I was also deeply hurt when I learned the loss of your first son who went to UC Davis. I give my warmest condolences. My heart goes out to you for every tragedy that you have gone through. God bless your soul.

I know that there is a good in every bad, and that bad things don't happen without a reason. I am sure, that you too, will find peace and comfort as a human being after these difficulties, and you will be able to (as you already have) change the lives of so many others, especially the youth, by passing on your story and your experience. I am glad to know there are still survivors out there of the Holocaust who can share their experiences, because that is something that high school teaching simply cannot provide or be able to deliver sentimentally. Your story had sentimental value, and that is severely lacking in our history and English classes. So I am grateful that you were able to bring forth lots of emotions, laughter and grief on the table that day.

Thank you so much! I am really grateful to you! And God always bless you and give you peace and comfort and sense of belonging.

AmenWarda Nawaz

February 13, 2009

Lillian Judd,

I would like to start off by saying, thank you so much for taking the time out of your daily schedule to attend our classroom at Santa Rosa High School. When you told us about your experience and your story, I had tears falling from my eyes, because I felt your pain. When your speech was over and you told us not to hate or feel sadness or anger, I really took your lectures into consideration and I am currently using your advice as a part of my daily life. My mother also went through similar experiences as yours and that's why I truly see you as an idol in my life. I really wish we could have had more time for you to talk to us some more. However, Thank you for coming and you are a true inspiration.

Thank you

Tanya Chavez

Imagine a school gym packed to capacity with hundreds of eighth grade students. Imagine, too, that they have been asked to remain seated in respectful silence for over two hours as a diminutive woman speaks to them in a soft, accented voice. Are you picturing it?

The image you have in your mind may be of some form of barely controlled (or uncontrolled) chaos; yet every year for over a decade the eighth grade students at Mountain Shadows Middle School have sat for hours in rapt, silent attention listening to Mrs. Judd share her powerful and life-changing story. You can hear a pin drop as you walk into the packed gym; and if you look at the crowd, you will no doubt see tears in more than one set of teenage eyes.

As part of the eighth grade curriculum in Rohnert Park, California, our eighth graders read Anne Frank's famous diary. For most, it is a deeply moving experience that is, in itself, a kind of awakening into adulthood. Nothing really prepares them, though, for the impact of hearing firsthand the story of this courageous and indomitable woman. We have many students come to us years after hearing Mrs. Judd's story to tell us how vividly they still remember her words. I have never heard a student speak of Mrs. Judd with anything less than respect, admiration, and affection. The affection, I think, comes mostly from their realization of how painful it must be for her to stand in front of them and relive those terrible years of her life; and what a selfless and loving gift it is for her to do so.

As she shares the story of her ordeal, Mrs. Judd has always impressed our students with three profound messages. The first is the inspiring power of the human will to survive. Her experience reminds our students to continue striving and believing in the future, no matter what their personal circumstances. The second is that hatred is an evil that destroys everyone in its wake; both the victim and the perpetrator of hatred ultimately suffer. Sadly, this message remains as relevant now as it was then. And of course, one central and resounding message rings in every word: the Holocaust must never be forgotten. For the thousands of students in Rohnert Park whose lives have been touched by Mrs. Judd's story, it never will be.

Amy Riebli   Rae Galeazzi   Sandy Bartholome
Mountain Shadows Middle School

February 26, 2004

9590 Laughlin Way
Redwood Valley, California 95470

Lillian Judd
1495 Rocklan Road
Santa Rosa, California 95410

Dear Lillian,

I would like to thank you so much for coming to talk to our school. I feel honored that you, one of the few survivors of the Holocaust, actually came to talk to our class! I know it must be hard to revive all of those horrible memories, and I appreciate that you gave us your time. During your talk, I couldn't help but picture myself in your situation, and, quite truthfully, started crying right away. You are such an unbelievingly strong woman, and I am glad that there are still such amazing people out there! I wish that the Holocaust had never happened, but I am glad that some people actually lived to tell the tale. There is so much more I want to hear from you! Your words mean a lot to me.

I was especially interested when you said that the Germans let you bring a few belongings with you from your house and then forbade you from taking them off the cattle cars with you. I would think that if you couldn't keep your things, then you would not be allowed to bring them in the first place. I also couldn't believe they showed such cruelty to you! It was inhumane, and I couldn't imagine someone with such a black heart as Hitler. Hitler did so many things that were too horrible to imagine. No human should be able to treat his/her own species as animals. How could the Germans do things like that to such a huge mass of people without feeling a thing? Why didn't anyone stand up for the Jews?

I would really love to read your book, but I don't know what it's called! What is the name of your book? A first-hand account of Auschwitz seems like a really valuable read. I look forward to reading it so that if something like that happens in the future, I will know more about it and might be able to do something in order to prevent it. Also, I wanted to know how you felt when you found out where your mother and sisters had gone; that you were never going to see them again. It must have been awful; I cannot even <u>begin</u>

to grasp the nightmarish experiences that you spoke about (and, quite honestly, do not wish to come across anything so horrible in my life). What kept you going? I know for sure that I would not have lasted, but I would have fought to the bitter end. I'm really glad that such a wonderful person survived to tell all the ignorant adolescents about what can happen from something started by a prejudiced opinion. Now that I know more about the Holocaust, I feel like my life is suddenly bigger. Small disagreements are less important, and easily mended. Thank you for giving me a new view of my life!

Sincerely,

Sarah Hardy

P.S. I just wanted to thank you again for inspiring me to do something with my life—to work hard for something and to get it.

Lillian Judd's memoir of suffering and survival is a work conceived in great courage and perseverance. Her decision to tell what happened to her in the years of World War II and the Holocaust and how she found the strength to rise from the ashes and live again, to become a wife and mother and an active member of society, is truly remarkable. As she relates her own story she also speaks for the many other survivors who have not recorded their own past and for the millions who perished and whose voices were silenced forever.

Lillian has lectured to students of all ages and to adult groups, and her true story has brought to vivid reality the statistics and dry facts found in textbooks. Now her words are available in book form. They deserve to be read by people of all ages, but especially by young people, for Lillian was a teenager, when her life and that of her family abruptly changed and plunged them into a nightmare of humiliation and deprivation. Let the Holocaust deniers read this text and find in it the complete refutation of their insulting, obscene claims. Here is vivid testimony to the strength of the human spirit that allows survival, revival and rebuilding through courage and deep faith.

Susanne M. Batzdorff, Librarian & Author.

Newspaper/Magazine Articles

Sonoma West Times & News

THE WINDSOR TIMES   The Healdsburg Tribune   SONOMA WEST

Discoveries

If you were mayor ...	Bridget's diary	Free harp music concert	Fisherman's Fest in Bodega
Eco•Logic B8	Screenings B1	Do Dates B4	Do Dates B2

ARTS & ENTERTAINMENT • DO DATES • CLASSIFIEDS • WINING & DINING • APRIL 18 & 19, 2001 • SECTION B

Remembering the Holocaust

A survivor tells her story as part of her own healing

"I still believe in destiny, and it wasn't my destiny to die there."
– *Lillian Judd, Holocaust survivor*

by Carol Vanek
Staff Writer

Lillian Judd is a survivor of the Holocaust. She, along with six other survivors, will light seven candles at the Holocaust Memorial Day Observance, or *Yom Hashoah*, on April 22 at Sonoma State University.

Six candles represent the murder of six million Jews during World War II, one candle represents the murder of all the others.

Judd, 77, is writing a 400-page book about her experiences of the Holocaust. The book, currently in the editing phase, has no publication date or title as of yet.

"Writing has been very healing for me," said Judd in her Czechoslovakian accent. "It has brought everything up — good and bad."

Judd, a Santa Rosa resident, was 14 years old when the Holocaust began in 1938. At 18 she, along with her father, mother and three sisters, were rounded up and sent to a ghetto. From there they were taken in 1944 to Auschwitz.

HOLOCAUST   from B1

began to take hold for Judd at Auschwitz where her mother and two sisters died in the gas chambers, and she watched as her pious father, upon reaching for his prayer items, was brutally murdered by an SS guard.

Judd and her sister, Herczi, were given the job of working in a factory braiding strips of rubber. "I don't know what they were used for but we braided meters and meters of them," said Judd. Later in the year, they received numbered tattoos on their left arms, which Judd still wears today. Her sister died three years ago.

A year later, Judd and her sister were taken to Bergen-Belsen where, for a short time, they endured this "terrible, dirty, crowded camp," said Judd. Their bodies and spirits weakened, they were sent to yet another camp via a covered truck. "The windows of the train were covered up and we could not see where we were being taken," said Judd.

"This is the first place that we were treated semi -human," said Judd. "There were actually bathrooms, showers, hot food and only two to a bunk, instead of five," she added. Once again, she was given a factory job, this time drilling holes in circular metal parts. "Probably something for the war effort," said Judd.

Upon leaving this "mysterious" camp, Judd and her sister were sent to other camps where food was scarce and Judd received frequent beatings on her head by other prisoners and criminals. As a result of those

beatings, she suffered severe headaches later in her life.

At the end of the war, in 1945, Judd and her sister were forced to take part in the horrendous "death march," along with 1,250 others. They were among 250 prisoners who survived.

"I have learned to live with my losses," said Judd. "I have decided not to have any hate inside me ... I have worked it out."

Reflecting on the Holocaust, Judd states, "It can happen anyplace. All it takes is a soapbox and a good speaker ... especially if the economy is poor."

> ## Reflecting on the Holocaust, Judd states, "It can happen anyplace. All it takes is a soapbox and a good speaker ... especially if the economy is poor."

Judd uses her computer to write. "The world does not want to hear me cry all the time," she said. " I write when I need to get the burden off of my chest."

On occasion, Judd is asked to speak at schools or other events about her experiences. In March, she spoke to the Sebastopol Rotary Club. At the end of April, she will speak to students at Comstock Junior High in Santa Rosa, and on May 20 she will speak at the Community Church of Sebastopol during their worship service at 10:30 a.m.

April 18 & 19, 2001 · **DISCOVERIES** B9

As a candle-lighter, Judd will participate in both a Holocaust Memorial on April 19 at 7:30 p.m. at Congregation Shomrei Torah in Santa Rosa, and then on April 22, from 2 to 3:30 p.m. in Warren Auditorium, Ives Hall at Sonoma State University in Rohnert Park.

"Hope" will be the theme of this year's observance at SSU, and will feature a benediction and invocation by Rabbi Jonathan Slater of Congregation Beth Ami, traditional chanting by Freddi Bloom of Congregation B'nai Israel and guest speaker Rev. Douglas K. Huneke of the Westminster Presbyterian Church of Tiburon. The Vuillaume String Quartet will perform.

Another way in which the county observes the memory of the Holocaust is through the Holocaust Lecture Series, now in its 18th year at Sonoma State University. Sponsored by the Alliance for the Study of the Holocaust, the series began on January 30 and continues

PHOTO BY GAIL SANDS

Lillian Judd will participate in both a Holocaust Memorial on April 19 at 7:30 p.m. at Congregation Shomrei Torah in Santa Rosa, and then on April 22, at Sonoma State University.

every Tuesday night through May 15. The free lectures are open to the public.

Joel Neuberg, Alliance for the Study of the Holocaust, is a West County resident and librarian at El Molino High School. He is also a part-time instructor in natural resources management at Santa Rosa Junior College. The alliance is a "community support group that raises funds and organizes people to speak," said Neuberg. He also organizes and conducts workshops for teachers, advising them how to tackle the subject of the Holocaust in the classroom.

The next lecture in the SSU series will take place on April 24, from 4 to 5:30 p.m. in Warren Auditorium. Jack Weinstein will present "Facing History and Ourselves." For more information on the Holocaust Lecture Series, call 664-4076. For more information on the Holocaust Memorial Day Observance at SSU, call 528-4222.

202

PubDate:**11/23**/2003 Page:**A1** Plate:**Composite** Filmed:**11/22/03** **23:55**

'NUTCRACKER'
Holiday classic takes stage **Q**

SUNNY AND COOL
Santa Rosa | High: 60 Low: 38
Petaluma | High: 60 Low: 35

The Sunday Press
DEMOCRAT

NOVEMBER 23, 2003 • SANTA ROSA, CALIFORNIA $1.25

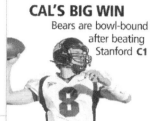

CAL'S BIG WIN
Bears are bowl-bound
after beating
Stanford **C1**

A CELEBRATION OF
Survival

PRISONER A-10946: How a Santa Rosa grandmother
endured Auschwitz — and finally had her bat mitzvah

CHRISTOPHER CHUNG / The Press Democrat

Lillian Judd, 80, is lifted into the air on a chair as she celebrates her bat mitzvah, which she had earlier in the day, during a dinner reception last weekend.

203

Lillian Judd exulted in song and dance, her radiant smile a testament to the completion of a ceremony — and a journey — marking her formal entry as an adult into Judaism. Typically, the bat mitzvah is a rite of passage reserved for 12-and 13-year-old girls. Judd is 80.

Lillian Judd, on the right with a kerchief on her head, arrives at the Auschwitz-Birkenau concentration camp in 1944 with other members of her family.

The unusual ceremony marked a life that has passed from unspeakable horror to unimaginable joy, a triumph of spirit and faith.

When she was coming of age in her native Czechoslovakia under Hitler's anti-Semitic laws, Judd's hopes for a bat mitzvah were overshadowed by a more pressing fight to stay alive.

By the time she was 21 and a prisoner at the Auschwitz concentration camp in Poland, she had witnessed Nazis beat her father to death and condemn her mother and two sisters to the gas chamber.

By CECILIA M. VEGA

THE PRESS DEMOCRAT

"I had other things to worry about," said Judd, the permanent reminder of her lost youth etched onto her wrinkled arm — A-10946.

Now a grandmother living in a Santa Rosa retirement community, she marked her 80th birthday last weekend by reclaiming part of that history through the long overdue bat mitzvah ceremony.

The sparkling red gown she wore to celebrate the event kept hidden the muddied black tattoo ink that is her witness to being a Holocaust survivor.

TURN TO **SURVIVAL**, PAGE A14

Lillian Judd leans on her son, Dennis, as she prays on the anniversary of the death of another son, Irving, at Congregation Beth Ami in Santa Rosa on Nov. 11. In prayer, Judd invited the spirits of her deceased husband, Emil, and son Irving to attend her bat mitzvah last weekend.

SURVIVAL: SR grandmother's rite of passage was more than a religious ceremony

Continued from page A1

"I worked out the bitterness and the hate. I got rid of it," she said in the Czech accent that still dominates her speech. "You have to create your own peace and spread that to other people."

Tradition prevented girls from having bat mitzvahs when Judd was a teen. At that time, only married women were allowed into temple on High Holidays. But it didn't stop her hoping.

She enviously watched her older brother prepare for his own bar mitzvah, the ceremony for boys, and memorized the Hebrew prayers with him, hopeful that it one day might be her turn.

But by 1938, when Judd was 15, Hitler's regime had control of her country and any youthful desire for a religious custom in her honor vanished.

"So many things happened that I never thought of a bat mitzvah," she said, sitting in her Santa Rosa living room where the walls bear smiling family photos of a new life in a new homeland.

By the time she finally was ready for the ceremony—nearly seven decades after her 13th birthday—it was a party marked by more than 200 guests, a band, caterers and dancing late into the night.

When Judd was a teenager, Jews in Europe were stripped of their most basic rights.

Business permits were revoked and her father was forced to abandon his job as a butcher. Judd, her brother, three sisters and their parents ate

Lillian Judd has her picture taken with her brother, Leonard Klein, as her granddaughter, Sarah Judd, watches at congregation Beth Ami before they all attended a dinner celebrating Lillian's mitzvah last weekend

whatever food they could grow on their small property.

Judd had just graduated from high school and was planning to take a business course for further studies, but the Czech schools soon closed. She took an illegal job as a seamstress out of desperation.

"I hated sewing, but there was nothing else. Everything was against the law for Jews, "she said.

The knock on the door

In 1944, a soldier knocked on the family's door in Uzhorod and ordered them to leave behind their home and belongings because they were being relocated.

All the Jews in the area were crammed into an outdoor brick factory where families slept on the ground or, if they were lucky, on the shelves used to dry bricks.

"I looked up and saw the old people bewildered, scared with tears in their eyes, "she said. "I thought, 'God, what is going on?

After six weeks, everyone was herded onto cattle cars for a four day train ride without food or bathroom

Photos by CHRISTOPHER CHUNG
THE PRESS DEMOCRAT

facilities. They had no idea where they were headed.

When the train finally stopped, the now infamous Auschwitz sign greeted them: "Arbeit macht frei." Work makes you free.

Decades after the war, Judd would learn that her initial reaction to the horror of the camp was documented by a Nazi soldier with a camera.

While thumbing through a brochure sent to her by the United States Holocaust Memorial Museum in Washington, she noticed a photograph of her mother, sisters and herself wedged into a crowd of people as they debarked from the train at Auschwitz.

The Press Democrat

Though Judd seems to be staring back at the camera, she does not recall her picture being taken that day. Her memory, instead, is clouded by the image of her father, who just moments after their arrival was beaten to death with a soldier's rifle butt as he reached for his prayer objects.

"There was so much shouting and pushing and shouting," Judd remembered. "My mother kept saying, 'If they take you away from me I'm as good as dead.' But I couldn't offer her any comfort because that's what I needed too."

205

Judd and a sister were separated into one line, her mother and two other sisters into another.

"I went to look back and say goodbye but they were gone," she said. "That was the last time I saw them. I never said goodbye."

She cried the entire first night in camp after being told by a guard that the red sky and stench was from smoldering bodies. "There are your families burning," she was told. Judd and a sister, Herczi, who died five years ago, spent about a year at Auschwitz and were sent briefly to four other labor camps. At the war's end in 1945, as the Nazis struggled to erase the evidence of their atrocities, Judd and her sister were among the 1,250 people sent on a death march from which only 250 survived.

"This kind of life takes a lot out of you. We weren't humans," she said. "We didn't know at the time how lucky we were."

Fighting to stay sane

Judd said she stayed sane knowing there was hope elsewhere. Shortly before Hitler took control of Czechoslovakia, her older brother, Leonard, had moved to the United States to live with family. Every day in the concentration camp she scribbled his address in the dirt so that she never forgot it. After she and her sister made it home from the death march and learned that their house had been taken over by another family, she sent him a telegram for help.

"I didn't think they were alive, but I knew what was happening," said her brother, who was serving in the U.S. military and stationed in Europe when he heard from his sister. "She's a real survivor," he said. He is now living in

Palm Springs, but came to Santa Rosa for his sister's bat mitzvah. Judd married in Czechoslovakia and soon after moved to Los Angeles, where she and her husband, Emil, who also was a concentration camp survivor, ran a restaurant before they retired to Santa Rosa in 1996. They had two sons, one of whom died in a car crash while in college. Her husband died six years ago. The days leading up to the bat mitzvah also brought painful memories of her eldest child's fatal Nov.11 accident. In a prayerful moment, she and her surviving son, Dennis, invited the spirits of her late son and late husband to attend her ceremony. For years after the war, Judd, who as a child was raised in a traditional orthodox home, was disconnected from her faith.

"When we came home from the concentration camps we were not so religious," she said. "It wasn't the most important thing in my life." There was a new country to adjust to, children to raise and a language to learn.

It was only when Judd's eldest son had his bar mitzvah that she became reconnected to her religion and years after that, as she wrote an unpublished memoir of her own experiences, she was able to clearly reflect on her past. Now, in speaking to schools and civic groups, she has told her story hundreds of times. But she still has trouble contemplating why it is that she survived, chalking it up to destiny and God's plan for her.

'Will to go on'

"As long as I'm alive I'll move forward and go on living," she said, during her bat mitzvah. "God has helped me get through the painful hurdles in my life and has given me

the strength and will to go on one day at a time."

Known in her family for being a free spirit—a polka lover who dances with more strength than those half her age—Judd said making her bat mitzvah at 80 simply was something she wanted to do before she died. Rabbi George Schlesinger of Congregation Beth Ami in Santa Rosa has watched her spend the past six months studying the complicated melodies and words of the Hebrew prayers that she recited during her bat mitzvah service. He suspects there's a deeper purpose.

"She really wants to be a role model. She's hoping that others look at her and say, 'I can do this too,'" he said.

A newsletter from the synagogue sent to members before Judd's bat mitzvah shows the striking difference between her life and the world of today's youngsters who have their bat mitzvahs at13.

"I am Lillian Judd...I am a Holocaust survivor," the newsletter entry begins.

Directly below is a photograph of a smiling eighth grader who would have her bat mitzvah two weeks later.

"My favorite subjects are math and drama," begins the teenager's entry.

Judd smiled at the contrast. "I don't want to live in the past," she said. "I want to live for the future."

You can reach Staff Writer Cecilia M. Vega at 521-5213 or cvega@pressdemocrat.com.

" I don't want to live in the past. I want to live for the future"
Lillian Judd, Holocaust Survivor

Community
sports digest

...........Page 6

Friday

Feb. 4, 2011

COMMUNITY
Local happening

....

INSIDE
World briefly
.......Page 14

7 58551 69301 0

A MediaNews Group NEWSPAPER

The Ukiah

Mendocino County's
local newspaper

DAILY JOURNAL

50 cents

14 pages. Volume 152 Number 301

AT POMOLITA MIDDLE SCHOOL

Holocaust survivor:
'tell people what happened'

Sarah Baldik/The Daily Journal

Lillian Judd, a Czechoslovakian-born Holocaust survivor, pulls up her sleeve to show an assembly of Pomolita middle school students the tattoo she received in a concentration camp during World War II, Thursday at the middle school.

By JUSTINE FREDERIKSEN
The Daily Journal

Lillian Judd remembers trying coffee for the first time in a German concentration camp. It wasn't good coffee, but when you're cold and hungry, any warm liquid is welcome.

"Today, I am still always starving, and always cold," said the 88-year-old Santa Rosa resident, who came to tell her story of surviving the Holocaust to students at Pomolita Middle School Thursday morning.

Born in Czechoslovakia, Judd remembers Hungary taking over her country when she was a teenager as part of Adolf Hitler's Nazi regime, and her father and the rest of the Jews being forced to close their businesses and wear yellow stars.

Every day, she said, there were

See SURVIVOR, Page 2

Judd receives a hug from student Hattie Sher after the presentation Thursday. "Please, talk about the Holocaust," she told the students, "because it did happen. I'm afraid when (all us survivors die) it will be forgotten."

207

Survivor

Continued from page 1

Continued from page 1

different orders from their occupiers, until one day in 1944 they were told they would be relocated.

"I will never forget that sight," Judd said of the morning everyone was emptied out of their homes in the cold, crying, shivering and scared. First Judd's family -her parents, three sisters and her, now 21 -- and their neighbors were taken to a former brick factory, where they were fed "watery soup" and left to build shelter outside with whatever bits of wood and cardboard they could find.

"It was raining all the time, and muddy," she recalled. "And there was nothing to do. Time moved very slowly."

Then one day, groups of people were told to get ready to move again. They walked to the train station and were crammed onto box cars where there was nothing to eat or drink, and nowhere to go to the bathroom.

"These trains were used to take animals to the butcher shop," she said. "Now we were in them." When the trains arrived at their destination, Judd said she and the others were ordered out by guards who yelled, hit and called them "terrible names."

The men and women were then separated, and in a horrific scene Judd says is burned in her memory, her father was beaten to death in front of her and dragged away.

"I never told my mother and sister what happened," said Judd, explaining that the women were lined up and marched in front of a man in a white uniform, whom she later learned was the infamous Nazi doctor Josef Mengele, who pointed some people to the left and some to the right.

Judd said her mother feared if she were separated from her daughters she would be killed, so she urged her younger sisters to hunch down so they would look smaller and might be able to stay with their mother.

As they approached Mengele, Judd said two of her sisters were sent with their mother in one direction, while she and her remaining sister went in the other direction.

Next, Judd said groups of five were taken into a large building. The floor was "covered with hair, and the guards were standing around laughing, telling us to take everything off."

Judd said she had never undressed in front of strangers and was worried about finding her clothes again, but she took them off. Then a woman shaved her head, she was given a piece of soap and sent into another room with her sister, who was also now bald.

"She was so pretty, but now, with no hair, she was so ugly," she recalled. Cold water was turned on and they were told to wash themselves. When the water turned off, Judd said they were not even given towels before they were pushed back outside in the cold.

"But we didn't know how lucky we were," she said. "Because the other group, they got gas instead of water. They were killed."

And now, Judd lives with the guilt of telling her other sisters to stay with their mother. Eventually, Judd said she was forced out of the concentration camp with 1,249 other people into a "death march" across Germany. By the time World War II ended and the Nazi soldiers scattered, Judd said 250 of the walkers were still alive. She and her sister both came to the United States and married, though her sister has since died. Judd said she comes to schools like Pomolita to make sure that no one forgets what happened.

"I really need your help, because we (survivors) are disappearing," Judd told the teens gathered. "Please, talk about the Holocaust, because it did happen. I'm afraid when (all us survivors die) it will be forgotten."

When she was done speaking, the teens crowded around Judd, coming up one by one to hug her and ask to take a photo with her.

Judd said she did not know why she survived when so many others didn't, but waved her arms at the crowd of teens and said, "Maybe it is so I can do this." *Justine Frederiksen can be reached at udjjf@pacific.net. or 468-3521.*

208

Myrna Goodman, Ph.D.

Professor of Sociology

Director Sonoma State University Center

for the Study of the Holocaust and Genocide

As a Holocaust scholar and educator, I have read and viewed the accounts of many Holocaust survivors' experiences. Lillian Judd's memoir is an outstanding example of memory in the service of tolerance and understanding.

Lillian has spoken to many of our Holocaust Lecture Series classes. Each time she related her experiences, our students were deeply touched. Her quiet, soft-spoken narrative brought home to them the reality of the loss and suffering she experienced during the Holocaust. Lillian's is a remarkable story, filled with so many people she lost, but it also reflects her deep understanding of the importance of preventing genocide and prejudice in our world.

This text is unique. Not only does Lillian relate wonderful details of her life, the book contains several unusual features. The photographs bring light to her story; several are remarkable and iconic (Lily arriving at Auschwitz). The copies of her wartime records demonstrate the extensive and wide-ranging madness of Nazi bureaucracy of destruction. Lillian's son Dennis' reflections as a member of the second generation add an important dimension to this work. It is a testament to the persistent impact of the Holocaust on survivors and their families.

This book is an important addition to the genre of survivor memoirs. Lillian's account of her life and experiences will be most appropriate for students of all ages, but the complexity and detail portrayed in the book should also engage a much wider audience.

I am continually thankful to Lillian for sharing her experiences with my students and grateful for her dedication to genocide prevention. Knowing her has been a blessing.

From Nightmare To Freedom

Renee   Hajnal   Iren   Herczi   Lili

This actual photograph of "Hungarian Jews arriving at Auschwitz" includes Lillian Klein Judd's family. It was taken just after her father Elemer was brutally murdered by a German SS Guard, and is the last photograph of her mother Hajnal and her two little sisters Renee and Iren alive before they were sent to the gas chambers.

Herczi   Iren   Hajnal   Renee   Elemer   Lili

This photograph is of the Klein family. Compare their faces with those in the above photograph.

Made in the USA
Charleston, SC
08 September 2011